CCNA Cyber Ops SECOPS

210-255

Official Cert Guide

OMAR SANTOS, CISSP No. 463598

JOSEPH MUNIZ, CISSP No. 344594

Cisco Press

800 East 96th Street

Indianapolis, IN 46240

CCNA Cyber Ops SECOPS 210-255 Official Cert Guide

Omar Santos, CISSP No. 463598
Joseph Muniz, CISSP No. 344594

Copyright© 2017 Pearson Education, Inc.

Published by:
Cisco Press
800 East 96th Street
Indianapolis, IN 46240 USA

Printed in the United States of America

1   17

Library of Congress Control Number: 2017937634

ISBN-13: 978-1-58714-703-6

ISBN-10: 1-58714-703-3

Warning and Disclaimer

This book is designed to provide information about the CCNA Cyber Ops SECOPS 210-255 exam. Every effort has been made to make this book as complete and as accurate as possible, but no warranty or fitness is implied.

The information is provided on an "as is" basis. The authors, Cisco Press, and Cisco Systems, Inc. shall have neither liability nor responsibility to any person or entity with respect to any loss or damages arising from the information contained in this book or from the use of the discs or programs that may accompany it.

The opinions expressed in this book belong to the author and are not necessarily those of Cisco Systems, Inc.

Trademark Acknowledgments

All terms mentioned in this book that are known to be trademarks or service marks have been appropriately capitalized. Cisco Press or Cisco Systems, Inc., cannot attest to the accuracy of this information. Use of a term in this book should not be regarded as affecting the validity of any trademark or service mark.

Special Sales

For information about buying this title in bulk quantities, or for special sales opportunities (which may include electronic versions; custom cover designs; and content particular to your business, training goals, marketing focus, or branding interests), please contact our corporate sales department at corpsales@pearsoned.com or (800) 382-3419.

For government sales inquiries, please contact governmentsales@pearsoned.com.
For questions about sales outside the U.S., please contact intlcs@pearson.com.

Feedback Information

At Cisco Press, our goal is to create in-depth technical books of the highest quality and value. Each book is crafted with care and precision, undergoing rigorous development that involves the unique expertise of members from the professional technical community.

Readers' feedback is a natural continuation of this process. If you have any comments regarding how we could improve the quality of this book, or otherwise alter it to better suit your needs, you can contact us through email at feedback@ciscopress.com. Please make sure to include the book title and ISBN in your message.

We greatly appreciate your assistance.

Editor-in-Chief: Mark Taub	**Business Operation Manager, Cisco Press:** Ronald Fligge
Product Line Manager: Brett Bartow	**Technical Editors:** Jeremy McGuinn, Justin Poole
Executive Editor: Mary Beth Ray	**Copy Editor:** Bart Reed
Managing Editor: Sandra Schroeder	**Editorial Assistant:** Vanessa Evans
Development Editor: Eleanor Bru	**Composition:** Bronkella Publishing
Project Editor: Mandie Frank	**Indexer:** Ken Johnson
Cover Designer: Chuti Prasertsith	

CISCO.

Americas Headquarters	**Asia Pacific Headquarters**	**Europe Headquarters**
Cisco Systems, Inc.	Cisco Systems (USA) Pte. Ltd.	Cisco Systems International BV Amsterdam,
San Jose, CA	Singapore	The Netherlands

Cisco has more than 200 offices worldwide. Addresses, phone numbers, and fax numbers are listed on the Cisco Website at **www.cisco.com/go/offices.**

Cisco and the Cisco logo are trademarks or registered trademarks of Cisco and/or its affiliates in the U.S. and other countries. To view a list of Cisco trademarks, go to this URL: www.cisco.com/go/trademarks. Third party trademarks mentioned are the property of their respective owners. The use of the word partner does not imply a partnership relationship between Cisco and any other company. (1110R)

About the Authors

Omar Santos is an active member of the cybersecurity community, where he leads several industry-wide initiatives and standards bodies. His active role helps businesses, academic institutions, state and local law enforcement agencies, and other participants dedicated to increasing the security of their critical infrastructures.

Omar is the author of more than a dozen books and video courses, as well as numerous white papers, articles, and security configuration guidelines and best practices. Omar is a principal engineer of the Cisco Product Security Incident Response Team (PSIRT), where he mentors and leads engineers and incident managers during the investigation and resolution of cybersecurity vulnerabilities. Additional information about Omar's current projects can be found at omarsantos.io, and you can follow Omar on Twitter @santosomar.

Joseph Muniz is an architect at Cisco Systems and security researcher. He has extensive experience in designing security solutions and architectures for the top Fortune 500 corporations and the U.S. government. Joseph's current role gives him visibility into the latest trends in cybersecurity, from both leading vendors and customers. Examples of Joseph's research include his RSA talk titled "Social Media Deception," which has been quoted by many sources (search for "Emily Williams Social Engineering"), as well as his articles in *PenTest Magazine* regarding various security topics.

Joseph runs The Security Blogger website, a popular resource for security, hacking, and product implementation. He is the author and contributor of several publications covering various penetration testing and security topics. You can follow Joseph at www.thesecurityblogger.com and @SecureBlogger.

About the Technical Reviewers

Jeremy McGuinn is a support engineer in the Applied Security Intelligence group at Cisco Systems where he focuses on the detection of cyber attacks. Before spending 10 years in security roles at Cisco, Jeremy was an enterprise systems administrator for both government and private sector networks. Jeremy was *Time*® magazine's person of the year in 2006 and lives in Raleigh, North Carolina.

Justin Poole, CCIE No. 16224 (R&S, Security), CISSP, is a consulting systems engineer at Cisco Systems, specializing in Cybersecurity, Secure Data Center, and Enterprise Network architectures and solutions. Justin supports customers across the U.S. public sector market. He has been at Cisco for 11 years and in the industry for more than 15 years.

Dedications

I would like to dedicate this book to my lovely wife, Jeannette, and my two beautiful children, Hannah and Derek, who have inspired and supported me throughout the development of this book.

I also dedicate this book to my father, Jose, and to the memory of my mother, Generosa. Without their knowledge, wisdom, and guidance, I would not have the goals that I strive to achieve today.

—Omar Santos

I would like to dedicate this book to the memory of my father, Raymond Muniz. He never saw me graduate from college or accomplish great things, such as writing this book. I would also like to apologize to him for dropping out of soccer in high school. I picked it back up later in life, and today play in at least two competitive matches a week. Your hard work paid off. Hopefully you somehow know that.

—Joseph Muniz

Acknowledgments

I would like to thank Joey Muniz for accepting to co-author this book with me. I really enjoyed working with Joey on this book and also on the CCNA Cyber Ops SECFND book as well. I would also like to thank the technical editors, Jeremy McGuinn and Justin Poole, for their time and technical expertise. They verified our work and contributed to the success of this book. I would also like to thank the Cisco Press team, especially Mary Beth Ray, Denise Lincoln, and Christopher Cleveland, for their patience, guidance, and consideration. Their efforts are greatly appreciated. Finally, I would like to acknowledge the Cisco Security Research and Operations teams, Cisco Advanced Threat Analytics, and Cisco Talos. Several leaders in the network security industry work there, supporting our Cisco customers, often under very stressful conditions, and working miracles daily. They are truly unsung heroes, and I am honored to have had the privilege of working side by side with them in the trenches while protecting customers and Cisco.

—Omar Santos

I would first like to thank Omar for including me on this project. I really enjoyed working with him and hope we can do more in the future. I also would like to thank the Cisco Press team and technical editors, Jeremy McGuinn and Justin Poole, for their fantastic support in making the writing process top quality and easy for everybody.

I would also like to thank all the great people in my life who make me who I am.

Finally, a message for Raylin Muniz (age 7): Hopefully one day you can accomplish your dreams like I have with this book.

—Joseph Muniz

Contents at a Glance

Elements Available on the Book Website

Contents

Command Syntax Conventions

The conventions used to present command syntax in this book are the same conventions used in the IOS Command Reference. The Command Reference describes these conventions as follows:

■ **Boldface** indicates commands and keywords that are entered literally as shown. In actual configuration examples and output (not general command syntax), boldface indicates commands that are manually input by the user (such as a **show** command).

■ *Italic* indicates arguments for which you supply actual values.

■ Vertical bars (|) separate alternative, mutually exclusive elements.

■ Square brackets ([ ]) indicate an optional element.

■ Braces ({ }) indicate a required choice.

■ Braces within brackets ([{ }]) indicate a required choice within an optional element.

Introduction

Congratulations! If you are reading this, you have in your possession a powerful tool that can help you to:

■ Improve your awareness and knowledge of cybersecurity operations

■ Increase your skill level related to operational security

■ Prepare for the CCNA Cyber Ops SECOPS certification exam

Whether you are preparing for the CCNA Cyber Ops certification or just changing careers to cybersecurity, this book will help you gain the knowledge you need to get started and prepared. When writing this book, we did so with you in mind, and together we will discover the critical ingredients that make up the recipe for a secure network and how to succeed in cybersecurity operations. By focusing on covering the objectives for the CCNA Cyber Ops SECOPS exam and integrating that with real-world best practices and examples, we created this content with the intention of being your personal tour guides as we take you on a journey through the world of network security.

The CCNA Cyber Ops: Implementing Cisco Cybersecurity Operations (SECOPS) 210-255 exam is required for the CCNA Cyber Ops certification. This book covers all the topics listed in Cisco's exam blueprint, and each chapter includes key topics and preparation tasks to assist you in mastering this information. Reviewing tables and practicing test questions will help you practice your knowledge in all subject areas.

About the 210-255 CCNA Cyber Ops SECOPS Exam

The CCNA Cyber Ops: Implementing Cisco Cybersecurity Operations (SECOPS) 210-255 exam is the second of the two required exams to achieve the CCNA Cyber Ops certification and is aligned with the job role of associate-level security operations center (SOC) security analyst. The SECOPS exam tests candidates' understanding of cybersecurity operation principles, foundational knowledge, and core skills needed to detect and respond to cybersecurity incidents and protect their organization from modern threats.

The CCNA Cyber Ops: Implementing Cisco Cybersecurity Operations (SECOPS) 210-255 exam is a computer-based test that has 50 to 60 questions and a 90-minute time limit. Because all exam information is managed by Cisco Systems and is therefore subject to change, candidates should continually monitor the Cisco Systems site for exam updates at https://learningnetwork.cisco.com/community/certifications/ccna-cyber-ops.

You can take the exam at Pearson VUE testing centers. You can register with VUE at www.vue.com/cisco.

210-255 CCNA Cyber Ops SECOPS Exam Topics

Table I-1 lists the topics of the 210-255 SECOPS exam and indicates the chapter in the book where they are covered.

Table I-1   *210-255 SECOPS Exam Topics*

Exam Topic	Chapter
1.0. Endpoint Threat Analysis and Computer Forensics	
1.1. Interpret the output report of a malware analysis tool such as AMP Threat Grid or Cuckoo Sandbox	*Chapter 1*
1.2. Describe these terms as they are defined in the CVSS 3.0	*Chapter 1*
1.2.a. Attack vector	Chapter 1
1.2.b. Attack complexity	Chapter 1
1.2.c. Privileges required	Chapter 1
1.2.d. User interaction	Chapter 1
1.2.e. Scope	Chapter 1
1.3. Describe these terms as they are defined in the CVSS 3.0	*Chapter 1*
1.3.a. Confidentiality	Chapter 1
1.3.b. Integrity	Chapter 1
1.3.c. Availability	Chapter 1
1.4. Define these items as they pertain to the Microsoft Windows file system	*Chapter 2*
1.4.a. FAT32	Chapter 2
1.4.b. NTFS	Chapter 2
1.4.c. Alternative data streams	Chapter 2
1.4.d. MACE	Chapter 2
1.4.e. EFI	Chapter 2
1.4.f. Free space	Chapter 2
1.4.g. Timestamps on a file system	Chapter 2
1.5. Define these terms as they pertain to the Linux file system	*Chapter 2*
1.5.a. Ext4	Chapter 2
1.5.b. Journaling	Chapter 2
1.5.c. MBR	Chapter 2
1.5.d. Swap file system	Chapter 2
1.5.e. MAC	Chapter 2
1.6. Compare and contrast three types of evidence	*Chapter 2*
1.6.a. Best evidence	Chapter 2
1.6.b. Corroborative evidence	Chapter 2
1.6.c. Indirect evidence	Chapter 2

Exam Topic	Chapter
1.7. Compare and contrast two types of image	*Chapter 2*
1.7.a. Altered disk image	Chapter 2
1.7.b. Unaltered disk image	Chapter 2
1.8. Describe the role of attribution in an investigation	*Chapter 2*
1.8.a. Assets	Chapter 2
1.8.b. Threat actor	Chapter 2
2.0. Network Intrusion Analysis	
2.1. Interpret basic regular expressions	Chapter 3
2.2. Describe the fields in these protocol headers as they relate to intrusion analysis	Chapter 3
2.2.a. Ethernet frame	Chapter 3
2.2.b. IPv4	Chapter 3
2.2.c. IPv6	Chapter 3
2.2.d. TCP	Chapter 3
2.2.e. UDP	Chapter 3
2.2.f. ICMP	Chapter 3
2.2.g. HTTP	Chapter 3
2.3. Identify the elements from a NetFlow v5 record from a security event	Chapter 4
2.4. Identify these key elements in an intrusion from a given PCAP file	Chapter 3
2.4.a. Source address	Chapter 3
2.4.b. Destination address	Chapter 3
2.4.c. Source port	Chapter 3
2.4.d. Destination port	Chapter 3
2.4.e. Protocols	Chapter 3
2.4.f. Payloads	Chapter 3
2.5. Extract files from a TCP stream when given a PCAP file and Wireshark	Chapter 3
2.6. Interpret common artifact elements from an event to identify an alert	Chapter 3
2.6.a. IP address (source / destination)	Chapter 3
2.6.b. Client and server port identity	Chapter 3
2.6.c. Process (file or registry)	Chapter 3
2.6.d. System (API calls)	Chapter 3

Exam Topic	Chapter
2.6.e. Hashes	Chapter 3
2.6.f. URI/URL	Chapter 3
2.7. Map the provided events to these source technologies	Chapter 3
2.7.a. NetFlow	Chapter 4
2.7.b. IDS/IPS	Chapter 3
2.7.c. Firewall	Chapter 3
2.7.d. Network application control	Chapter 3
2.7.e. Proxy logs	Chapter 3
2.7.f. Antivirus	Chapter 3
2.8. Compare and contrast impact and no impact for these items	Chapter 3
2.8.a. False Positive	Chapter 3
2.8.b. False Negative	Chapter 3
2.8.c. True Positive	Chapter 3
2.8.d. True Negative	Chapter 3
2.9. Interpret a provided intrusion event and host profile to calculate the impact flag generated by Firepower Management Center (FMC)	Chapter 3
3.0. Incident Response	
3.1. Describe the elements that should be included in an incident response plan as stated in NIST.SP800-61 r2	Chapter 5
3.2. Map elements to these steps of analysis based on the NIST.SP800-61 r2	Chapter 5
3.2.a. Preparation	Chapter 5
3.2.b. Detection and analysis	Chapter 5
3.2.c. Containment, eradication, and recovery	Chapter 5
3.2.d. Post-incident analysis (lessons learned)	Chapter 5
3.3. Map the organization stakeholders against the NIST IR categories (C2M2, NIST.SP800-61 r2)	Chapter 5
3.3.a. Preparation	Chapter 5
3.3.b. Detection and analysis	Chapter 5
3.3.c. Containment, eradication, and recovery	Chapter 5
3.3.d. Post-incident analysis (lessons learned)	Chapter 5
3.4. Describe the goals of the given CSIRT	Chapter 6
3.4.a. Internal CSIRT	Chapter 6

Exam Topic	Chapter
3.4.b. National CSIRT	Chapter 6
3.4.c. Coordination centers	Chapter 6
3.4.d. Analysis centers	Chapter 6
3.4.e. Vendor teams	Chapter 6
3.4.f. Incident response providers (MSSP)	Chapter 6
3.5. Identify these elements used for network profiling	Chapter 8
3.5.a. Total throughput	Chapter 8
3.5.b. Session duration	Chapter 8
3.5.c. Ports used	Chapter 8
3.5.d. Critical asset address space	Chapter 8
3.6. Identify these elements used for server profiling	Chapter 8
3.6.a. Listening ports	Chapter 8
3.6.b. Logged in users/service accounts	Chapter 8
3.6.c. Running processes	Chapter 8
3.6.d. Running tasks	Chapter 8
3.6.e. Applications	Chapter 8
3.7. Map data types to these compliance frameworks	Chapter 7
3.7.a. PCI	Chapter 7
3.7.b. HIPAA (Health Insurance Portability and Accountability Act)	Chapter 7
3.7.c. SOX	Chapter 7
3.8. Identify data elements that must be protected with regard to a specific standard (PCI-DSS)	Chapter 7
4.0. Data and Event Analysis	
4.1. Describe the process of data normalization	Chapter 9
4.2. Interpret common data values into a universal format	Chapter 9
4.3. Describe 5-tuple correlation	Chapter 9
4.4. Describe the 5-tuple approach to isolate a compromised host in a grouped set of logs	Chapter 9
4.5. Describe the retrospective analysis method to find a malicious file, provided a file analysis report	Chapter 9
4.6. Identify potentially compromised hosts within the network based on a threat analysis report containing malicious IP address or domains	Chapter 9
4.7. Map DNS logs and HTTP logs together to find a threat actor	Chapter 9

Exam Topic	Chapter
4.8. Map DNS, HTTP, and threat intelligence data together	Chapter 9
4.9. Identify a correlation rule to distinguish the most significant alert from a given set of events from multiple data sources using the Firepower Management Console	Chapter 9
4.10. Compare and contrast deterministic and probabilistic analysis	Chapter 9
5.0. Incident Handling	
5.1. Classify intrusion events into these categories as defined in the Diamond Model of Intrusion	Chapter 10
5.1.a. Reconnaissance	Chapter 10
5.1.b. Weaponization	Chapter 10
5.1.c. Delivery	Chapter 10
5.1.d. Exploitation	Chapter 10
5.1.e. Installation	Chapter 10
5.1.f. Command and control	Chapter 10
5.1.g. Action on objectives	Chapter 10
5.2. Apply the NIST.SP800-61 r2 incident handling process to an event	Chapter 10
5.3. Define these activities as they relate to incident handling	Chapter 10
5.3.a. Identification	Chapter 10
5.3.b. Scoping	Chapter 10
5.3.c. Containment	Chapter 10
5.3.d. Remediation	Chapter 10
5.3.e. Lesson-based hardening	Chapter 10
5.3.f. Reporting	Chapter 10
5.4. Describe these concepts as they are documented in NIST SP 800-86	Chapter 10
5.4.a. Evidence collection order	Chapter 10
5.4.b. Data integrity	Chapter 10
5.4.c. Data preservation	Chapter 10
5.4.d. Volatile data collection	Chapter 10
5.5. Apply the VERIS schema categories to a given incident	Chapter 5

About the CCNA Cyber Ops SECOPS #210-255 Official Cert Guide

This book maps to the topic areas of the 210-255 SECOPS exam and uses a number of features to help you understand the topics and prepare for the exam.

Objectives and Methods

This book uses several key methodologies to help you discover the exam topics on which you need more review, to help you fully understand and remember those details, and to help you prove to yourself that you have retained your knowledge of those topics. So, this book does not try to help you pass the exams only by memorization, but by truly learning and understanding the topics. This book is designed to help you pass the SECOPS exam by using the following methods:

- Helping you discover which exam topics you have not mastered

- Providing explanations and information to fill in your knowledge gaps

- Supplying exercises that enhance your ability to recall and deduce the answers to test questions

- Providing practice exercises on the topics and the testing process via test questions on the companion website

Book Features

To help you customize your study time using this book, the core chapters have several features that help you make the best use of your time:

- **"Do I Know This Already?" quiz:** Each chapter begins with a quiz that helps you determine how much time you need to spend studying that chapter.

- **Foundation Topics:** These are the core sections of each chapter. They explain the concepts for the topics in that chapter.

- **Exam Preparation Tasks:** After the "Foundation Topics" section of each chapter, the "Exam Preparation Tasks" section lists a series of study activities that you should do at the end of the chapter. Each chapter includes the activities that make the most sense for studying the topics in that chapter:

  - **Review All the Key Topics:** The Key Topic icon appears next to the most important items in the "Foundation Topics" section of the chapter. The "Review All the Key Topics" activity lists the key topics from the chapter, along with their page numbers. Although the contents of the entire chapter could be on the exam, you should definitely know the information listed in each key topic, so you should review these.

  - **Complete the Tables and Lists from Memory:** To help you memorize some lists of facts, many of the more important lists and tables from the chapter are included in a document on the companion website. This document lists only partial information, allowing you to complete the table or list.

- **Define Key Terms:** Although the exam is unlikely to ask you to define a term, the CCNA Cyber Ops exams do require that you learn and know a lot of networking terminology. This section lists the most important terms from the chapter, asking you to write a short definition and compare your answer to the glossary at the end of the book.

- **Q&A:** Confirm that you understand the content you just covered.

- **Web-based practice exam:** The companion website includes the Pearson Test Prep practice test software, which allows you to take practice exam questions. Use it to prepare with a sample exam and to pinpoint topics where you need more study.

How This Book Is Organized

This book contains 10 core chapters—Chapters 1 through 10. Chapter 11 includes some preparation tips and suggestions for how to approach the exam. Each core chapter covers a subset of the topics on the CCNA Cyber Ops SECOPS exam. The core chapters are organized into parts. They cover the following topics:

Part I   Threat Analysis and Computer Forensics

- **Chapter 1: Threat Analysis** covers details about the vectors, complexity, scope, and required privileges of cyber attacks in respect to the Common Vulnerability Scoring System version 3 (CVSSv3). This chapter also describes the confidentiality, integrity, and availability impacts of cyber attacks.

- **Chapter 2: Forensics** covers fundamentals about forensics in Windows and Linux-based systems. It covers the Windows file system, defines terms as they pertain to the underlying operating system, master boot record, and other architectural components.

Part II   Network Intrusion Analysis

- **Chapter 3: Fundamentals of Intrusion Analysis** covers the common artifact elements and sources of security events. In this chapter, you will gain an understanding of regular expressions, protocol headers, and intrusion analysis. You will also learn how to use packet captures for intrusion analysis.

- **Chapter 4: NetFlow for Cybersecurity** covers the details about NetFlow, all NetFlow versions, and how to use NetFlow for cybersecurity operations.

Part III   Incident Response

- **Chapter 5: Introduction to Incident Response and the Incident Handling Process** provides an introduction to incident response, the incident response plan, the incident response process, and details about information sharing and incident coordination. This chapter covers the different incident response team structures.

- **Chapter 6: Incident Response Teams** covers the different types of incident response teams, including Computer Security Incident Response Teams (CSIRTs), Product Security Incident Response Teams (PSIRTs), national CSIRTs, and Computer Emergency Response Teams (CERTs), coordination centers, and incident response providers and managed security service providers (MSSPs).

- **Chapter 7: Compliance Frameworks** provides an introduction to the different industry compliance frameworks, including the Payment Card Industry Data Security Standard (PCI DSS), Health Insurance Portability and Accountability Act (HIPAA), and the Sarbanes-Oxley Act of 2002 (SOX).

- **Chapter 8: Network and Host Profiling** covers how to perform network and host profiling. The results of these profiling methodologies may be used to determine the access rights that will be granted to the system, to identify potentially malicious behavior, to troubleshoot, to audit for compliance, and so on.

Part IV   Data and Event Analysis

- **Chapter 9: The Art of Data and Event Analysis** covers how to normalize security event data and also how to use the 5-tuple correlation to respond to security incidents. This chapter also covers what retrospective analysis is and identifying malicious files with different security tools in the industry, such as Cisco AMP. In this chapter, you will also learn how to map threat intelligence with DNS and other artifacts to respond to security incidents and identify malicious files and transactions in your network. At the end of this chapter, you will learn the difference between deterministic and probabilistic analysis.

Part V   Incident Handling

- **Chapter 10: Intrusion Event Categories** covers the different intrusion event categories. You will learn what the Diamond Model of Intrusion is as well as how to apply the VERIS schema categories to a given incident.

Part VI: Final Preparation

- **Chapter 11: Final Preparation** identifies the tools for final exam preparation and helps you develop an effective study plan. It contains tips on how to best use the web-based material to study.

Part VII   Appendixes

- **Appendix A: Answers to "Do I Know This Already?" Quizzes and Q&A Questions** includes the answers to all the questions from Chapters 1 through 10.

- **Appendix B: Memory Tables and Lists** (a website-only appendix) contains the key tables and lists from each chapter, with some of the contents removed. You can print this appendix and, as a memory exercise, complete the tables and lists. The goal is to help you memorize facts that can be useful on the exam. This appendix is available in PDF format on the book website; it is not in the printed book.

- **Appendix C: Memory Tables and Lists Answer Key** (a website-only appendix) contains the answer key for the memory tables in Appendix B. This appendix is available in PDF format on the book website; it is not in the printed book.

- **Appendix D: Study Planner** (a website-only appendix) is a spreadsheet with major study milestones, where you can track your progress throughout your study.

Companion Website

Register this book to get access to the Pearson Test Prep practice test software and other study materials, plus additional bonus content. Check this site regularly for new and updated postings written by the authors that provide further insight into the more troublesome topics on the exam. Be sure to check the box that you would like to hear from us to receive updates and exclusive discounts on future editions of this product or related products.

To access this companion website, follow these steps:

1.   Go to www.pearsonITcertification.com/register and log in or create a new account.

2.   Enter the ISBN 9781587147036.

3.   Answer the challenge question as proof of purchase.

4.   Click the "Access Bonus Content" link in the Registered Products section of your account page, to be taken to the page where your downloadable content is available.

Please note that many of our companion content files can be very large, especially image and video files.

If you are unable to locate the files for this title by following the steps, please visit www.pearsonITcertification.com/contact and select the "Site Problems/ Comments" option. Our customer service representatives will assist you.

Pearson Test Prep Practice Test Software

As noted previously, this book comes complete with the Pearson Test Prep practice test software containing two full exams. These practice tests are available to you either online or as an offline Windows application. To access the practice exams that were developed with this book, please see the instructions in the card inserted in the sleeve in the back of the book. This card includes a unique access code that enables you to activate your exams in the Pearson Test Prep software.

Accessing the Pearson Test Prep Software Online

The online version of this software can be used on any device with a browser and connectivity to the Internet, including desktop machines, tablets, and smartphones. To start using your practice exams online, simply follow these steps:

1.   Go to http://www.PearsonTestPrep.com.

2.   Select **Pearson IT Certification** as your product group.

3.   Enter your email/password for your account. If you don't have an account on PearsonITCertification.com or CiscoPress.com, you will need to establish one by going to PearsonITCertification.com/join.

4.   In the My Products tab, click the **Activate New Product** button.

5. Enter the access code printed on the insert card in the back of your book to activate your product.

6. The product will now be listed in your My Products page. Click the **Exams** button to launch the exam settings screen and start your exam.

Accessing the Pearson Test Prep Software Offline

If you wish to study offline, you can download and install the Windows version of the Pearson Test Prep software. There is a download link for this software on the book's companion website, or you can just enter the following link in your browser:

http://www.pearsonitcertification.com/content/downloads/pcpt/engine.zip

To access the book's companion website and the software, simply follow these steps:

1. Register your book by going to PearsonITCertification.com/register and entering the ISBN 978158714706.

2. Respond to the challenge questions.

3. Go to your account page and select the **Registered Products** tab.

4. Click the **Access Bonus Content** link under the product listing.

5. Click the **Install Pearson Test Prep Desktop Version** link under the Practice Exams section of the page to download the software.

6. Once the software finishes downloading, unzip all the files on your computer.

7. Double-click the application file to start the installation and then follow the onscreen instructions to complete the registration.

8. Once the installation is complete, launch the application and select the **Activate Exam** button on the My Products tab.

9. Click the **Activate a Product** button in the Activate Product Wizard.

10. Enter the unique access code found on the card in the sleeve in the back of your book and click the **Activate** button.

11. Click **Next** and then the **Finish** button to download the exam data to your application.

12. You can now start using the practice exams by selecting the product and clicking the **Open Exam** button to open the exam settings screen.

Note that the offline and online versions will synch together, so saved exams and grade results recorded on one version will be available to you on the other as well.

Customizing Your Exams

Once you are in the exam settings screen, you can choose to take exams in one of three modes:

- Study mode

- Practice Exam mode

- Flash Card mode

Study mode allows you to fully customize your exams and review answers as you are taking the exam. This is typically the mode you would use first to assess your knowledge and identify information gaps. Practice Exam mode locks certain customization options, as it is presenting a realistic exam experience. Use this mode when you are preparing to test your exam readiness. Flash Card mode strips out the answers and presents you with only the question stem. This mode is great for late-stage preparation when you really want to challenge yourself to provide answers without the benefit of seeing multiple-choice options. This mode will not provide the detailed score reports that the other two modes will, so it should not be used if you are trying to identify knowledge gaps.

In addition to these three modes, you will be able to select the source of your questions. You can choose to take exams that cover all of the chapters or you can narrow your selection to just a single chapter or the chapters that make up a specific part in the book. All chapters are selected by default. If you want to narrow your focus to individual chapters, simply deselect all the chapters then select only those on which you wish to focus in the Objectives area.

You can also select the exam banks on which to focus. Each exam bank comes complete with a full exam of questions that cover topics in every chapter. The two exams printed in the book are available to you as well as two additional exams of unique questions. You can have the test engine serve up exams from all four banks or just from one individual bank by selecting the desired banks in the exam bank area.

There are several other customizations you can make to your exam from the exam settings screen, such as the time of the exam, the number of questions served up, whether to randomize questions and answers, whether to show the number of correct answers for multiple-answer questions, and whether to serve up only specific types of questions. You can also create custom test banks by selecting only questions that you have marked or questions on which you have added notes.

Updating Your Exams

If you are using the online version of the Pearson Test Prep software, you should always have access to the latest version of the software as well as the exam data. If you are using the Windows desktop version, every time you launch the software, it will check to see if there are any updates to your exam data and automatically download any changes that were made since the last time you used the software. This requires that you are connected to the Internet at the time you launch the software.

Sometimes, due to many factors, the exam data may not fully download when you activate your exam. If you find that figures or exhibits are missing, you may need to manually update your exam.

To update a particular exam you have already activated and downloaded, simply select the **Tools** tab and select the **Update Products** button. Again, this is only an issue with the desktop Windows application.

If you wish to check for updates to the Pearson Test Prep exam engine software, Windows desktop version, simply select the **Tools** tab and select the **Update Application** button. This will ensure you are running the latest version of the software engine.

This chapter covers the following topics:

- Defining and understanding confidentiality, integrity, and availability
- Understanding threat modeling
- Defining and analyzing the attack vector
- Understanding the attack complexity
- Understanding privileges and user interaction
- Understanding the attack scope

CHAPTER 1

Threat Analysis

In this chapter, you will learn the fundamentals of threat analysis. *Cyber threat analysis* is a process that evaluates internal and external threats and vulnerabilities and matches them against real-world attacks. Ultimately, the desired result of a threat assessment is to develop best practices on how to protect your organization's assets and their availability, confidentiality, and integrity, without hindering usability and functionality.

"Do I Know This Already?" Quiz

The "Do I Know This Already?" quiz helps you identify your strengths and deficiencies in this chapter's topics. The 10-question quiz, derived from the major sections in the "Foundation Topics" portion of the chapter, helps you determine how to spend your limited study time. Table 1-1 outlines the major topics discussed in this chapter and the "Do I Know This Already?" quiz questions that correspond to those topics.

Table 1-1 "Do I Know This Already?" Foundation Topics Section-to-Question Mapping

Foundation Topics Section	Questions Covered in This Section
What Is the CIA Triad: Confidentiality, Integrity, and Availability?	1–2
Threat Modeling	3–5
Defining and Analyzing the Attack Vector	6–7
Understanding the Attack Complexity	8
Privileges and User Interaction	9
The Attack Scope	10

1. You must have adequate control mechanisms in order to enforce and ensure that data is only accessed by the individuals who should be allowed to access it and nobody else. Which of the following techniques can be used to prevent any attacks that could impact confidentiality?

   a. Secure routing protocols

   b. Network scanners

   c. Encryption

   d. Metasploit

2. Which of the following statements is not true about integrity protection?

   a. Integrity protection encompasses only data and information.

   b. Integrity protection encompasses more than just data; it not only protects data, but also operating systems, applications, and hardware from being altered by unauthorized individuals.

   c. Integrity protection encompasses more than just data; it not only protects data, but also operating systems, applications, and hardware from being altered by authorized individuals.

   d. Integrity protection can only be applied to protect operating systems, applications, and hardware from being altered by unauthorized individuals.

3. Which of the following are examples of threat modeling techniques? (Select all that apply.)

   a. STRIDE

   b. STRIKE

   c. DREAD

   d. THREAD

4. Which of the following is not a component of DREAD?

   a. Damage potential

   b. Reproducibility

   c. Prosecution

   d. Discoverability

5. Which of the following is not a component of STRIDE?

   a. SQL injection

   b. Tampering

   c. Repudiation

   d. Information disclosure

   e. Denial of service

6. Which of the following are examples of attack vectors? (Select all that apply.)

   a. A malicious email attachment or a malicious link on an email

   b. Malicious web page content

   c. A vulnerable or compromised network service used maliciously

   d. The Common Vulnerability Scoring System (CVSS)

7. Which of the following is not an example of a tool that can help analyze the attack surface of a system?

   a. Web application scanner

   b. Fuzzer

   c. The Common Vulnerability Assessment Language (CVAL)

   d. Network scanner

8. Which of the following is true about the attack complexity in terms of threat analysis?

   a. The attack complexity is categorized as high when specialized access conditions or mitigating circumstances do not exist.

   b. The attack complexity is categorized as low when specialized access conditions or mitigating circumstances do not exist.

   c. The attack complexity is changed if the attacker fails to launch the attack.

   d. The attack complexity is dependent on the attack scope.

9. Which of the following is not true about privileges and user interaction in terms of threat analysis?

   a. The risk is considered low if the attacker is required to have privileges or system credentials on the system, in order to launch the attack.

   b. The risk is considered high if the attacker is already authorized or is required to have privileges on the system.

   c. The risk is high if the attack does not require the attacker to be authenticated or have significant (for example, administrative) control over the vulnerable system.

   d. CVSS version 3 also includes the requirements of privileges in its base metrics.

10. What is an example of a vulnerability that could lead to an attack scope change?

    a. VM injection

    b. VM escape

    c. Denial of service

    d. SQL injection

Foundation Topics

What Is the CIA Triad: Confidentiality, Integrity, and Availability?

The three fundamental security control principles are confidentiality, integrity, and availability. Collectively, these are often referred to as the "CIA triad." This threat is illustrated in Figure 1-1.

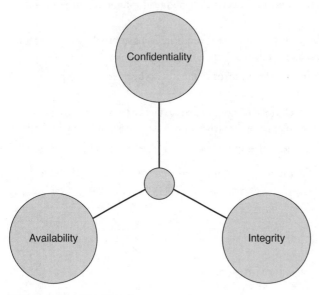

Figure 1-1 *CIA Triad*

Threat analysis embraces the identification of threats that can negatively impact the availability, integrity, and confidentiality of assets and also identifies protection and mitigation capabilities.

Confidentiality

Confidentiality is the promise that data is not unveiled to unauthorized users, applications, or processes. Depending on the type of information, a higher level of confidentiality might be required, depending on how sensitive it is. You must have adequate control mechanisms in place to enforce and ensure that data is only accessed by the individuals who should be allowed to access it and no one else. Also, you must enforce what the users can do with that data once they have accessed it. Another important part of confidentiality is that all sensitive data needs to be controlled, audited, and monitored at all times. Here are some examples of sensitive data:

- Social security numbers
- Bank and credit card account information
- Criminal records

- Patient and health records
- Trade secrets
- Source code
- Military secrets

The following are examples of security mechanisms designed to preserve confidentiality:

- Logical and physical access controls
- Encryption (in motion and at rest)
- Database views
- Controlled traffic routing

Data classification is important when you're deciding how to protect data. By having a good data classification methodology, you can enhance the way you secure your data across your network and systems.

Many organizations deploy virtual private networks (VPNs) between their sites using IPSec. In some cases, they also use internal site-to-site tunnels to protect their sensitive data. The VPN tunnel is an example of encryption while data is in motion.

Integrity

Integrity is the next component of the CIA triad. It is very important that systems and the data they maintain are accurate, complete, and protected from unauthorized modification. Integrity protection encompasses more than just data; it not only protects data, but also operating systems, applications, and hardware from being altered by unauthorized individuals. For example, what if a router is modified to send data to a destination that it was not intended to? What if a confidential email is modified by an attacker before it reaches its originally intended recipient? What if an Internet of Things (IoT) device, such as an IP camera, is modified to send crafted packets to a victim and cause a denial-of-service condition? All these are examples of integrity compromises of a system or data.

Availability

The last component of the CIA triad is availability, which states that systems, applications, and data must be available to users without impacting productivity. The most common attack against availability is a denial-of-service (DoS) attack. User productivity can be greatly affected, and companies can lose a lot of money if data is not available. For example, if you are an online retailer or a cloud service provider and your ecommerce site or service is not available to your users, you could potentially lose current or future business, thus impacting revenue.

You have to understand the various security technologies, methodologies, policies, and procedures that can provide different levels of availability, integrity, and confidentiality protection. Your security goals must be evaluated to ensure the proper security mechanisms are put into place to always protect against threats that could affect the CIA triad.

Threat Modeling

Risk analysis is crucial. You need to know what you are protecting and how you are protecting it. What are your critical systems and assets? What constitutes your organization today? These are some initial questions you should ask yourself when starting any risk analysis process. You must know the difference between threats and vulnerabilities. *Threats* are occurrences that can affect a system or an organization as a whole. Examples of threats include fraud, theft of information, and physical theft. *Vulnerabilities* are flaws that make a system, an individual, or an organization exposed and susceptible to a threat or an attack.

> **TIP**   It is very important that you "think" like an attacker to better understand the safeguards needed in order to protect your systems and data.

Typically, when you ask security engineers, managers, architects, and executives to list or describe the critical systems of their organization, their answers are contradictory. One of the main goals that members of an organization should have is to understand their environment to better comprehend what they are trying to protect and what risks are most imminent.

Several methods of risk analysis have been published in books, websites, magazines, and blogs. Some take the quantitative approach, some take the qualitative approach, and others measure impact versus probability.

 The primary goal of any threat modeling technique is to develop a formal process while identifying, documenting, and mitigating security threats. This process has a huge impact on any organization because it is basically a methodology used to understand how attacks can take place and how they will impact the network, systems, and users. Organizations have adopted several threat modeling techniques. For example, Microsoft uses the DREAD model. The DREAD acronym defines five key areas:

- Damage potential
- Reproducibility
- Exploitability
- Affected users
- Discoverability

In the DREAD model, the first step is to quantify or estimate the damage potential of a specific threat. This estimate can include monetary and productivity costs, followed by a probability study on the reproducibility and exploitability of the vulnerability at hand. In addition, the first step should identify which users and systems will be affected and how easily the threat can be discovered and identified.

You can find more information about Microsoft threat modeling at https://msdn.microsoft.com/en-us/library/ff648644.aspx. Microsoft also has a threat modeling tool at https://www.microsoft.com/en-us/download/details.aspx?id=49168.

Another very popular threat modeling technique is STRIDE, which stands for spoofing, tampering, repudiation, information disclosure, denial of service, and elevation of privilege. STRIDE was created by Loren Kohnfelder and Praerit Garg. This is a framework designed to help software developers identify the types of threats against the applications they are creating. The following are the different components of STRIDE:

- **Spoofing:** Sometimes referred to as *identify spoofing*. Attackers can disguise themselves as someone else. They can also disguise their systems as some other systems. For instance, in many distributed denial-of-service (DDoS) attacks, attackers can spoof the source of the attacks (that is, the IP addresses of the attacking machines or bots) in order to carry out the attack and maintain anonymity. This is why systems should have protection in place against spoofing attacks—and not just for DDoS. In general, users should not be able to become any other users or assume the attributes of other users, period.

- **Tampering:** This ties into the discussion earlier in this chapter about integrity. Users must not be able to tamper with data, applications, or systems. In threat modeling, you must understand what threats could allow an attacker to tamper with data, applications, or systems in your organization.

- **Repudiation:** You must consider if the system or applications requires nonrepudiation controls, such as system logs, web access logs, and audit trails. Another consideration is that an application should run with the user's privileges, not more.

- **Information disclosure:** You must make sure that a system or application does not disclose information that is not intended. For example, a web application should not store usernames and passwords in its source. Also, user credentials should not be stored in logs or in any other configuration or troubleshooting feature in plain text.

- **Denial of service:** You should evaluate what threats can cause a denial-of-service condition. This is beyond just performance testing and should employ methodologies such as fuzzing (sending random data to an application or protocol).

- **Elevation of privilege:** It is very important that you ensure in any application or system that users cannot elevate their privileges. Many organizations develop an authorization matrix to ensure that only authorized users and roles can access privileged functionality.

Another threat modeling technique is to create attack trees. Bruce Schneier, the chief technology officer of Counterpane Internet Security and the inventor of the Blowfish and Twofish encryption algorithms, initially introduced this method. Attack trees represent attacks against a system or network in a hierarchical tree structure. The root node describes a goal, and the leaf nodes are various ways of reaching such a goal. For example, the main goal of a specific attack may be to interrupt the services of an ecommerce web server farm. This goal will be the root of the tree. Each subsequent "tree branch or leaf" describes the methods used to take down that web server farm (such as sending millions of spoofed TCP packets, compromising zombies on the Internet to launch DDoS attacks, and so on).

A detailed white paper on attack trees by Bruce Schneier is posted at http://www.schneier.com/paper-attacktrees-ddj-ft.html.

Several other threat modeling techniques suggest the use and understanding of system and device roles. You need to identify what the network devices do and how they are used and placed within the infrastructure. You should also document and identify their functionality in the context of the organization as a whole; furthermore, you need to configure them according to their role. For example, the configuration used for Internet-edge routers is not suitable for data center devices. In addition, you should create easy-to-understand architecture diagrams that describe the composition and structure of your infrastructure and its devices, and then elaborate the diagram by adding details about the trust boundaries, authentication, and authorization mechanisms.

The following are great resources that you should become familiar with and that may help you study for the exam:

- **OWASP threat modeling site**: https://www.owasp.org/index.php/Threat_Risk_Modeling
- **SANS threat modeling whitepaper**: https://www.sans.org/reading-room/whitepapers/securecode/threat-modeling-process-ensure-application-security-1646
- **SANS practical analysis and threat modeling spreadsheet**: https://cyber-defense.sans.org/blog/2009/07/11/practical-risk-analysis-spreadsheet
- **NIST Special Publication 800-154: Guide to Data-Centric System Threat Modeling**: http://csrc.nist.gov/publications/drafts/800-154/sp800_154_draft.pdf

Defining and Analyzing the Attack Vector

According to NIST, an *attack vector* is "a segment of the entire pathway that an attack uses to access a vulnerability. Each attack vector can be thought of as comprising a source of malicious content, a potentially vulnerable processor of that malicious content, and the nature of the malicious content itself." The following are a few examples of attack vectors:

- A malicious email attachment or a malicious link on an email.
- Malicious web page content
- A vulnerable or compromised network service used maliciously
- A social engineering conversation by a threat actor done in person or by phone, email, text, or instant messaging to obtain sensitive information from the user, such as credentials, date of birth, account information, social security numbers, and so on.
- Personal information gathered by a threat actor from social media to carry out a targeted attack.
- An open port on a system that could lead to services being exposed to an attacker.
- A database with default or no credentials.
- An infrastructure device with default or easily guessable credentials.

Many other terms are used when describing attack vectors. In addition to studying and understanding attack vectors is analyzing all of the attack vectors directly against a particular system. This methodology is often referred to as the system's "attack surface."

In order to measure and understand the attack surface, you can read through the source code of an application and identify different points of entry and exit, including the following:

- Application programming interfaces (APIs)
- Databases

- Email or other kinds of messages
- Files
- Other local storage
- Runtime arguments
- User interface (UI) forms and fields

It is important to understand that the total number of different attack entry or exit points can be numbered in the dozens, hundreds, or even thousands, depending on the system or application's complexity. Sometimes this will feel like an unmanageable task. In order to make this task more manageable, you can break the model into different categories, depending on the function, design, and technology. Here are some examples:

- Admin interfaces
- Business workflows
- Data entry (CRUD) forms
- Inquiries and search functions
- Interfaces with other applications/systems
- Login/authentication entry points
- Operational command and monitoring interfaces/APIs
- Transactional interfaces/APIs

Several tools can accelerate your analysis of the overall attack surface of a system or application. These include network and vulnerability scanners such as the following:

- nmap
- Nessus
- Nexpose
- Qualys

You can also use web application scanners such as these:

- OWASP_Zed_Attack_Proxy_Project
- Arachni
- Skipfish
- w3af
- Several commercial dynamic testing and vulnerability scanning tools such as IBM AppScan

NOTE   You learned different examples of network and application scanners while preparing for the CCNA Cyber Ops SECFND exam.

Understanding the Attack Complexity

The attack complexity describes the conditions beyond the attacker's control that must exist in order to exploit a given vulnerability. For example, an attacker may need to collect additional information about the target, including network topologies, specific system configurations, and computational exceptions. The Common Vulnerability Scoring System (CVSS) base metrics analyze the attack complexity. CVSS is an industry standard maintained by the Forum of Incident Response and Security Teams (FIRST) that is used by many product security incident response teams (PSIRTs) to convey information about the severity of the vulnerabilities they disclose to their customers.

> **TIP**   Although you learned about CVSS when studying for the CCNA Cyber Ops SECFND exam, Chapter 6 includes additional details about the standard. For the SECOPS exam, you must also be familiar with the CVSS metrics, as covered in Chapter 6 and also at FIRST's website at https://www.first.org/cvss/specification-document.

The attack complexity is categorized as low when specialized access conditions or mitigating circumstances do not exist. When the attack complexity is low, the attacker or threat actor can carry out the attack in a consistent and repeatable manner. When the attack complexity is considered high, the attack depends on conditions beyond the attacker's control. For instance, a successful attack probably cannot be executed successfully or a vulnerability exploited without the attacker having to invest some time and effort in preparing and orchestrating the attack. Here are a few examples:

- The need for the attacker to obtain additional configuration information, sequence numbers, and credentials.

- The need for an attacker to "win" a race condition and/or overcome advanced exploit mitigation techniques.

- The need for the threat actor to place him- or herself into the logical network path between the victim and the destination or resource that victim is trying to access. This is done in order to read and/or modify network communications, and is referred to as a *man-in-the-middle attack*.

 ## Privileges and User Interaction

The risk of a specific threat or vulnerability can increase depending on the requirements around privileges and user interaction—in other words, depending on if the attacker needs to have user credentials prior to successfully launching the attack or if the attacker can launch the attack without authentication. The risk is considered low if the attacker is required to have privileges or system credentials on the system in order to launch the attack. On the contrary, the risk is high if the attack does not require the attacker to be authenticated or have significant (for example, administrative) control over the vulnerable system.

CVSS version 3 also includes the requirements of privileges in its base metrics.

The Attack Scope

It is also important that you understand the attack scope and how an attack or vulnerability can impact resources beyond the attacker's means or privileges. The attack scope is also represented in CVSS by the base metric Authorization Scope, or simply Scope. CVSS defines scope as "when the vulnerability of a software component governed by one authorization scope is able to affect resources governed by another authorization scope, a Scope change has occurred."

A good example of a scope change is when an attacker is able to break out of a sandbox. Another example is when an attacker can perform a virtual machine (VM) escape (see Figure 1-2). In other words, when the attacker compromises a VM and then is able to access, modify, or delete files on the host operating system (hypervisor), thereby getting access to all VMs on the host machine.

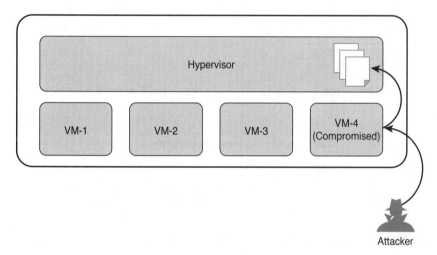

Figure 1-2 *VM Escape*

If an attack or exploited vulnerability can only affect resources managed by the same authority, the scope is not changed. When such a vulnerability can affect resources beyond the authorization privileges intended by the vulnerable component, then the scope is considered to be changed.

Exam Preparation Tasks

Review All Key Topics

Review the most important topics in the chapter, noted with the Key Topic icon in the outer margin of the page. Table 1-2 lists these key topics and the page numbers on which each is found.

Table 1-2   Key Topics

Key Topic Element	Description	Page
Summary	What is confidentiality?	6
Summary	What is integrity?	7
Summary	What is availability?	7
Summary	Threat modeling	8
Paragraph	What is DREAD?	8
Paragraph	What is STRIDE?	9
Paragraph	What are attack trees?	9
Paragraph	What is an attack vector?	10
Summary	Understanding the attack complexity	12
Summary	Attacks, privileges, and user interaction	12
Paragraph	Define and understand the scope of an attack	13

Complete Tables and Lists from Memory

Print a copy of Appendix B, "Memory Tables and Lists," (found on the book website), or at least the section for this chapter, and complete the tables and lists from memory. Appendix C, "Memory Tables and Lists Answer Key," also on the website, includes completed tables and lists to check your work.

Define Key Terms

Define the following key terms from this chapter, and check your answers in the glossary:

confidentiality, integrity, availability, attack vector, STRIDE

Q&A

The answers to these questions appear in Appendix A, "Answers to the 'Do I Know This Already' Quizzes and Q&A." For more practice with exam format questions, use the exam engine on the website.

1. A denial-of-service attack against a web server affects which of the following?
   a. Availability
   b. Confidentiality
   c. Integrity
   d. Repudiation

2. An attacker is able to compromise a system and change files in the affected system. Which of the following is affected?
   a. Availability
   b. Confidentiality
   c. Integrity
   d. Repudiation

3. An attacker is able to eavesdrop on the conversation between two users launching a man-in-the-middle attack. Which of the following is affected?
   a. Availability
   b. Confidentiality
   c. Integrity
   d. Repudiation

4. Which of the following is an example of an attack whose scope has been potentially changed?
   a. An attack against a VM escape vulnerability
   b. A denial-of-service attack
   c. A spoofing attack
   d. A man-in-the-middle attack

5. Which of the following are examples of thread modeling techniques? (Select all that apply.)
   a. STRIDE
   b. DREAD
   c. SREAD
   d. SDL

6. Which of the following is not an attack vector?
   a. Malicious web page content
   b. A malicious email attachment or a malicious link on an email
   c. DDoS
   d. Social engineering conversation by a threat actor done in person or by phone, email, text, or instant messaging to obtain sensitive information from the user such as credentials, date of birth, account information, social security numbers, and so on.

This chapter covers the following exam topics:

- Introduction to cybersecurity forensics
- The role of attribution in a cybersecurity investigation
- The use of digital evidence
- Fundamentals of Microsoft Windows forensics
- Fundamentals of Linux forensics

CHAPTER 2

Forensics

This chapter introduces cybersecurity forensics and defines the role of attribution in a cybersecurity investigation. You will also learn the use of digital evidence as well as the fundamentals of Microsoft Windows and Linux forensics.

"Do I Know This Already?" Quiz

The "Do I Know This Already?" quiz helps you identify your strengths and deficiencies in this chapter's topics. The 10-question quiz, derived from the major sections in the "Foundation Topics" portion of the chapter, helps you determine how to spend your limited study time. Table 2-1 outlines the major topics discussed in this chapter and the "Do I Know This Already?" quiz questions that correspond to those topics.

Table 2-1 "Do I Know This Already?" Foundation Topics Section-to-Question Mapping

Foundation Topics Section	Questions Covered in This Section
Introduction to Cybersecurity Forensics	1–2
The Role of Attribution in a Cybersecurity Investigation	3
The Use of Digital Evidence	4
Fundamentals of Microsoft Windows Forensics	5–7
Fundamentals of Linux Forensics	8–10

1. Which of the following are the three broad categories of cybersecurity investigations?

   a. Public, private, and individual investigations

   b. Judiciary, private, and individual investigations

   c. Public, private, and corporate investigations

   d. Government, corporate, and private investigations

2. In addition to cybercrime and attacks, evidence found on a system or network may be presented in a court of law to support accusations of crime or civil action, including which of the following?

   a. Fraud, money laundering, and theft

   b. Drug-related crime

   c. Murder and acts of violence

   d. All of the above

3. Which of the following is true about attribution in a cybersecurity investigation?

    a. A suspect-led approach is often accepted in supreme courts.

    b. A suspect-led approach is pejorative and often biased to the disadvantage of those being investigated.

    c. A suspect-led approach is mostly used in corporate investigations.

    d. A suspect-led approach is mostly used in private investigations.

4. Which of the following is *not* true regarding the use of digital evidence?

    a. Digital forensics evidence provides implications and extrapolations that may assist in proving some key fact of the case.

    b. Digital evidence helps legal teams and the court develop reliable hypotheses or theories as to the committer of the crime or threat actor.

    c. The reliability of the digital evidence is vital to supporting or refuting any hypothesis put forward, including the attribution of threat actors.

    d. The reliability of the digital evidence is not as important as someone's testimony to supporting or refuting any hypothesis put forward, including the attribution of threat actors.

5. Which of the following statements is true about processes and threads?

    a. Each thread starts with a single process, known as the primary process, but can also create additional processes from any of its services.

    b. Each service starts with a single hive, known as the primary hive, but can also create additional threads from any of its hives.

    c. Each process starts with a single thread, known as the primary thread, but can also create additional threads from any of its threads.

    d. Each hive starts with a single thread, known as the primary thread, but can also create additional threads from any of its threads.

6. What is a job in Microsoft Windows?

    a. A job is a group of threads.

    b. A job is a group of hives.

    c. A job is a group of services.

    d. A job is a group of processes.

7. Which of the following file systems is more secure, scalable, and advanced?

    a. FAT32

    b. FAT64

    c. uFAT

    d. NTFS

8. Which of the following Linux file systems not only supports journaling but also modifies important data structures of the file system, such as the ones destined to store the file data for better performance and reliability?

   a. GRUB

   b. LILO

   c. Ext4

   d. FAT32

9. Which of the following are examples of Linux boot loaders?

   a. GRUB

   b. ILOS

   c. LILO

   d. Ubuntu BootPro

10. Which of the following is true about journaling?

   a. The journal is the least used part of the disk, making the blocks that form part of it more prone to hardware failure.

   b. The journal is the most used part of the disk, making the blocks that form part of it less prone to hardware failure.

   c. The journal is the most used part of the disk, making the blocks that form part of it more prone to hardware failure.

   d. The journal is the least used part of the disk, making the blocks that form part of it less prone to hardware failure.

Foundation Topics

Introduction to Cybersecurity Forensics

Cybersecurity forensics (or digital forensics) has been of growing interest among many organizations and individuals due to the large number of breaches during the last few years. Many folks choose digital forensics as a career path in law enforcement and corporate investigations. During the last few years, many technologies and forensic processes have been designed to meet the growing number of cases relying on digital evidence. There is a shortage of well-trained, experienced personnel who are experts in cybersecurity forensics.

Cybersecurity forensic practitioners are at a crossroads in terms of changes affecting evidence recovery and management. Forensic evidence is often used in a court of law. This is why it is extremely important for digital forensic experts to perform an excellent analysis and collect and maintain reliable evidence. Also, the huge increase in cybercrime has accelerated the need for enhanced information security management. It also requires forensics experts to help remediate the network and affected systems and try to reveal the responsible threat actor. This is often called *threat actor attribution*. Desktops, laptops, mobile devices, servers, firewall logs, and logs from network infrastructure devices are rich in information of evidentiary value that can assist forensics experts in reconstructing the attack and gain a better understanding of the threat actor responsible for the attack.

There are three broad categories of cybersecurity investigations:

- **Public investigations:** These investigations are resolved in the court of law.
- **Private investigations:** These are corporate investigations.
- **Individual investigations:** These investigations often take the form of ediscovery.

In addition to cybercrime and attacks, evidence found on a system or network may be presented in a court of law to support accusations of crime or civil action, including but not limited to the following:

- Extortion
- Domestic violence
- Fraud, money laundering, and theft
- Drug-related crime
- Murder and acts of violence
- Pedophilia and cyber stalking
- Sabotage
- Terrorism

Usually, criminal investigations and prosecutions involve government agencies that work within the framework of criminal law. Cybersecurity forensic practitioners are expected to provide evidence that may help the court make their decision in the investigated case. Also, practitioners must constantly be aware of and comply with regulations and laws during case examination and evidence presentation. It is important to know that factors detrimental to the disclosure of digital evidence include the knowledge of exculpatory evidence that would challenge the evidence.

The Role of Attribution in a Cybersecurity Investigation

One of the key topics in cybersecurity forensics is attribution of assets and threat actors. There is undeniable motivation to support an evidence-led approach to cybersecurity forensics to achieve good attribution. A suspect-led approach is pejorative and often biased to the disadvantage of those being investigated. Due to the large number of technical complexities, it is often impractical for cybersecurity forensics experts to determine fully the reliability of endpoints, servers, or network infrastructure devices and provide assurances to the court about the soundness of the processes involved and the complete attribution to a threat actor.

The forensics expert needs to ensure that not one part of the examination process is overlooked or repetitive. In addition, cybersecurity forensic experts are often confronted with the inefficacy of traditional security processes in systems and networks designed to preserve documents and network functionality—especially because most systems are not designed to enhance digital evidence recovery. There is a need for appropriate cybersecurity forensic tools, including software imaging and the indexing of increasingly large datasets in order to successfully reconstruct an attack and attribute the attack to an asset or threat actor. One thing to keep in mind is that traditional digital forensics tools are typically designed to obtain the "lowest-hanging fruit" and encourage security professionals to look for the evidence that is easiest to identify and recover. Often, these tools do not have the capability to even recognize other, less-obvious evidence.

The Use of Digital Evidence

During cybersecurity investigations, the forensics expert may revisit portions of the evidence to determine its validity. As a result, additional investigation might be required, which often can be a tedious process. In some cases, the complexity of the network and the time required for the investigation can affect the efficacy of the cybersecurity forensics professional to reconstruct and provide an accurate interpretation of the evidence. From a practical and realistic perspective, the amount of time and effort involved in the digital forensic process should pass an acceptable "reasonableness test." In other words, all imaginable effort shouldn't be put into finding all conceivable traces of evidence and then seizing and analyzing it. This is especially becoming more challenging for the cybersecurity forensics expert as the volume of data to be analyzed becomes too big.

Evidence in cybersecurity investigations that go to court is used to prove (or disprove) facts that are in dispute, as well as to prove the credibility of disputed facts (in particular, circumstantial evidence or indirect evidence). Digital forensics evidence provides implications and extrapolations that may assist in proving some key fact of the case. Such evidence helps legal teams and the court develop reliable hypotheses or theories as to the committer of the crime (threat actor). The reliability of the evidence is vital to supporting or refuting any hypothesis put forward, including the attribution of threat actors.

Defining Digital Forensic Evidence

Digital forensic evidence is information in digital form found on a wide range of endpoint, server, and network devices—basically, any information that can be processed by a computing device or stored on other media. Evidence tendered in legal cases, such as criminal trials, is classified as witness testimony or direct evidence, or as indirect evidence in the form of an object, such as a physical document, the property owned by a person, and so forth. Cybersecurity forensic evidence can take many forms, depending on the conditions of each case and the devices from which the evidence was collected.

Understanding Best, Corroborating, and Indirect or Circumstantial Evidence

There are three general types of evidence:

- Best evidence
- Corroborating evidence
- Indirect or circumstantial evidence

Historically, the term *best evidence* refers to evidence that can be presented in court in the original form (for example, an exact copy of a hard disk drive). However, in cyber forensics, what is the original when it comes to digital photography, copier machines, computer storage, and cloud storage? Typically, properly collected system images and appropriate copies of files can be used in court.

Corroborating evidence (or corroboration) is evidence that tends to support a theory or an assumption deduced by some initial evidence. This corroborating evidence confirms the proposition.

Indirect or circumstantial evidence relies on an extrapolation to a conclusion of fact (such as fingerprints, DNA evidence, and so on). This is, of course, different from direct evidence. Direct evidence supports the truth of a proclamation without need for any additional evidence or interpretation. Forensic evidence provided by an expert witness is typically considered circumstantial evidence. Indirect or circumstantial evidence is often used in civil and criminal cases that lack direct evidence.

> **TIP** Digital information that is stored in electronic databases and computer-generated audit logs and does not contain information generated by humans has been challenged in some court trials. Law enforcement and courts can also demand proof that the creation and storage of evidence records are part of the organization's business activities.

Collecting Evidence from Endpoints and Servers

Again, cybersecurity forensic evidence can take many forms, depending on the conditions of each case and the devices from which the evidence was collected. To prevent or minimize contamination of the suspect's source device, you can use different tools, such as a piece of hardware called a write blocker, on the specific device so you can copy all the data (or an image of the system).

The imaging process is intended to copy all blocks of data from the computing device to the forensics professional evidentiary system. This is sometimes referred to as a "physical copy" of all data, as distinct from a logical copy, which only copies what a user would normally see. Logical copies do not capture all the data, and the process will alter some file metadata to the extent that its forensic value is greatly diminished, resulting in a possible legal challenge by the opposing legal team. Therefore, a full bit-for-bit copy is the preferred forensic process. The file created on the target device is called a forensic image file. The following are the most common file types for forensic images:

- .AFF
- .ASB
- .E01
- .DD or raw image files
- Virtual image formats such as .VMDK and .VDI

The benefit of being able to make an exact copy of the data is that the data can be copied and the original device can be returned to the owner or stored for trial, normally without having to be examined repeatedly. This reduces the likelihood of drive failure or evidence contamination.

SANS has a good resource that goes over disk imaging tools in cyber forensics at https://www.sans.org/reading-room/whitepapers/incident/overview-disk-imaging-tool-computer-forensics-643.

In short, imaging or disk imaging is the process of making a forensically sound copy to media that can retain the data for an extended amount of time. One of the things to be careful about is to make sure that the disk imaging does not alter the layout of the copy or even omit free and deleted space. It is very important to have a forensically sound copy of the original evidence and only work from that copy to avoid making changes or altering the original image. In addition, you must use appropriate media to avoid any alteration or contamination of the evidence. The original copy should be placed in secure storage or a safe.

There is also the process of file deletion and its degradation and eventual erasure through system operation. This results in many files being partly stored in the unallocated area of a system's hard disk drive. Typically, such fragments of files can only be located and "carved out" manually using a hex editor that's able to identify file headers, footers, and segments held in the image. This is because the file system allocation information is not typically available and results in a very labor-intensive and challenging operation for the forensics professional. File carving continues to be an important process that's used in many cases where the recovery of alleged deleted files is required. Different forensic tools are available, such as ILookIX, EnCase, and others. These tools provide features that allow you to locate blocks and sectors of hard disk drives that could contain deleted information that's important. Recovering files from unallocated space is usually referred to as *data carving*.

It is very important to make sure that the timestamps of all files on a system being analyzed during any cyber forensics investigation are reliable. This is critical for making a valid reconstruction of key events of the attack or security incident.

Collecting Evidence from Mobile Devices

Mobile devices such as cell phones, wearables, and tablets are not imaged in the same way as desktops. Also, today's Internet of Things (IoT) world is very different from just a few years ago. Now we have to worry about collecting evidence from low-power and low-resource devices (including sensors, fog edge devices, and so on). The hardware and interfaces of these devices, from a forensic perspective, are very different. For example, an iPhone cannot be accessed unless you know the manufacturing password from Apple. Apple uses a series of encrypted sectors located on microchips, making it difficult to access the raw data inside the phone. Newer Android versions similarly prevent more than a backup being taken of the device and no longer allow physical dumps to be recovered.

In some cases, not only does evidence need to be collected from mobile devices, but also from mobile device management (MDM) applications and solutions.

Collecting Evidence from Network Infrastructure Devices

You can collect a lot of information from network infrastructure devices, such as routers, switches, wireless LAN controllers, load balancers, firewalls, and many others that can be very beneficial for cybersecurity forensics investigations. Collecting all this data can be easier said than done, which is why it is important to have one or more systems as a central log repository and to configure all your network devices to forward events to this central log analysis tool. You should also make sure it can hold several months' worth of events. As you learned during your preparation for the SECFND exam, syslog is often used to central-ize events. You should also increase the types of events that are logged—for example, DHCP events, NetFlow, VPN logs, and so on.

Another important thing to keep in mind is that network devices can also be compromised by threat actors. Subsequently, the data generated by these devices can also be assumed to be compromised and manipulated by the attacker. Finding forensic evidence for these inci-dents can become much harder.

Network infrastructure devices can be compromised by different attack methods, including the following:

- Leftover troubleshooting commands
- Manipulating Cisco IOS images
- Security vulnerabilities

Cisco has several good resources that go over device integrity assurance and verification. These resources can be found at the following links:

- **Cisco IOS Software Integrity Assurance**

    http://www.cisco.com/c/en/us/about/security-center/integrity-assurance.html

- **Cisco IOS XE Software Integrity Assurance**

    http://www.cisco.com/web/about/security/intelligence/ios-xe-integrity-assurance.html

- **Cisco Guide to Harden Cisco IOS Devices**

    http://www.cisco.com/c/en/us/support/docs/ip/access-lists/13608-21.html

- **Cisco IOS Image Verification**

  http://www.cisco.com/web/about/security/intelligence/iosimage.html

- **Offline Analysis of IOS Image Integrity Blog**

  http://blogs.cisco.com/security/offline-analysis-of-ios-image-integrity

- **Securing Tool Command Language on Cisco IOS**

  http://www.cisco.com/web/about/security/intelligence/securetcl.html

- **Cisco Security Vulnerability Policy**

  http://www.cisco.com/web/about/security/psirt/security_vulnerability_policy.html

- **Use of the Configuration Register on All Cisco Routers**

  http://www.cisco.com/c/en/us/support/docs/routers/10000-series-routers/50421-config-register-use.html

- **Digitally Signed Cisco Software**

  http://www.cisco.com/c/en/us/td/docs/ios-xml/ios/sys-image-mgmt/configuration/15-mt/sysimgmgmt-15-mt-book/sysimgmgmt-dgtly-sgnd-sw.html

- **Cisco IOS Software Checker**

  http://tools.cisco.com/security/center/selectIOSVersion.x

- **Creating Core Dumps**

  http://www.cisco.com/en/US/docs/internetworking/troubleshooting/guide/tr19aa.html

- **Cisco IOS Configuration Guide**

  http://www.cisco.com/c/en/us/support/ios-nx-os-software/ios-15-3m-t/products-installation-and-configuration-guides-list.html

- **MD5 File Validation**

  http://www.cisco.com/c/en/us/td/docs/ios-xml/ios/sys-image-mgmt/configuration/15-mt/sysimgmgmt-15-mt-book/sysimgmgmt-md5.html

- **Image Verification**

  http://www.cisco.com/c/en/us/td/docs/ios-xml/ios/sec_usr_cfg/configuration/15-mt/sec-usr-cfg-15-mt-book/sec-image-verifctn.html

- **Telemetry-Based Infrastructure Device Integrity Monitoring**

  http://www.cisco.com/web/about/security/intelligence/network-integrity-monitoring.html

- **Cisco Supply Chain Security**

  http://www.cisco.com/web/about/doing_business/trust-center/built-in-security/supply-chain-security.html

These documents go over numerous identification techniques, including the following:

- Image file verification using the Message Digest 5 file validation feature
- Using the image verification feature
- Using offline image file hashes
- Verifying authenticity for digitally signed images
- Cisco IOS runtime memory integrity verification using core dumps

- Creating a known-good text region
- Text memory section export
- Cisco address space layout randomization considerations
- Different indicators of compromise
- Unusual and suspicious commands
- Checking that Cisco IOS software call stacks are within the text section boundaries
- Checking command history in the Cisco IOS core dump
- Checking the command history
- Checking external accounting logs
- Checking external syslog logs
- Checking booting information
- Checking the ROM monitor variable
- Checking the ROM monitor information

You can take several preventive steps to facilitate a forensic investigation of network devices, including the following security best practices:

- Maintaining Cisco IOS image file integrity
- Implementing change control
- Hardening the software distribution server
- Keeping Cisco IOS software updated
- Deploying digitally signed Cisco IOS images
- Using Cisco Secure Boot
- Using Cisco Supply Chain Security
- Leveraging the Latest Cisco IOS security protection features
- Using authentication, authorization, and accounting
- Using TACACS+ authorization to restrict commands
- Implementing credentials management
- Implementing configuration controls
- Protecting interactive access to devices
- Gaining traffic visibility with NetFlow
- Using centralized and comprehensive logging

Chain of Custody

Chain of custody is the way you document and preserve evidence from the time that you started the cyber forensics investigation to the time the evidence is presented in court. It is extremely important to be able to show clear documentation of the following:

- How the evidence was collected
- When it was collected

- How it was transported
- How is was tracked
- How it was stored
- Who had access to the evidence and how it was accessed

TIP   If you fail to maintain proper chain of custody, it is likely you will not be able to use the evidence in court. It is also important to know how to dispose of evidence after an investigation.

When you collect evidence, you must protect its integrity. This involves making sure that nothing is added to the evidence and that nothing is deleted or destroyed (this is known as *evidence preservation*).

TIP   A method often used for evidence preservation is to only work with a copy of the evidence—in other words, you do not want to work directly with the evidence itself. This involves creating an image of any hard drive or any storage device.

Several forensics tools are available on the market. The following are two of the most popular:

- Guidance Software's EnCase (https://www.guidancesoftware.com/)
- AccessData's Forensic Toolkit (http://accessdata.com/)

Another methodology used in evidence preservation is to use write-protected storage devices. In other words, the storage device you are investigating should immediately be write-protected before it is imaged and should be labeled to include the following:

- Investigator's name
- The date when the image was created
- Case name and number (if applicable)

Additionally, you must prevent electronic static or other discharge from damaging or erasing evidentiary data. Special evidence bags that are antistatic should be used to store digital devices. It is very important that you prevent electrostatic discharge (ESD) and other electrical discharges from damaging your evidence. Some organizations even have cyber forensic labs that control access to only authorized users and investigators. One method often used involves constructing what is called a Faraday cage. This "cage" is often built out of a mesh of conducting material that prevents electromagnetic energy from entering into or escaping from the cage. Also, this prevents devices from communicating via Wi-Fi or cellular signals.

What's more, transporting the evidence to the forensics lab or any other place, including the courthouse, has to be done very carefully. It is critical that the chain of custody be maintained during this transport. When you transport the evidence, you should strive to secure it in a lockable container. It is also recommended that the responsible person stay with the evidence at all times during transportation.

Fundamentals of Microsoft Windows Forensics

This section covers the fundamentals of Windows forensics and related topics.

Processes, Threads, and Services

While preparing for the CCNA Cyber Ops SECFND exam, you learned that a **process** is a program that the system is running. Each process provides the required resources to execute a program. A process is made up of one or more *threads*, which are the basic unit an operating system allocates process time to. A thread can be executed during any part of the application runtime, including being executed by another thread. Each process starts with a single thread, known as the primary thread, but can also create additional threads from any of its threads.

Processes can be grouped together and managed as a unit. This is called a *job object* and can be used to control attributes of the processes they are associated with. Grouping processes together simplifies impacting a group of processes because any operation performed on a specific job object will impact all associated processes. A *thread pool* is a group of worker threads that efficiently execute asynchronous callbacks for the application. This is done to reduce the number of application threads and to manage the worker threads. A *fiber* is a unit of execution that is manually scheduled by an application. Threads can schedule multiple fibers; however, fibers do not outperform properly designed multithreaded applications.

It is important to understand how these components all work together when developing applications and later securing them. There are many threats to applications (known as *vulnerabilities*) that could be abused to change the intended outcome of an application. This is why it is critical to include security in all stages of developing applications to ensure these and other application components are not abused.

Windows services are long running executable applications that run in their own Windows session. Basically, they are services that run in the background. Services can automatically kick on when a computer boots up. Services are ideal for running things within a user security context, starting applications that should always be run for a specific user, and long running functionally that doesn't interface with other users who are working on the same computer. An example would be the desire to have an application that monitors if the storage is consumed past a certain threshold. The programmer would create a Windows service application that monitors storage space and set it to automatically start at boot, so it is continuously monitoring for the critical condition. If the user chooses not to monitor their system, they could open the services windows and change the Startup type to manual, meaning it must be manually turned on or they could just stop the service. The services inside the service control manager can be started, stopped, or triggered by an event. Because services operate in their own user account, they can operate when a user is not logged in to the system, meaning the monitor storage space application example could be set to automatically run for a specific user or for any users including when there isn't a user logged in.

Windows administrators can manage services using services snap-in, Sc.exe, or Windows PowerShell. The *services snap-in* is built in with the services management console and can connect to a local or remote computer on a network enabling the administrator to perform some of the following actions.

- View installed services
- Start, stop, or restart services
- Change the startup type for a service
- Specify service parameters when available
- Change the startup type
- Change the user account context where the service operates
- Configure recovery actions in the event a service fails
- Inspect service dependencies for troubleshooting
- Export the list of services

The *Sc.exe*, also known as the Service Control utility, is a command-line version of the services snap-in. This means it can do everything the services snap-in can do, as well as install and uninstall services. *Windows PowerShell* can also manage Windows services using the following commands, also called cmdlets:

- **Get-Service:** Gets the services on a local or remote computer
- **New-Service:** Creates a new Windows service
- **Restart-Service:** Stops and then starts one or more services
- **Resume-Service:** Resumes one or more suspended (paused) services
- **Set-Service:** Starts, stops, and suspends a service and changes its properties
- **Start-Service:** Starts one or more stopped services
- **Stop-Service:** Stops one or more running services
- **Suspend-Service:** Suspends (pauses) one or more running services.

Other tools that can manage Windows services are Net.exe, Windows Task Manager, and MSConfig; however, their capabilities are limited compared to the other tools mentioned. For example, MSConfig can enable or disable Windows services while Windows Task manager can show a list of installed services as well as start or stop them.

Like other aspects of Windows, services are targeted by attackers. Windows has improved securing services in later versions of the operating system after finding various attack methods compromising and completely owning older versions of Windows. Windows, however, is not perfect, so best practice dictates securing services such as disabling the following services unless they are needed:

- **TCP 53:** DNS Zone Transfer
- **TCP 135:** RPC Endpoint Mapper
- **TCP 139:** NetBIOS Session Service
- **TCP 445:** SMB Over TCP
- **TCP 3389:** Terminal Services
- **UDP 137:** NetBIOS Name Service

- **UDP 161:** Simple Network Management Protocol
- **TCP/UDP 389:** Lightweight Directory Access Protocol

In addition, you should enable host security solutions such as the Windows Firewall filters services from outsiders. Enforcing least privilege access, using restricted tokens, and access control can reduce the damages that could occur if an attacker successfully compromised a Windows system's services. Basically applying best practices to secure hosts and your network will also apply to reducing the risk of attacks against Microsoft Windows system services.

The list that follows highlights the key concepts concerning processes and threads:

- A process is a program that the system is running and is made of one or more threads.
- A thread is a basic unit an operating system allocates process time to.
- A job is a group of processes.
- A thread pool is a group of worker threads that efficiently execute asynchronous call-backs for the application.
- Microsoft Windows services are long running executable applications that run in their own Windows session
- Services are ideal for running things within a user security context, starting applications that should always be run for a specific user, and long running functionally that doesn't interface with other users who are working on the same computer
- Windows administrators can manage services using Services snap-in, Sc.exe, or Windows PowerShell

When performing forensics investigations in Windows or any other operating system, you should look for orphan and suspicious processes and services on the system. Malware could create processes running in your system.

Memory Management

Memory can be managed different ways, which is referred to as memory allocation or memory management. *Static memory allocation* is when a program allocates memory at compile time. *Dynamic memory allocation* is when a program allocates memory at runtime. Memory can be assigned to blocks representing portions of allocated memory dedicated to a running program. A program will request a block of memory, which the memory manager will assign to the program. When the program completes whatever it's doing, the allocated memory blocks are released and available for other uses.

A *stack* is the memory set aside as scratch space for a thread of execution. A *heap* is memory set aside for dynamic allocation, meaning where you put data on the fly. Unlike a stack, there isn't an enforced pattern to the allocation and deallocation of blocks from the heap. With heaps, you can allocate a block at any time and free it at any time. Stacks are best when you know how much memory is needed, whereas heaps are better for when you don't know how much data you will need at runtime or if you need to allocate a lot of data. Memory allocation happens in hardware, in the operating system, and in programs and applications.

There are various approaches to how Windows allocates memory. The ultimate result is the same; however, the approaches are slightly different. *VirtualAlloc* is a specialized allocation of the OS virtual memory system, meaning it is allocated straight into virtual memory via reserved blocks of memory. Typically, it is used for special-purpose type allocation because the allocation has to be very large, needs to be shared, needs a specific value, and so on. Allocating memory in the virtual memory system is the most basic form of memory allocation. Typically, VirtualAlloc manages pages in the Windows virtual memory system.

HeapAlloc allocates any size of memory that is requested dynamically. It is designed to be very fast and used for general-purpose allocation. Heaps are set up by VirtualAlloc used to initially reserve allocation space from the OS. Once the memory space is initialized by the VirtualAlloc, various tables, lists, and other data structures are built to maintain operation of the heap. Heaps are great for smaller objects; however, due to having a guaranteed thread allocation, they can cause performance issues. HeapAlloc is a Windows API function.

The next memory examples are more programing focused and not Windows dependent. *Malloc* is a standard C and C++ library function that allocates memory to a process using the C runtime heap. Malloc will usually require one of the operating system APIs to create a pool of memory when the application starts running and then allocate from that pool as there are Malloc requests for memory. Malloc therefore has the disadvantage of being run-time dependent.

It is important to note that Malloc is part of a standard, meaning it is portable, whereas HeapAlloc is not portable, meaning it's a Windows API function.

Another programing-based memory allocator is *New*, which is a standard C++ operator that allocates memory and then calls constructors on that memory. New has the disadvantage of being compiler dependent and language dependent, meaning other programing languages may not support New. One final programing-based memory allocator is *CoTaskMemAlloc*, which has the advantage of working well in either C, C++, or Visual Basic. It is not important for the SECFND to know the details of how each memory allocator functions. The goal is to have a general understanding of memory allocation.

The list that follows highlights the key memory allocation concepts:

- Volatile memory is memory that loses its contents when the computer or hardware storage device loses power.
- Nonvolatile memory, or NVRAM, holds data with or without power.
- Static memory allocation is when a program allocates memory at compile time.
- Dynamic memory allocation is when a program allocates memory at runtime.
- A heap is memory set aside for dynamic allocation.
- A stack is memory set aside as scratch space for a thread of execution.
- *VirtualAlloc* is a specialized allocation of the OS virtual memory system, meaning it's allocated straight into virtual memory via reserved blocks of memory.
- *HeapAlloc* allocates any size of memory that is requested.
- *Malloc* is a standard C and C++ library function that allocates memory to a process using the C runtime heap.
- New and *CoTaskMemAlloc* are also programing-based memory allocators.

Windows Registry

Pretty much anything performed in Windows refers to or is recorded into the registry, meaning any actions taken by a user reference the Windows registry. Therefore, a definition for the Windows registry could be a hierarchical database used to store information necessary to configure the system for one or more users, applications, and hardware devices.

Some functions of the registry are to load device drivers, run startup programs, set environment variables, and store user settings and operating system parameters. You can view the Windows registry by typing the command **regedit** in the Run window.

The Windows registry can contain very valuable information that is useful to cyber forensic professionals. It can contain information about recently run programs, programs that have been installed or uninstalled, users who perhaps have been removed or created by a threat actor, and much more.

The Windows subsystem that manages the registry is called the Configuration Manager. The Windows registry appears as a single hierarchy in tools such as **regedit**; however, it is actually composed of a number of different binary files, called *hives*, on disk. The hive files themselves are broken into fixed-sized bins of 0 × 1000 bytes, and each bin contains variable-length cells. These cells hold the actual registry data. References in hive files are made by the cell index. The cell index is a value that can be used to determine the location of the cell containing the referenced data. The structure of the registry data is typically composed of two distinct data types: key nodes and value data.

The structure of the registry is similar to a file system. The key nodes are similar to directories or folders, and the values can be compared to files. On the other hand, data in the registry always has an unequivocal associated type, unlike data on a file system. To work with registry data in memory, it is necessary to find out where in memory the hives have been loaded and know how to translate cell indexes to memory addresses. It will also be helpful to understand how the Windows Configuration Manager works with the registry internally, and how we can make use of its data structures to tell us what the operating system itself maintains about the state of the registry.

The folders listed on the left start with the five hierarchal folders called hives, each beginning with the term HKEY (meaning "handle to a key"). Two of the hives are real locations: HKEY_USERS (HKU) and HKEY_LOCAL_MACHINE (HKLM). The remaining three are shortcuts to other elements within the HKU and HKLM hives. Each of these main five hives is composed of keys, which contain values and subkeys. Values are the names of specific values pertaining to the operation system or applications within a key. One way to think of the Windows registry is to compare it to an application containing folders. Inside an application, folders hold files. Inside the Windows registry, the hives hold values.

The following list defines the function of the five hives within the Windows registry:

- **HKEY_CLASSES_ROOT (HKCR):** HKCR information ensures that the correct programs open when executed in Windows Explorer. HKCR also contains further details on drag-and-drop rules, shortcuts, and information on the user interface. The reference location is HKLM\Software\Classes.

- **HKEY_CURRENT_USER (HKCU):** HKCU contains configuration information for any user who is currently logged in to the system, including the user's folders, screen colors, and Control Panel settings. The reference location for a specific user is HKEY_USERS. The reference for a general user is HKU\.DEFAULT.

- **HKEY_CURRENT_CONFIG (HCU):** HCU stores information about the system's current configuration. The reference for HCU is HKLM\Config\profile.

- **HKEY_LOCAL_MACHINE (HKLM):** HKLM contains machine hardware-specific information that the operating system runs on. This includes a list of drives mounted on the system and generic configurations of installed hardware and applications. HKLM is a hive that isn't referenced from within another hive.

- **HKEY_USERS (HKU):** HKU contains configuration information of all user profiles on the system. This includes application configurations and visual settings. HKU is a hive that isn't referenced from within another hive.

Some interesting data points can be abstracted from analyzing the Windows registry. All registries contain a value called LastWrite time, which is the last modification time of a file. This can be used to identify the approximate date and time an event occurred. Autorun locations are registry keys that launch programs or applications during the boot process. This is extremely important to protect because Autorun could be used by an attacker for executing malicious applications. The most recently used (MRU) list contains entries made due to actions performed by the user. The purpose of an MRU is to contain a list of items in the event the user returns to them in the future. Think of an MRU as similar to how a cookie is used in a web browser. The UserAssist key contains information about what resources the user has accessed.

Many other things, such as network settings, USB devices, and mounted devices, have registry keys that can be pulled up to identify activity within the operating system.

The registry can specify whether applications start automatically when the system is booted or when a user logs in. A good reference about this is the following Microsoft Sysinternals document: https://technet.microsoft.com/en-us/sysinternals/bb963902. Malware can change the registry to automatically start a program when the system is booted or when a user logs in.

A good example of Windows registry categories related to program execution and other functions can be found at https://blogs.sans.org/computer-forensics/files/2012/06/SANS-Digital-Forensics-and-Incident-Response-Poster-2012.pdf.

The Security hive is one of the Windows registry hives that includes information that is related to the running and operations of the system. The information available in this and other hives is all about the system, rather than specific users on the system. The Windows Registry Security hive contains useful information regarding the system configuration and settings.

Information about local users on a system is maintained in the SAM "database" or hive file. In corporate environments, the SAM hive may not have a great deal of useful information.

User information may be found on a domain controller or LDAP server. However, in environments where the users access their system using local accounts, this hive file can provide great information.

In some cases, during investigations you may need to crack a user's password—for instance, a user created by a threat actor and used in malware. There are several free password cracking tools available, including Cain & Abel (http://www.oxid.it/cain.html), OphCrack (http://ophcrack.sourceforge.net), and John the Ripper (http://www.openwall.com/john).

The System hive contains a great deal of configuration information about the system and devices that were included in it and have been attached to it.

The Windows File System

Before learning the different file system structures, you need to understand the different parts in a partitioned hard drive.

Master Boot Record (MBR)

The master boot record (MBR) is the first sector (512 bytes) of the hard drive. It contains the boot code and information about the hard drive itself. The MBR contains the partition table, which includes information about the partition structure in the hard disk drive. The MBR can tell where each partition starts, its size, and the type of partition. While performing forensics analysis, you can verify the existing partition with the information in the MBR and the printed size of the hard drive for a match. If there is some missing space, you can assume a potential compromise or corruption of the system.

The Master File Table (MFT)

The first sector (512 bytes) of each partition contains information, such as the type of the file system, the booting code location, the sector size, and the cluster size in reference to the sector.

If you formatted the partition with FAT or NTFS, some sectors at the beginning of the partition will be reserved for the master file table (MFT), which is the location that contains the metadata about the files in the system. Each entry is 1 KB in size, and when a user deletes a file, the file's entry in the MFT is marked as unallocated. On the other hand, the file's information still exists until another file uses this MFT entry and overwrites the previous file's information.

Data Area and Free Space

The rest of the partition space after the file system's area has been reserved will be available for data. Each unit of the data area is called a cluster or block. If files are deleted from the hard drive, the clusters that contain data related to this file will be marked as unallocated. Subsequently, the data will exist until new data that is related to a new file overwrites it.

The following are a few facts about clusters:

■ **Allocated cluster:** Holds data that is related to a file that exists and has an entry in the file system's MFT area.

- **Unallocated cluster**: A cluster that has not been connected to an existing file and may be empty or "not empty," thus containing data that is related to a deleted file and still hasn't been overwritten with a new file's data.

When you run a backup tool for the system, it backs up only the files that exist in the current file system's MFT area and identifies its related cluster in the data area as allocated. Typically, when you back up your hard drive, the backup software compresses the data. On the other hand, when you are collecting a forensic image, the size of the collected image must be exactly equal to the size of the source.

FAT

The File Allocation Table (FAT) was the default file system of the Microsoft DOS operating system back in the 1980s. Then other versions were introduced, including FAT12, FAT16, FAT32, and exFAT. Each version overcame some of the limitations of the file system until the introduction of the New Technology File System (NTFS).

FAT partitions include the following main areas:

- Boot sector, which is the first sector of the partition that is loaded in memory. The boot sector includes the following information:
  - Jump code, which is the location of the bootstrap and the operating system initialization code
  - Sector size
  - Cluster size
  - The total number of sectors in the partition
  - Number of root entries (FAT12 and FAT16 only)
- The File Allocation Table (FAT), which is the actual file system
- Another copy of the FAT table if the first FAT table has been corrupted
- Root directory entries
- The address of the first cluster, which contains the file's data
- The data area

One of FAT's limitations is that no modern properties can be added to the file, such as compression, permissions, and encryption.

The number after each FAT version, such as FAT12, FAT16, or FAT32, represents the number of bits that are assigned to address clusters in the FAT table:

- **FAT12**: This is a maximum of $2^{12} = 4,096$ clusters.
- **FAT16**: This is a maximum of $2^{16} = 65,536$ clusters.
- **FAT32**: This is a maximum of $2^{32} = 4,294,967,296$ clusters, but it has 4 reserved bits, so it is actually 28 bits, which means a maximum of $2^{28} = 268,435,456$.
- **exFAT**: This uses the whole 32 bits for addressing.

NTFS

NTFS is the default file system in Microsoft Windows since Windows NT and is a more secure, scalable, and advanced file system compared to FAT. NTFS has several components. The boot sector is the first sector in the partition, and it contains information about the file system itself, such as the start code, sector size, cluster size in sectors, and the number of reserved sectors. The file system area contains many files, including the master file table (MFT). The MFT includes metadata of the files and directories in the partition. The data area holds the actual contents of the files, and it is divided in clusters with a size assigned during formatting and recorded in the boot sector.

MFT

NTFS has a file called $MFT. In this file is an entry for each file in the partition. This entry is 1,024 bytes in size. It even has an entry for itself. Each entry has a header of 42 bytes at the beginning and a signature of 0xEB52904E, which is equivalent to FILE in ASCII. The signature also can be BAD, which in this case indicates that an error has occurred. After the header is another 982 bytes left to store the file metadata. If there is space left to store the file contents, the file's data is stored in the entry itself and no space in the data area is used by this file. MFT uses attributes to stockpile the metadata of the file. Different attribute types can be used in a single MFT entry and are assigned to store different information.

Timestamps, MACE, and Alternate Data Streams

NTFS keeps track of lots of timestamps. Each file has a timestamp for Modify, Access, Create, and Entry Modified (commonly referred to as the MACE values).

NTFS includes a feature referred to as Alternate Data Streams (ADS). This feature has also been referred to as "multiple data streams" as well as "alternative data streams." ADS exists with the goal of supporting the resource forks employed by the Hierarchal File System (HFS) employed by Apple Macintosh systems.

Microsoft File System Resource Manager (FSRM) also uses ADS as part of "file classification."

> **NOTE**   Cybersecurity forensics experts use tools such as EnCase and ProDiscover to collect evidence from systems. These tools display the ADS found in acquired images in red.

EFI

The EFI system partition (ESP) is a partition on a hard disk drive or solid-state drive whose main purpose is to interact with the Unified Extensible Firmware Interface (UEFI). UEFI firmware loads files stored on the EFI system partition to start the operating system and different utilities. An EFI system partition needs to be formatted with a file system whose specification is based on the FAT file system and maintained as part of the UEFI specification. The EFI system partition specification is independent from the original FAT specification. It includes the boot loaders or kernel images for all installed operating systems that are present in other partitions. It also includes device driver files for hardware devices present in a system and used by the firmware at boot time, as well as system utility programs that run before an operating system is loaded. The EFI system partition also contains data files, including error logs.

The Unified Extensible Firmware Interface Forum at http://www.uefi.org has a lot of great information about Secure Boot, UEFI operations, specifications, tools, and much more.

Fundamentals of Linux Forensics

This section covers cyber forensics fundamentals of Linux-based systems. Most of these concepts also apply to the Mac OS X operating system.

Linux Processes

In Linux, there are two methods for starting a process—starting it in the foreground and starting it in the background. You can see all the processes in UNIX by using the command **ps ()** in a terminal window, also known as **shell**. What follows **ps** are the details of what type of processes should be displayed. Example 2-1 includes the output of the **ps** command in a Linux system.

Example 2-1   *Output of the ps Command in Linux*

```
omar@odin:~$ ps awux
USER         PID %CPU %MEM    VSZ    RSS TTY       STAT START    TIME COMMAND
root           1  0.0  0.1 120416   6432 ?         Ss   Oct27    0:30 /lib/systemd/systemd
--system --deserialize 20
daemon       867  0.0  0.0  26044   1928 ?         Ss   Oct27    0:00 /usr/sbin/atd -f
root         938  0.0  0.0  19472    252 ?         Ss   Oct27    3:22 /usr/sbin/irqbalance
--pid=/var/run/irqbalance.pid
root        1027  0.0  0.1  65520   5760 ?         Ss   Oct27    0:00 /usr/sbin/sshd -D
root        1040  0.0  0.4 362036  16752 ?         Ssl  Oct27   33:00 /usr/bin/dockerd -H
fd://
redis       1110  0.0  0.1  40136   6196 ?         Ssl  Oct27   63:44 /usr/bin/redis-server
127.0.0.1:6379
mysql       1117  0.0  3.2 1300012 127632 ?        Ssl  Oct27   41:24 /usr/sbin/mysqld
root        1153  0.0  0.0   4244    580 ?         Ss   Oct27    0:00 runsv nginx
root        1230  0.0  0.0  15056   1860 ?         Ss   Oct27    0:00 /usr/sbin/xinetd
-pidfile /run/xinetd.pid -stayalive -inetd_compat -
root        1237  0.0  0.1 142672   4396 ?         Ssl  Oct27    3:01 docker-containerd -l
unix:///var/run/docker/libcontainerd/docker-con
root        1573  0.0  0.0  65408   3668 ?         Ss   Oct27    0:42 /usr/lib/postfix/
sbin/master
postfix     1578  0.0  0.0  67644   3852 ?         S    Oct27    0:15 qmgr -l -t unix -u
root        4039  0.0  0.0      0      0 ?         S    19:08    0:00 [kworker/0:1]
root        4478  0.0  0.0  43976   3544 ?         Ss   Nov27    0:02 /lib/systemd/systemd-
udevd
root        4570  0.0  0.1 275876   6348 ?         Ssl  Nov27    0:55 /usr/lib/accountsser-
vice/accounts-daemon
root        5477  0.0  0.0      0      0 ?         S    19:29    0:00 [kworker/u8:1]
bind        6202  0.0  1.5 327604  59748 ?         Ssl  Nov02   17:04 /usr/sbin/named -f -u
bind
```

```
postfix   7371  0.0  0.1  67476   4524 ?        S    19:57   0:00 pickup -l -t unix -u
-c
root      7413  0.0  0.0      0      0 ?        S    19:58   0:00 [kworker/u8:0]
root      7580  0.0  0.0   4508    700 ?        Ss   20:00   0:00 /bin/sh /opt/gitlab/
embedded/bin/gitlab-logrotate-wrapper
root      8267  0.0  0.0   4380    660 ?        S    20:10   0:00 sleep 3000
root      8346  0.0  0.1 111776   7496 ?        Ss   20:11   0:00 sshd: omar [priv]
omar      8358  0.0  0.0 118364   1640 ?        S    20:12   0:00 sshd: omar [priv]
omar      8359  0.0  0.1  45368   5084 ?        Ss   20:12   0:00 /lib/systemd/systemd
--user
root      8362  0.0  0.0      0      0 ?        S    20:12   0:00 [kworker/1:0]
root      8364  0.0  0.0      0      0 ?        S    20:12   0:00 [kworker/0:0]
omar      8365  0.0  0.0 162192   2860 ?        S    20:12   0:00 (sd-pam)
omar      8456  0.0  0.0 111776   3492 ?        R    20:12   0:00 sshd: omar@pts/0
omar      8457  0.1  0.1  22576   5136 pts/0    Ss   20:12   0:00 -bash
root      8497  0.0  0.0      0      0 ?        S    20:12   0:00 [kworker/u8:2]
git       8545  0.0  0.0   4380    672 ?        S    20:13   0:00 sleep 1
omar      8546  0.0  0.0  37364   3324 pts/0    R+   20:13   0:00 ps awux
gitlab-+ 13342  1.2  0.2  39720   9320 ?        Ssl  Nov27 580:31 /opt/gitlab/embedded/
bin/redis-server 127.0.0.1:0
gitlab-+ 13353  0.0  1.2 1053648 50132 ?        Ss   Nov27   0:32 /opt/gitlab/embedded/
bin/postgres -D /var/opt/gitlab/postgresql/data
gitlab-+ 13355  0.0  0.3 1054128 11908 ?        Ss   Nov27   0:00 postgres: check-
pointer process
gitlab-+ 13356  0.0  0.2 1054128  9788 ?        Ss   Nov27   0:16 postgres: writer
process
gitlab-+ 13357  0.0  0.1 1054128  4092 ?        Ss   Nov27   0:15 postgres: wal writer
process
gitlab-+ 13358  0.0  0.1 1055100  4884 ?        Ss   Nov27   0:53 postgres: autovacuum
launcher process
systemd+ 32717  0.0  0.0 100324   2280 ?        Ssl  Nov27   0:02 /lib/systemd/systemd-
timesyncd
```

Several other tools are great for displaying not only the processes running in the system but also the resource consumption (CPU, memory, network, and so on). Two widely used tools are **top** and **htop**. Example 2-2 shows the output of **top**, and Example 2-3 shows the output of **htop**.

Example 2-2 *The top Command in Linux*

```
top - 20:20:25 up 64 days,  5:17,  1 user,  load average: 0.09, 0.06, 0.01
Tasks: 197 total,   2 running, 195 sleeping,   0 stopped,   0 zombie
%Cpu(s):  1.5 us,  0.0 sy,  0.0 ni, 98.5 id,  0.0 wa,  0.0 hi,  0.0 si,  0.0 st
KiB Mem :  3914932 total,   195108 free,  2008376 used,  1711448 buff/cache
KiB Swap:  4058620 total,  3994692 free,    63928 used.  1487784 avail Mem

  PID USER       PR  NI    VIRT    RES    SHR S  %CPU %MEM     TIME+ COMMAND
13465 git        20   0  731848 496408  15184 S   2.0 12.7  1105:01 bundle
13342 gitlab-+   20   0   39720   9320   2896 S   1.3  0.2 580:36.88 redis-server
```

```
 9039 omar       20   0    41800    3772    3112 R   0.7  0.1   0:00.02 top
    1 root       20   0   120416    6432    3840 S   0.0  0.2   0:30.43 systemd
    2 root       20   0        0       0       0 S   0.0  0.0   0:00.21 kthreadd
    3 root       20   0        0       0       0 S   0.0  0.0   0:11.62 ksoftirqd/0
    5 root        0 -20        0       0       0 S   0.0  0.0   0:00.00 kworker/0:0H
    7 root       20   0        0       0       0 S   0.0  0.0  58:43.51 rcu_sched
    8 root       20   0        0       0       0 S   0.0  0.0   0:00.00 rcu_bh
    9 root       rt   0        0       0       0 S   0.0  0.0   0:29.90 migration/0
   10 root       rt   0        0       0       0 S   0.0  0.0   0:16.00 watchdog/0
   11 root       rt   0        0       0       0 S   0.0  0.0   0:16.03 watchdog/1
   12 root       rt   0        0       0       0 S   0.0  0.0   0:29.83 migration/1
   13 root       20   0        0       0       0 S   0.0  0.0   0:17.28 ksoftirqd/1
   15 root        0 -20        0       0       0 S   0.0  0.0   0:00.00 kworker/1:0H
   16 root       20   0        0       0       0 S   0.0  0.0   0:00.00 kdevtmpfs
   17 root        0 -20        0       0       0 S   0.0  0.0   0:00.00 netns
   18 root        0 -20        0       0       0 S   0.0  0.0   0:00.00 perf
   19 root       20   0        0       0       0 S   0.0  0.0   0:02.84 khungtaskd
   20 root        0 -20        0       0       0 S   0.0  0.0   0:00.00 writeback
   21 root       25   5        0       0       0 S   0.0  0.0   0:00.00 ksmd
   22 root       39  19        0       0       0 S   0.0  0.0   0:14.74 khugepaged
   23 root        0 -20        0       0       0 S   0.0  0.0   0:00.00 crypto
   24 root        0 -20        0       0       0 S   0.0  0.0   0:00.00 kintegrityd
   25 root        0 -20        0       0       0 S   0.0  0.0   0:00.00 bioset
   26 root        0 -20        0       0       0 S   0.0  0.0   0:00.00 kblockd
   27 root        0 -20        0       0       0 S   0.0  0.0   0:00.00 ata_sff
```

Example 2-3 *The htop Linux Utility*

```
  1  [|||||                                    1.0%]   4  [  0.0%]
  2  [|                                        0.0%]   5  [|  1.3%]
  3  [                                         0.0%]   6  [  0.0%]
  Mem[|||||||||||||||||||||||||||||||||||||||||||||||748M/15.6G]   Tasks: 47, 108 thr;
1 running
  Swp[|                                        29.7M/15.9G]   Load average: 0.00
0.00 0.00
                                                       Uptime: 47 days,
08:00:26
  PID USER      PRI  NI  VIRT   RES   SHR S CPU% MEM%   TIME+  Command
17239 omar       20   0 24896  4112  3248 R  1.3  0.0  0:00.07 htop
 1510 root       35  15 1812M  115M  4448 S  0.0  0.7  1h26:51 Plex Plug-in [com.plex-
app.system] /usr/lib/plexmediaserver/Resources/P
    1 root       20   0  117M  6012  3416 S  0.0  0.0  0:28.91 /lib/systemd/systemd
--system --deserialize 19
  432 root       20   0 35420  7316  7032 S  0.0  0.0  7:00.23 /lib/systemd/systemd-
journald
  475 root       20   0  100M  3180   944 S  0.0  0.0  0:00.00 /sbin/lvmetad -f
  938 root       20   0  4396  1308  1220 S  0.0  0.0  0:00.04 /usr/sbin/acpid
  964 syslog     20   0  250M  3916  2492 S  0.0  0.0  0:58.03 /usr/sbin/rsyslogd -n
```

```
  965 syslog     20   0  250M  3916  2492 S  0.0  0.0  0:00.00 /usr/sbin/rsyslogd -n
  966 syslog     20   0  250M  3916  2492 S  0.0  0.0  1:05.88 /usr/sbin/rsyslogd -n
  943 syslog     20   0  250M  3916  2492 S  0.0  0.0  2:04.34 /usr/sbin/rsyslogd -n
  967 root       20   0  273M 14348  9176 S  0.0  0.1  0:03.84 /usr/lib/snapd/snapd
  968 root       20   0  273M 14348  9176 S  0.0  0.1  0:00.00 /usr/lib/snapd/snapd
  969 root       20   0  273M 14348  9176 S  0.0  0.1  0:00.63 /usr/lib/snapd/snapd
 1041 root       20   0  273M 14348  9176 S  0.0  0.1  0:00.75 /usr/lib/snapd/snapd
 1043 root       20   0  273M 14348  9176 S  0.0  0.1  0:00.77 /usr/lib/snapd/snapd
 1045 root       20   0  273M 14348  9176 S  0.0  0.1  0:00.00 /usr/lib/snapd/snapd
11707 root       20   0  273M 14348  9176 S  0.0  0.1  0:00.64 /usr/lib/snapd/snapd
  947 root       20   0  273M 14348  9176 S  0.0  0.1  0:06.68 /usr/lib/snapd/snapd
 1040 root       20   0  302M  2924  1384 S  0.0  0.0  0:11.12 /usr/bin/lxcfs /var/
lib/lxcfs/
 1042 root       20   0  302M  2924  1384 S  0.0  0.0  0:11.26 /usr/bin/lxcfs /var/
lib/lxcfs/
20680 root       20   0  302M  2924  1384 S  0.0  0.0  0:11.19 /usr/bin/lxcfs /var/
lib/lxcfs/
 6250 root       20   0  302M  2924  1384 S  0.0  0.0  0:07.26 /usr/bin/lxcfs /var/
lib/lxcfs/
  953 root       20   0  302M  2924  1384 S  0.0  0.0  0:40.87 /usr/bin/lxcfs /var/
lib/lxcfs/
  958 root       20   0 28632  3020  2640 S  0.0  0.0  0:04.29 /lib/systemd/systemd-
logind
F1Help  F2Setup F3SearchF4FilterF5Tree  F6SortByF7Nice -F8Nice +F9Kill  F10Quit
```

Just like in Windows or any other operating system, looking for orphan, zombie, and suspicious processes is one of the tasks in Linux forensics. For instance, if you find a process running with open network sockets that doesn't show up on a similar system, there may be something suspicious on that system. You may find network saturation originating from a single host (by way of tracing its Ethernet address or packet counts on its switch port) or a program eating up 100% of the CPU but nothing in the file system with that name.

Ext4

You should also become familiar with the Linux file system. Ext4 is one of the most used Linux file systems. It has several improvements over its predecessors Ext3 and Ext2. Ext4 not only supports journaling (covered in the next section), but also modifies important data structures of the file system, such as the ones destined to store the file data. This is done for better performance, reliability, and additional features.

Ext3 supported 16 TB of maximum file system size, and 2 TB of maximum file size. Ext4 supports a maximum of 1 exabyte (EB), which equals 1,048,576 TB. The maximum possible number of sub directories contained in a single directory in Ext3 is 32,000. Ext4 allows an unlimited number of sub directories. It uses a "multiblock allocator" (*mballoc*) to allocate many blocks in a single call, instead of a single block per call. This feature avoids a lot of overhead and improves system performance.

Becoming familiar with the Linux file system is recommended for any cyber forensics practitioner. For example, in a compromised system, you may find a partition showing 100% utilization, but if you use the **du** command, the system may only show 30% utilization.

Two popular tools are used to analyze the Linux file system for cyber forensics: the Sleuth Kit and Autopsy. These tools are designed to analyze hard disk drives, solid-state drives (SSDs), and mobile devices. You can download the software and obtain more information about these tools at http://www.sleuthkit.org.

Journaling

Ext4 and Ext3 are journaling file systems. A journaling file system maintains a record of changes not yet committed to its main part. This data structure is referred to as a "journal," which is a circular log. One of the main features of a file system that supports journaling is that if the system crashes or experiences a power failure, it can be restored back online a lot quicker while also avoiding system corruption. A journaling file system may only keep track of stored metadata, but this depends on the implementation. Keeping track of only stored metadata improves performance but increases the possibility of data corruption.

The journal is the most used part of the disk, making the blocks that form part of it more prone to hardware failure. One of the features of Ext4 is that it checksums the journal data to know if the journal blocks are failing or becoming corrupted. Journaling ensures the integrity of the file system by keeping track of all disk changes, but it introduces a bit of overhead.

Linux MBR and Swap File System

As you learned earlier in this chapter, the MBR is a special type of boot sector that contains 512 or more bytes located in the first sector of the drive. The MBR includes instructions about how the logical partitions that have file systems are organized on the drive. It also has executable code to load the installed operating system.

The most common boot loaders in Linux are Linux Loader (LILO), Load Linux (LOADLIN), and the Grand Unified Bootloader (GRUB).

Figure 2-1 illustrates the Linux boot process in detail.

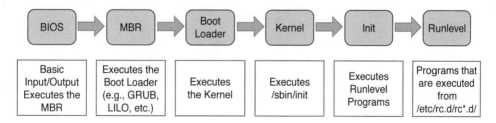

Figure 2-1   *The Linux Boot Process*

There are two main partitions on a Linux system:

- The data partition, which contains all Linux system data, including the root partition
- The swap partition, which is extra memory on the hard disk drive or SSD that is an expansion of the system's physical memory

The swap space (otherwise known as just "swap") is only accessible and viewable by the system itself. The swap makes sure that the operating system keeps working. Windows, Mac OS X, and other operating systems also use swap or virtual memory. The swap space is slower than real physical memory (RAM), but it helps the operating system immensely. A general rule of thumb is that Linux typically counts on having twice the amount of swap than physical memory.

One interesting point related to cyber forensics is that pretty much everything in RAM has the potential of being stored in swap space at any given time. Subsequently, you may find interesting system data such as plaintext data, encryption keys, user credentials, emails, and other sensitive information—especially due to the weaknesses in some applications that allow unencrypted keys to reside in memory.

Exam Preparation Tasks

Review All Key Topics

Review the most important topics in the chapter, noted with the Key Topic icon in the outer margin of the page. Table 2-2 lists these key topics and the page numbers on which each is found.

Table 2-2   Key Topics

Key Topic Element	Description	Page
Paragraph	The Role of Attribution in a Cyber Security Investigation	21
Paragraph	The Use of Digital Evidence	21
Paragraph	What is best evidence?	22
Paragraph	Defining what digital forensic evidence is.	22
Paragraph	What is corroborating evidence?	22
Paragraph	What is indirect or circumstantial evidence?	22
Paragraph	Collecting evidence from endpoints and servers.	22
Paragraph	Collecting evidence from mobile devices.	24
Paragraph	Collecting evidence from network infrastructure devices.	24
Paragraph	Chain of Custody	26
Paragraph	What are processes, threads, and services?	28
Paragraph	Understanding memory management.	30
Paragraph	Understanding the Windows registry.	32
Paragraph	The Windows file system.	34
Paragraph	What is FAT?	35
Paragraph	What is NTFS?	36
Paragraph	What is MFT?	36
Paragraph	Understanding Timestamps, MACE, and Alternate Data Streams	36
Paragraph	What is EFI?	36
Paragraph	Understanding Linux processes.	37
Paragraph	What is Ext4 and the Linux file system?	40
Paragraph	What is journaling?	41
Paragraph	Linux MBR and the swap file system.	41

Define Key Terms

Define the following key terms from this chapter and check your answers in the glossary:

FAT, NTFS, Ext4, master boot record, swap space, journaling

Q&A

The answers to these questions appear in Appendix A, "Answers to the 'Do I Know This Already?' Quizzes and Q&A." For more practice with exam format questions, use the exam engine on the website.

1. Which of the following is true about *VirtualAlloc*?

   a. It is a specialized allocation of the Windows virtual memory system, meaning it allocates straight into virtual memory via reserved blocks of memory.

   b. It is another name for swap space.

   c. It is a specialized allocation of the Linux virtual memory system, meaning it allocates straight into virtual memory via reserved blocks of memory.

   d. It is a specialized allocation of the Mac OS X virtual memory system, meaning it allocates straight into virtual memory via reserved blocks of memory.

2. Which of the following is true about *HeapAlloc*?

   a. It allocates any size of memory that is requested dynamically in Mac OS X. It is designed to be slow and used for special-purpose memory allocation.

   b. It allocates any size of memory that is requested dynamically in Microsoft Windows. It is designed to be slow and used for special-purpose memory allocation.

   c. It allocates any size of memory that is requested dynamically in Linux-based operating systems. It is designed to be very fast and used for general-purpose allocation.

   d. It allocates any size of memory that is requested dynamically in Microsoft Windows. It is designed to be very fast and used for general-purpose allocation.

3. In cyber forensics, the storage device you are investigating should immediately be write-protected before it is imaged and should be labeled to include which of the following? (Choose two.)

   a. Investigator's name

   b. Victim's name

   c. The date when the image was created

   d. NetFlow record ID

4. Which of the following is a benefit in cyber forensics of being able to make an exact copy of the data being investigated?

   a. The original device can be returned to the owner or stored for trial, normally without having to be examined repeatedly.

   b. The original device can be returned to the owner or stored for trial, typically always having to be examined repeatedly.

   c. A backup of the data can be performed so that the case manager and investigator can retrieve any lost records.

   d. A backup of the data can be performed so that the victim can retrieve any lost records.

5. What is best evidence?

   a. Evidence that can be presented in court in the original form.

   b. Evidence that tends to support a theory or an assumption deduced by some initial evidence. This best evidence confirms the proposition.

   c. Evidence that cannot be presented in court in the original form.

   d. Evidence that can be presented in court in any form.

6. Which of the following is extra memory on the hard disk drive or SSD that is an expansion of the system's physical memory?

   a. MBR

   b. MFT

   c. Swap

   d. RAM partition

7. Which of the following is true about journaling?

   a. A journaling file system provides less security than the alternatives.

   b. Journaling file systems are slow and should be avoided.

   c. A journaling file system maintains a record of changes not yet committed to the file system's main part.

   d. A journaling file system does not maintain a record of changes not yet committed to the file system's main part.

8. Which type of evidence relies on an extrapolation to a conclusion of fact (such as fingerprints, DNA evidence, and so on)?

   a. Indirect or circumstantial evidence

   b. Secondary evidence

   c. Corroborating evidence

   d. Best evidence

9. Which of the following is one of the most used Linux file systems that has several improvements over its predecessors and that supports journaling?

   a. NTFS

   b. exFAT

   c. Ext5

   d. Ext4

10. Which of the following statements is true about heaps in Windows?

    a. Heaps are set up by *Malloc* and are used to initially reserve allocation space from the operating system.

    b. Heaps are set up by swap and are used to initially reserve allocation space at bootup from the operating system.

    c. Heaps are set up by GRUB and are used to initially reserve allocation space from the operating system.

    d. Heaps are set up by *VirtualAlloc* and are used to initially reserve allocation space from the operating system.

This chapter covers the following topics:

- Common artifact elements and sources of security events

- Understanding regular expressions

- Protocols, protocol headers, and intrusion analysis

- Using packet captures for intrusion analysis

CHAPTER 3

Fundamentals of Intrusion Analysis

This chapter covers the common artifact elements and sources of security events and how you can use regular expressions to analyze security event data. You will learn the details about different protocols, protocol headers, and how they relate to intrusion analysis. You will also learn how to use packet captures for intrusion analysis.

"Do I Know This Already?" Quiz

The "Do I Know This Already?" quiz helps you identify your strengths and deficiencies in this chapter's topics. The seven-question quiz, derived from the major sections in the "Foundation Topics" portion of the chapter, helps you determine how to spend your limited study time. Table 3-1 outlines the major topics discussed in this chapter and the "Do I Know This Already?" quiz questions that correspond to those topics.

Table 3-1 "Do I Know This Already?" Foundation Topics Section-to-Question Mapping

Foundation Topics Section	Questions Covered in This Section
Common Artifact Elements and Sources of Security Events	1–2
Understanding Regular Expressions	3–4
Protocols, Protocol Headers, and Intrusion Analysis	5
Using Packet Captures for Intrusion Analysis	6–7

1. Source and destination IP addresses are usually shown in NetFlow records and security events. What other artifacts are part of NetFlow records? (Select all that apply.)

   a. Destination ports

   b. Usernames

   c. Signature IDs

   d. Source ports

2. Which of the following are artifacts that are usually shown in IDS and IPS events? (Select all that apply.)

   a. Signature IDs

   b. Passwords

   c. PII

   d. Source and destination IP addresses

3. Which of the following regular expressions will match the word *cat*, *bat*, or *rat*?

    a. [bcr]at

    b. ^at

    c. brc(at)

    d. brc[at]

4. Which of the following regular expressions will match any IP address on the 10.1.2.0/24 network?

    a. %10.1.2\.$

    b. 10\.1\.2\..*

    c. ^10.1.2.0

    d. 10.[1..2].0

5. Which of the following is true about protocol header analysis?

    a. Protocol header analysis has several drawbacks over IDS systems because it has less detection capabilities for both known and unknown attacks. This is because protocol header analysis tools cannot match traffic using signatures of security vulnerability exploits.

    b. Protocol header analysis has several benefits over more primitive security techniques because it has better detection of both known and unknown attacks. This is done by matching traffic on signatures of security vulnerability exploits.

    c. Protocol header analysis has several benefits over more primitive security techniques because it has better detection of both known and unknown attacks. This is done by alerting and blocking traffic on anomalies within the protocol transactions, instead of just simply matching traffic on signatures of security vulnerability exploits.

    d. Protocol header analysis is a primitive security technique that does not allow an IDS or IPS device to match traffic using signatures of security vulnerability exploits.

6. Which of the following is an example of a packet capture program?

    a. Wireshark

    b. Packetshark

    c. PacketReal

    d. NetFlow

7. Refer to the following output of **tcpdump**. Which of the following statements are true of this packet capture? (Select all that apply.)

```
23:52:36.664771 IP omar.cisco.com.33498 > www1.cisco.com.http: Flags [S], seq
2841244609, win 29200,

options [mss 1460,sackOK,TS val 1193036826 ecr 0,nop,wscale 7], length 0

23:52:36.694193 IP www1.cisco.com.http > omar.cisco.com.33498: Flags [S.], seq
1686130907,

ack 2841244610, win 32768, options [mss 1380], length 0

23:52:36.694255 IP omar.cisco.com.33498 > www1.cisco.com.http: Flags [.], ack 1,
win 29200, length 0

23:52:36.694350 IP omar.cisco.com.33498 > www1.cisco.com.http: Flags [P.], seq
1:74, ack 1, win 29200,

length 73: HTTP: GET / HTTP/1.1

23:52:36.723736 IP www1.cisco.com.http > omar.cisco.com.33498: Flags [.], ack
74, win 32695, length 0

23:52:36.724590 IP www1.cisco.com.http > omar.cisco.com.33498: Flags [P.], seq
1:505, ack 74,

win 32768, length 504: HTTP: HTTP/1.1 301 Moved Permanently

23:52:36.724631 IP omar.cisco.com.33498 > www1.cisco.com.http: Flags [.], ack
505, win 30016, length 0

23:52:36.724871 IP omar.cisco.com.33498 > www1.cisco.com.http: Flags [F.], seq
74, ack 505, win 30016,

length 0

23:52:36.754313 IP www1.cisco.com.http > omar.cisco.com.33498: Flags [F.], seq
505, ack 75, win 15544,

length 0

23:52:36.754364 IP omar.cisco.com.33498 > www1.cisco.com.http: Flags [.], ack
506, win 30016, length 0
```

   a. The source host is omar.cisco.com and the destination is www1.cisco.com.

   b. These are UDP transactions.

   c. These are TCP transactions.

   d. This is SIP redirect via HTTP.

Foundation Topics

Common Artifact Elements and Sources of Security Events

There are numerous artifact elements and sources of security event information. Figure 3-1 lists the common artifact elements found in security events.

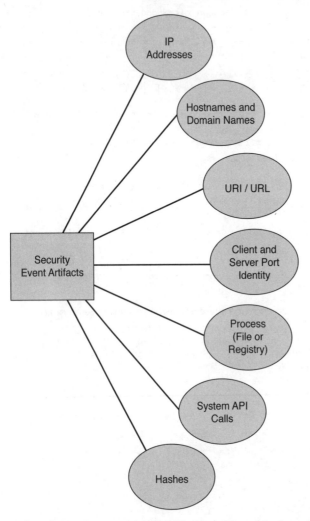

Figure 3-1 *Common Artifact Elements Found in Security Events*

Source and destination IP addresses are usually shown in network security events. Figure 3-2 shows the Intrusion Events panel of the summary dashboard of the Cisco Firepower Management Center (FMC). In Figure 3-2, you can see the top attackers' and top targets' IP addresses.

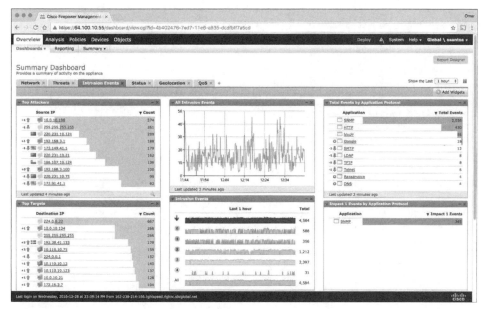

Figure 3-2 *Cisco FMC Intrusion Events*

Figure 3-3 shows a more detailed list of events in the Cisco FMC displaying the source and destination IP addresses of each system involved in each event.

Figure 3-3 *Cisco FMC Events by Priority and Classification*

Figure 3-4 shows the Cisco ASA logs in the Cisco Adaptive Security Device Manager (ASDM). You can see that all of the logs are mostly around the 5-tuple (source and destination IP addresses, source and destination ports, and protocols).

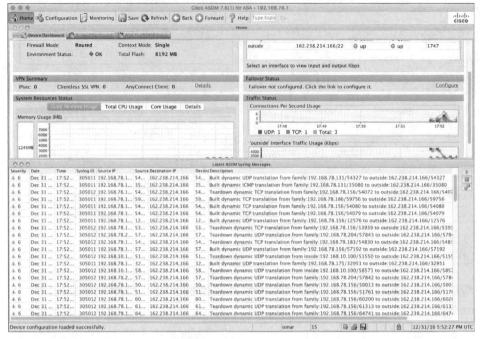

Figure 3-4 *Cisco ASA ASDM Syslogs*

Services are also part of many security event logs. Figure 3-5 shows the Cisco ASDM firewall dashboard, where you can see statistics about the top services and top destinations under attack.

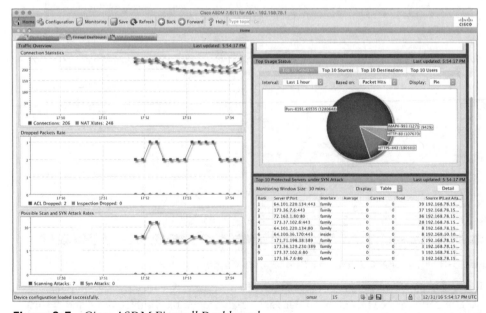

Figure 3-5 *Cisco ASDM Firewall Dashboard*

Security threat intelligence is extremely useful for correlating events and to gain an insight of what known threats are in your network. Figure 3-6 shows different security threat intelligence events in the Cisco FMC.

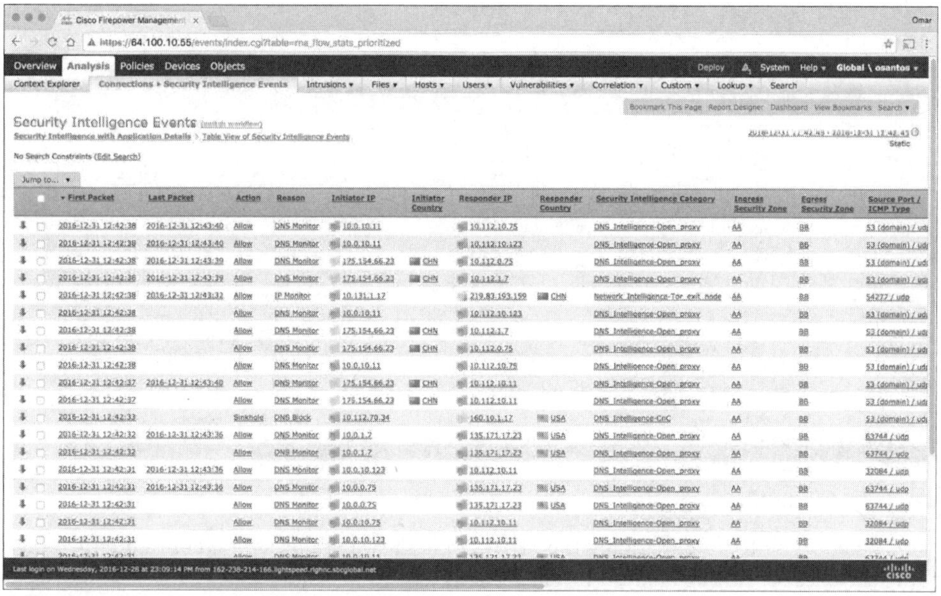

Figure 3-6   *Cisco FMC Security Intelligence Events*

DNS intelligence and URL reputation are also used in many security solutions, such as the Firepower appliances, Firepower Threat Defense (FTD), the Cisco Web and Email security appliances, and many more. Figure 3-7 shows many security events in the Cisco FMC that list several communications to known-malicious command-and-control (CnC) servers based on DNS intelligence.

File hashes are also part of many security event logs. For example, the Cisco Advanced Malware Protection (AMP) for Networks (A4N) and Cisco AMP for Endpoints (A4E) examine, record, track, and send files to the cloud. The Cisco AMP for Networks creates an SHA-256 hash of the file and compares it to the local file cache. If the hash is not in the local cache, it queries the Cisco FMC. The Cisco FMC has its own cache of all the hashes it has seen before, and if it hasn't previously seen this hash, the Cisco FMC queries the cloud. Unlike with AMP for Endpoints, when a file is new, it can be analyzed locally and doesn't have to be sent to the cloud for an analysis. Also, the file is examined and stopped in transit, as it is traversing the appliance.

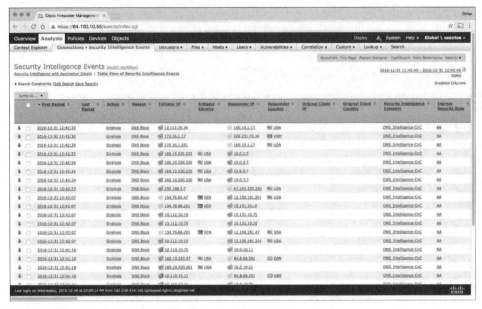

Figure 3-7   *Cisco FMC DNS Intelligence CnC Communication*

It's very important to note that only the SHA-256 hash is sent unless you configure the policy to send files for further analysis in Threat Grid.

Figure 3-8 shows the Cisco AMP for Endpoints console. In Figure 3-8, you can see a file (iodnxvg.exe) that was determined to be malware. There you can see the SHA-256 hash (fingerprint) of the file.

Figure 3-8   *Cisco AMP for Endpoints and Malware Hashes*

Cisco AMP can also provide retrospective analysis. The Cisco AMP for Networks appliance keeps data from what occurred in the past. When a file's disposition is changed, Cisco AMP provides a historical analysis of what happened, tracing the incident/infection. With the help of Cisco AMP for Endpoints, retrospection can reach out to that host and remediate the bad file, even though that file was permitted in the past. Figure 3-9 shows the retrospective analysis capabilities of the Cisco FMC.

Figure 3-9   *Cisco FMC Retrospective Analysis*

Figure 3-9 shows the network file trajectory in the Cisco FMC. To view this screen, you can navigate to **Analysis, Files, Network File Trajectory**. You can also access a file's trajectory from the Context Explorer, dashboard, or event views with file information.

You can also search SHA-256 hash values, host IP addresses, or the name of a file you want to track.

On the trajectory map, you can locate the first time a file event occurred involving an IP address. This highlights a path to that data point, as well as any intervening file events and IP addresses related to the first file event. The corresponding event in the Events table is also highlighted. The map scrolls to that data point if not currently visible.

You can also click any data point to highlight a path that includes all data points related to the selected data point, tracking a file's progress through the network. You can click the arrow icon to view all events not displayed in the File Summary event view. If you hover your mouse over the event icon, you can view summary information for the event. If you click any event summary information link, the first page of the File Events default workflow appears in a new window, with all the extra events constrained based on the file type.

False Positives, False Negatives, True Positives, and True Negatives

The term *false positive* is a broad term that describes a situation in which a security device triggers an alarm but there is no malicious activity or an actual attack taking place. In other words, false positives are "false alarms," and they are also called "benign triggers." False positives are problematic because by triggering unjustified alerts, they diminish the value and urgency of real alerts. If you have too many false positives to investigate, it becomes an operational nightmare and you most definitely will overlook real security events.

There are also *false negatives*, which is the term used to describe a network intrusion device's inability to detect true security events under certain circumstances—in other words, a malicious activity that is not detected by the security device.

A *true positive* is a successful identification of a security attack or a malicious event. A *true negative* is when the intrusion detection device identifies an activity as acceptable behavior and the activity is actually acceptable.

Traditional IDS and IPS devices need to be tuned to avoid false positives and false negatives. Next-generation IPSs do not need the same level of tuning compared to traditional IPS. Also, you can obtain much deeper reports and functionality, including advanced malware protection and retrospective analysis to see what happened after an attack took place.

Traditional IDS and IPS devices also suffer from many evasion attacks. The following are some of the most common evasion techniques against traditional IDS and IPS devices:

- **Fragmentation:** When the attacker evades the IPS box by sending fragmented packets.
- **Using low-bandwidth attacks:** When the attacker uses techniques that use low-bandwidth or a very small amount of packets in order to evade the system.
- **Address spoofing/proxying:** Using spoofed IP addresses or sources, as well as using intermediary systems such as proxies to evade inspection.
- **Pattern change evasion:** Attackers may use polymorphic techniques to create unique attack patterns.
- **Encryption:** Attackers can use encryption to hide their communication and information.

Understanding Regular Expressions

If you are a security professional, network engineer, or software developer, you are most definitely familiar with regular expressions because they are considered "a Swiss army knife" for many uses. A regular expression (sometimes referred to as "regex") is a text string for describing a search pattern. Regular expressions go beyond regular wildcards (such as *.mp3 to find all .mp3 files in a folder). Regular expressions can do a lot more. They are used in programming languages such as Perl, Python, PHP, Java, .NET, and several others. They are also commonly used to create intrusion detection signatures and search patterns in security tools.

Let's take a look at a few quick basic examples. Example 3-1 shows a list of files on a Linux system.

Example 3-1 *List of Several Text Files*

```
omar@odin:~/cyberOps$ ls -1
apple.txt
banana.txt
grape.txt
omar.txt
orange.txt
pear.txt
```

In Example 3-2, the **grep** command is used with the regular expression ^o to list all files that start with the letter o. In this case, the files that start with an *o* are omar.txt and orange.txt.

Example 3-2 *Files Starting with an o*

```
omar@odin:~/cyberOps$ ls -1 | grep ^o
omar.txt
orange.txt
```

Let's take a look at a more practical example. In Example 3-3, we have a file called packets. txt that has hundreds of transactions between hosts in the network (the complete output was omitted for brevity).

Example 3-3 *The Contents of packets.txt*

```
omar@odin:~/cyberOps$ cat packets.txt
15:46:15.551728 IP 192.168.78.8.ssh > 192.168.10.100.59657: Flags [P.], seq
3299992344:3299992544,
ack 4159081141, win 389, length 200
15:46:15.602341 IP 192.168.10.100.59657 > 192.168.78.8.ssh: Flags [.], ack 200, win
2065, length 0
15:46:15.700150 01:80:c2:00:00:01 (oui Unknown) > Broadcast, ethertype Unknown
(0x8874), length 60:
        0x0000:  e100 676a 11f5 e211 d51f e040 0000 0000  ..gj.......@....
        0x0010:  0000 0000 0000 0000 0000 0000 0000 0000  ................
        0x0020:  0000 0000 0000 0000 0000 0000 0000       .............
15:46:15.942336 ARP, Request who-has 192.168.78.24 tell 192.168.78.7, length 46
15:46:16.540072 IP 192.168.78.8.51800 > resolver1.opendns.com.domain: 50883+ PTR?
100.10.168.192.in-addr.arpa. (45)
15:46:16.554415 IP resolver1.opendns.com.domain > 192.168.78.8.51800: 50883* 0/1/0
(104)
15:46:16.554631 IP 192.168.78.8.43662 > resolver1.opendns.com.domain: 18373+ PTR?
8.78.168.192.in-addr.arpa. (43)
15:46:16.569193 IP resolver1.opendns.com.domain > 192.168.78.8.43662: 18373* 0/1/0
(102)
15:46:16.569373 IP 192.168.78.8.35694 > resolver1.opendns.com.domain: 53427+ PTR?
24.78.168.192.in-addr.arpa. (44)
15:46:16.583627 IP resolver1.opendns.com.domain > 192.168.78.8.35694: 53427* 0/1/0
(103)
```

```
15:46:16.583735 IP 192.168.78.8.53838 > resolver1.opendns.com.domain: 39294+ PTR?
7.78.168.192.in-addr.arpa. (43)

15:46:16.598422 IP resolver1.opendns.com.domain > 192.168.78.8.53838: 39294* 0/1/0 (102)

15:46:16.598528 IP 192.168.78.8.35167 > resolver1.opendns.com.domain: 6469+ PTR?
22.78.168.192.in-addr.arpa. (44)

15:46:16.612963 IP resolver1.opendns.com.domain > 192.168.78.8.35167: 6469* 0/1/0 (103)

15:46:16.617261 IP 192.168.78.8.58139 > resolver1.opendns.com.domain: 45553+ PTR?
23.78.168.192.in-addr.arpa. (44)

15:46:16.631734 IP resolver1.opendns.com.domain > 192.168.78.8.58139: 45553* 0/1/0 (103)

15:46:16.942294 ARP, Request who-has 192.168.78.24 tell 192.168.78.7, length 46

15:46:16.962249 ARP, Request who-has 192.168.78.22 tell 192.168.78.7, length 46

15:46:17.065729 IP 192.168.78.122.3451 > 255.255.255.255.5246: UDP, length 181

15:46:17.066197 IP 192.168.78.122.3451 > 255.255.255.255.5246: UDP, length 181

15:46:17.336147 IP 192.168.10.100.59657 > 192.168.78.8.ssh: Flags [P.], seq 1:41, ack
200, win 2065, length 40

15:46:17.336356 IP 192.168.78.8.ssh > 192.168.10.100.59657: Flags [P.], seq 200:240, ack
41, win 389, length 40

15:46:17.387069 IP 192.168.10.100.59657 > 192.168.78.8.ssh: Flags [.], ack 240, win
2065, length 0

15:46:17.462246 ARP, Request who-has 192.168.78.23 tell 192.168.78.7, length 46

15:46:17.577756 IP 192.168.10.100.59657 > 192.168.78.8.ssh: Flags [.], ack 280, win
2065, length 0

15:46:17.581627 IP resolver1.opendns.com.domain > 192.168.78.8.33813: 54875* 0/1/0 (104)


***output omitted for brevity***
```

Let's say that we want to display any transactions of the host with IP address 192.168.78.8 that took place at 15:46:15. We can use the **grep** command with a regular expressions like **cat packets.txt | grep ^15\:46:15.*78\.8**, as shown in Example 3-4. Of course, there are numerous other ways you can use regular expressions to display the same contents and manipulate that file.

Example 3-4 *Searching Using grep and Regular Expressions for Contents in packets.txt*

```
omar@odin:~/cyberOps$ cat packets.txt | grep ^15\:46:15.*78\.8
15:46:15.551728 IP 192.168.78.8.ssh > 192.168.10.100.59657: Flags [P.], seq
3299992344:3299992544,
ack 4159081141, win 389, length 200
15:46:15.602341 IP 192.168.10.100.59657 > 192.168.78.8.ssh: Flags [.], ack 200, win
2065, length 0
```

You must be familiar with regular expressions for the exam. If you are not familiar with the basic concepts of regular expressions, the following are several great resources:

- **MIT's regex Cheat Sheet**: http://web.mit.edu/hackl/www/lab/turkshop/slides/regex-cheatsheet.pdf

- **Regexp Security Cheat Sheet**: https://github.com/attackercan/regexp-security-cheat-sheet

- **Regular Expressions Info**: http://www.regular-expressions.info

- **Fun regular expression exercises**: https://regexcrossword.com

Protocols, Protocol Headers, and Intrusion Analysis

Traditional IDS and IPS, as well as next-generation IPS, can perform protocol analysis. The security device understands how various protocols, such as TCP, HTTP, TLS, Ethernet Frames, and many more, are supposed to work. They also ensure that the traffic that is inspected is compliant with the expected behavior for that protocol. In order to be able to inspect and enforce protocol compliance, the security device must look at the protocol headers. Traditional and next-generation firewalls also provide protocol inspection capabilities to make sure that such protocols are compliant. Protocol header analysis has several benefits over more primitive security techniques because it has better detection of both known and unknown attacks. This is done by alerting and blocking traffic on anomalies within the protocol transactions, instead of just simply matching traffic on signatures of security vulnerability exploits. Additionally, protocol analysis–based signatures are more difficult for threat actors to evade.

For example, if you search on the Internet for IPSec-based vulnerabilities, you will find dozens of results and examples. Traditional IDS and IPS systems leverage signatures based on the technical aspects of each vulnerability. On the other hand, by also having protocol analysis capabilities, the security device can alert on any misuse or anomaly of IPSec transactions.

Using Packet Captures for Intrusion Analysis

In the previous section, you learned about protocol analysis. One of the best ways to understand protocols and become familiar with the ins and outs of the packets traversing your network is to use *sniffers*, also called packet capture utilities. Packet captures can be used for security event research and analysis. They also confirm false positives and true positives. You can store all network traffic, including packet payload. On the other hand, one of the major disadvantages of full packet capture is that it requires large amounts of storage space and resources to analyze such data.

One of the most popular packet capture programs (or sniffers) is Wireshark. Figure 3-10 shows the Wireshark software displaying the details about a packet between source IP address 192.168.10.100 and the destination host with the IP address of 192.168.78.8.

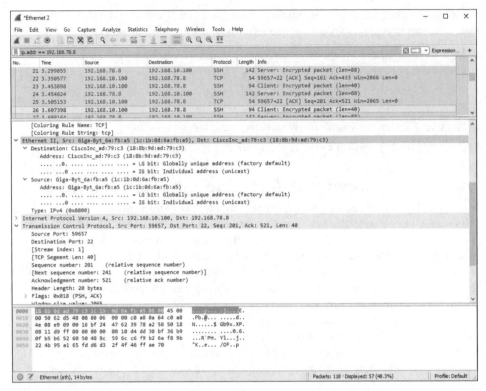

Figure 3-10 *Packet Captures in Wireshark*

In Figure 3-10, you can also see that this packet is an encrypted SSH packet that's 40 bytes long. Under the Ethernet header section that's highlighted both in the middle panel and in the lower hexadecimal dump of the packet, you can see Layer 2 details such as the MAC address of the network interface card of the source host (1c:1b:0d:6a:fb:a5) and the device in between that host and the final destination. In this case, that device is a Cisco ASA firewall with the MAC address 18:8b:9d:ad:79:c3.

Figure 3-11 shows the details about the TCP session highlighted in the middle panel and in the hexadecimal representation below it. You can see that the source port is 59657 and the destination port is the default SSH port (port 22). You can see details about the TCP header, which is 40 bytes long, as well as the TCP sequence number, acknowledge (ACK) number, TCP flags, Window size value, and much more.

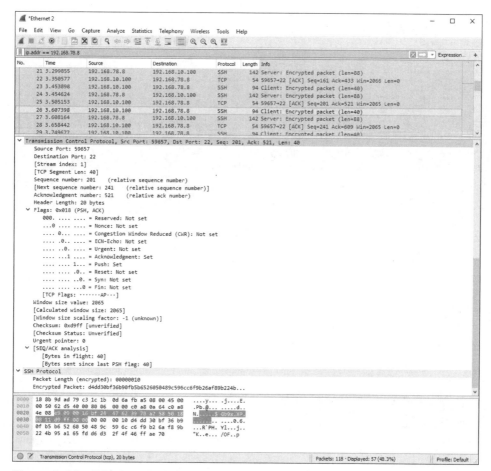

Figure 3-11   *TCP Session Information in a Full Packet Capture*

In Figure 3-11, you can also see the SSH protocol information. As you can see there, the payload of the packet is encrypted.

Packet capture tools such as Wireshark come with tons of protocol decoding capabilities and also allow you to filter packets to better analyze the ones you capture. Another great feature is the ability to follow a TCP stream in the way the application layer sees it. For example, you may not want to see just the low-level details about one packet but rather all the packets in that stream or session. In order to do this, you can select a TCP packet in the packet list of the stream you want to analyze and then select the **Follow TCP Stream** menu item from the Wireshark **Analyze** menu, as illustrated in Figure 3-12. Alternatively, you can right-click the packet and click **Follow, TCP Stream**.

Figure 3-12 *Following a TCP Stream in Wireshark*

After you select to follow the TCP stream, the screen shown in Figure 3-13 is displayed. There, you can see the details about the transactions of that stream and all the associated packets. In Figure 3-13, you can see that the session is an HTTP session. You can see the HTTP GET being sent to the HTTP server (192.168.78.8). You can even see that the server is running the NGINX web server.

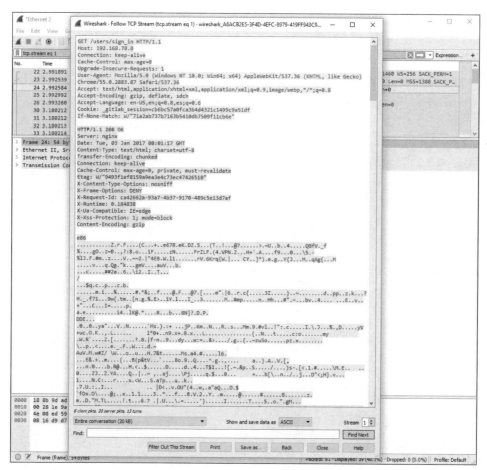

Figure 3-13   *Details about the TCP Stream in Wireshark*

Wireshark even provides capabilities that allow you to create command-line ACL rules for many different firewall products, including Cisco IOS, Linux Netfilter (iptables), OpenBSD PF, and Windows Firewall (via netsh), as shown in Figure 3-14.

Other, more scalable packet capture utilities are available. For example, Moloch is an open source full packet capture utility that provides indexing and a database in which you can store your packet captures. You can download and obtain more information about Moloch at https://github.com/aol/moloch.

Examples of commercial packet capture software are Symantec Blue Coat Security Analytics and Packet Capture (https://www.bluecoat.com/products-and-solutions/security-analytics-and-incident-response) and RSA NetWitness (https://www.rsa.com/en-us/products/threat-detection-and-response/network-monitoring-and-forensics).

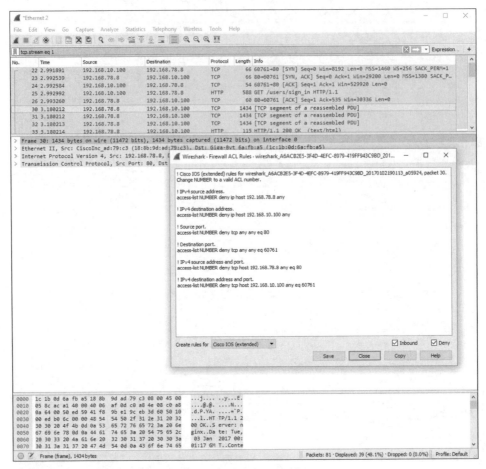

Figure 3-14   *Firewall ACL Suggestions in Wireshark*

Mapping Security Event Types to Source Technologies

You learned while preparing for the CCNA Cyber Ops SECFND exam that many different security technologies and products can be used in the security operations center (SOC) and in many organizations. It is really important to understand what products and technologies are used for what types of security events and how to analyze these events. Let's start with intrusion detection and prevention. Figure 3-15 shows the different types of analysis and features provided by intrusion detection and prevention systems as well as some sample products.

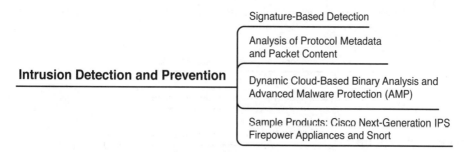

Figure 3-15 *Tools for the SOC: IDS and IPS*

Figure 3-16 shows the different types of analysis and features provided by anomaly detection systems as well as some sample products.

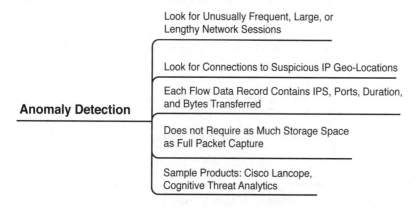

Figure 3-16 *Tools for the SOC: Anomaly Detection*

Figure 3-17 shows the different types of analysis and features provided by malware analysis technologies as well as some sample products.

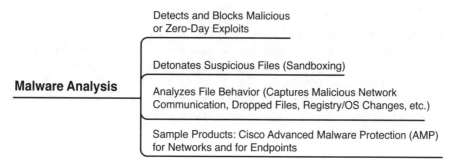

Figure 3-17 *Tools for the SOC: Malware Analysis*

Figure 3-18 shows the different types of analysis and features provided by full packet capture solutions as well as some sample products.

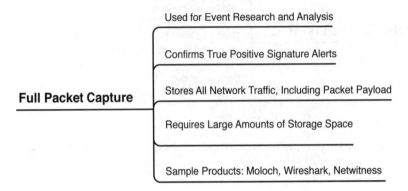

Figure 3-18   *Tools for the SOC: Full Packet Capture*

Figure 3-19 shows the different types of analysis and features provided by protocol and packet metadata solutions as well as some sample products.

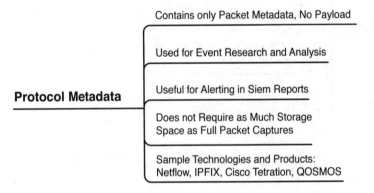

Figure 3-19   *Tools for the SOC: Protocol and Packet Metadata*

Depending on the technology and products used, you may need to analyze thousands upon thousands of logs and events. Some tools provide capabilities to see the overall health of your network, but also allow you to dive deeply into the details about each security event and potential intrusion. For instance, the Cisco Firepower Management Center (FMC) has drill-down views and a table view of events that share some common characteristics you can use to narrow a list of events. You can then concentrate your analysis on a group of related events, as shown in Figure 3-20.

Figure 3-20 *Cisco FMC Events by Priority and Classification*

In Figure 3-20, you can see two different message types related to SNMP and the number of times these events were encountered in the network. To access an intrusion event workflow in the FMC, you can navigate to **Analysis, Intrusions, Events.**

You can optionally limit the number of intrusion events that appear on the event views, as described in **Intrusion Event Drill-Down Page Constraints** or **Intrusion Event Table View Constraints.**

Figure 3-21 shows all the different events that matched the first message type or threat illustrated in Figure 3-20. In Figure 3-21 you can see detailed information about the source and destination IP addresses, geo-location information, source and destination ports, and many other types of information.

You can click each of the items shown in Figure 3-21 and either download the packets to your local system or view the packet details, as shown in Figure 3-22.

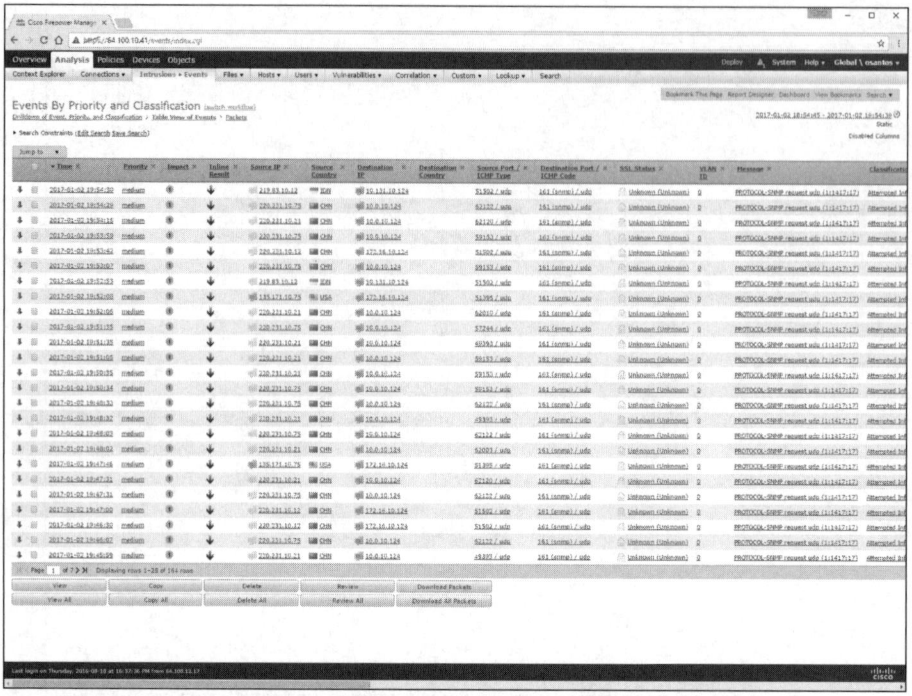

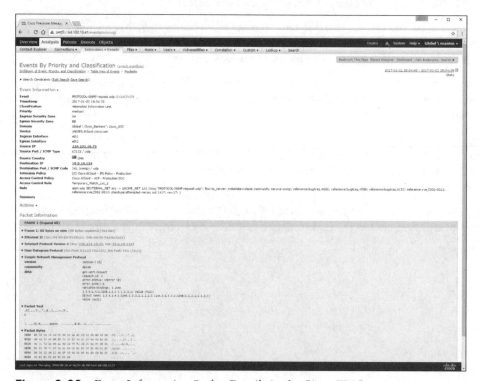

Figure 3-21   *Events by Priority and Classification Drill Down*

Figure 3-22   *Event Information Packet Details in the Cisco FMC*

Exam Preparation Tasks

Review All Key Topics

Review the most important topics in the chapter, noted with the Key Topic icon in the outer margin of the page. Table 3-2 lists a reference of these key topics and the page numbers on which each is found.

Table 3-2   Key Topics

Key Topic Element	Description	Page
Summary	Understanding the common artifact elements and sources of security events.	52
Summary	What are false positives, false negatives, true positives, and true negatives?	58
Summary	What are regular expressions?	58
Summary	Understanding protocols, protocol headers, and intrusion analysis.	61
Summary	Using Packet Captures for Intrusion Analysis	61
Summary	Mapping security event types to source technologies.	66

Complete Tables and Lists from Memory

Print a copy of Appendix B, "Memory Tables," (found on the book website), or at least the section for this chapter, and complete the tables and lists from memory. Appendix C, "Memory Tables Answer Key," also on the website, includes completed tables and lists to check your work.

Define Key Terms

Define the following key terms from this chapter, and check your answers in the glossary:

false positive, false negative, true positive, true negative, regular expression, sniffer

Q&A

The answers to these questions appear in Appendix A, "Answers to the 'Do I Know This Already' Quizzes and Q&A." For more practice with exam format questions, use the exam engine on the website.

1. Refer to the following packet capture. Which of the following statements is true about this packet capture?

```
00:00:04.549138 IP omar.cisco.com.34548 > 93.184.216.34.telnet: Flags [S], seq
3152949738, win 29200,

options [mss 1460,sackOK,TS val 1193148797 ecr 0,nop,wscale 7], length 0

00:00:05.547084 IP omar.cisco.com.34548 > 93.184.216.34.telnet: Flags [S], seq
3152949738, win 29200,

options [mss 1460,sackOK,TS val 1193149047 ecr 0,nop,wscale 7], length 0

00:00:07.551078 IP omar.cisco.com.34548 > 93.184.216.34.telnet: Flags [S], seq
3152949738, win 29200,

options [mss 1460,sackOK,TS val 1193149548 ecr 0,nop,wscale 7], length 0

00:00:11.559081 IP omar.cisco.com.34548 > 93.184.216.34.telnet: Flags [S], seq
3152949738, win 29200,

options [mss 1460,sackOK,TS val 1193150550 ecr 0,nop,wscale 7], length 0
```

   a. The host with the IP address 93.184.216.34 is the source.

   b. The host omar.cisco.com is the destination.

   c. This is a Telnet transaction that is timing out and the server is not responding.

   d. The server omar.cisco.com is responding to 93.184.216.34 with four data packets.

2. Which of the following is a successful identification of a security attack or a malicious event?

   a. True positive

   b. True negative

   c. False positive

   d. False negative

3. Which of the following is when the intrusion detection device identifies an activity as acceptable behavior and the activity is actually acceptable?

   a. True positive

   b. True negative

   c. False positive

   d. False negative

4. Which of the following terms describes a situation in which a security device triggers an alarm but there is no malicious activity or an actual attack taking place?

   a. True positive

   b. True negative

   c. False positive

   d. False negative

5. Which of the following has been used to evade IDS and IPS devices?

    a. SNMP

    b. HTTP

    c. TNP

    d. Fragmentation

6. Which of the following is not an example of an element in an IDS alert or event?

    a. Signature ID

    b. Protocol ID or number

    c. Flow record

    d. Source and destination ports

7. Which of the following are not components of the 5-tuple of a flow in NetFlow? (Select all that apply.)

    a. Source IP address

    b. Flow record ID

    c. Gateway

    d. Source port

    e. Destination port

The chapter covers the following exam topics:

- Introduction to NetFlow

- NetFlow versions

- Configuring NetFlow

- Understanding IPFIX

- NetFlow for cybersecurity and incident response

- NetFlow analysis tools

CHAPTER 4

NetFlow for Cybersecurity

This chapter starts with an introduction to NetFlow and then covers details about all the different NetFlow versions. In this chapter, you will learn how to configure basic NetFlow in a Cisco device. You will also learn about the industry standard IPFIX as well as how NetFlow is used for cybersecurity and incident response. This chapter also covers examples of commercial and open source NetFlow analysis tools.

"Do I Know This Already?" Quiz

The "Do I Know This Already?" quiz helps you identify your strengths and deficiencies in this chapter's topics. The 10-question quiz, derived from the major sections in the "Foundation Topics" portion of the chapter, helps you determine how to spend your limited study time. Table 4-1 outlines the major topics discussed in this chapter and the "Do I Know This Already?" quiz questions that correspond to those topics.

Table 4-1 "Do I Know This Already?" Foundation Topics Section-to-Question Mapping

Foundation Topics Section	Questions Covered in This Section
Introduction to NetFlow	1–3
NetFlow Versions	4–5
IPFIX	6
NetFlow for Cybersecurity and Incident Response	7–8
NetFlow Analysis Tools	9–10

1. Which of the following are some common uses of NetFlow? (Choose three.)

    a. To see what is actually happening across the entire network

    b. To identify DoS attacks

    c. To quickly identify compromised endpoints and network infrastructure devices

    d. To perform network scans to detect vulnerabilities

2. Flexible NetFlow, Cisco's next-generation NetFlow, can track a wide range of Layer 2, IPv4, and IPv6 flow information. Which of the following are examples of that information? (Choose four.)

    a. Source and destination IPv4 or IPv6 addresses

    b. Source and destination ports

    c. Packet and byte counts

    d. Flow timestamps

    e. Usernames

    f. Application ID

3. NetFlow supports different types of cache. Which of the following are the NetFlow cache types? (Choose three.)

   a. Normal

   b. Flexible

   c. Immediate

   d. Permanent

4. IPFIX is a flow standard based on what version of NetFlow?

   a. Version 1

   b. Version 5

   c. Version 7

   d. Version 9

5. What is one of the benefits of NetFlow templates?

   a. Templates make flow records more organized and better structured.

   b. Templates provide a vendor-neutral support for companies that create applications that provide collector or analysis capabilities for NetFlow so that they are not required to reinvent their product each time a new NetFlow feature is added.

   c. Templates provide a faster way of processing NetFlow records.

   d. Templates can be used to detect zero-day attacks faster because they provide support for indicators of compromise.

6. What protocol is used by IPFIX for packet transport?

   a. SNMP

   b. HTTPS

   c. SCTP

   d. TLS

7. NetFlow is a great tool for anomaly and DDoS detection. Before implementing these detection capabilities, you should perform which of the following tasks?

   a. Enable NetFlow in more than two interfaces.

   b. Enable BGP for route redirection.

   c. Develop a traffic baseline.

   d. Enable anti-spoofing protection.

8. Many network telemetry sources can also be correlated with NetFlow when responding to security incidents and performing network forensics. Which of the following are examples of other telemetry sources that can be correlated with NetFlow? (Choose two.)

   a. Dynamic Host Configuration Protocol (DHCP) logs

   b. VPN logs

   c. Core dumps

   d. Process utilization and hardware inventory logs

9. Which of the following are examples of open source tools that can be used for NetFlow analysis? (Choose three.)

   a. SiLK

   b. Elasticsearch, Logstash, Kibana (ELK)

   c. Lancope

   d. Graylog

10. Which of the following are components of the Cisco Lancope StealthWatch solution?

   a. StealthWatch Management Console

   b. FlowCollector

   c. FlowConnector

   d. ISE Connector

4

Foundation Topics

Introduction to NetFlow

NetFlow is a Cisco technology that provides comprehensive visibility into all network traffic that traverses a Cisco-supported device. Cisco invented NetFlow and is the leader in IP traffic flow technology. NetFlow was initially created for billing and accounting of network traffic and to measure other IP traffic characteristics such as bandwidth utilization and application performance. NetFlow has also been used as a network-capacity planning tool and to monitor network availability. NetFlow is used by many cybersecurity professionals as a network security tool because its reporting capabilities provide nonrepudiation, anomaly detection, and investigative capabilities. As network traffic traverses a NetFlow-enabled device, the device collects traffic flow information and provides a network administrator or security professional with detailed information about such flows.

NetFlow provides detailed network telemetry that allows the administrator to do the following:

- See what is actually happening across the entire network.
- Identify DoS attacks.
- Quickly identify compromised endpoints and network infrastructure devices.
- Monitor network usage of employees, contractors, or partners.
- Obtain network telemetry during security incident response and forensics.
- Detect firewall misconfigurations and inappropriate access to corporate resources.

NetFlow supports both IP version 4 (IPv4) and IP version 6 (IPv6), and it plays a crucial role in the following:

- Network planning
- Network security
- Network troubleshooting
- Traffic engineering

> **TIP**   Do not confuse the feature in Cisco IOS software called IP Accounting with NetFlow. IP Accounting is a great Cisco IOS tool, but it is not as robust or as well known as NetFlow.

What Is a Flow in NetFlow?

A *flow* is a unidirectional series of packets between a given source and destination. In a flow, the same source and destination IP addresses, source and destination ports, and IP protocol are shared. This is often referred to as the 5-tuple. Figure 4-1 shows an example of a flow between a client and a server.

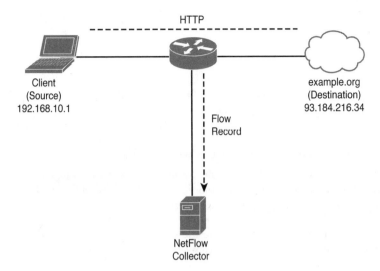

Figure 4-1 *Basic NetFlow Example*

In Figure 4-1, the client (source) establishes a connection to the server (destination). When the traffic traverses the router (configured for NetFlow), it generates a flow record. At the very minimum, the 5-tuple is used to identify the flow in the NetFlow database of flows kept on the device. This database is often called the NetFlow cache.

Table 4-2 shows the 5-tuple for the basic flow represented in Figure 4-1.

Table 4-2 NetFlow 5-Tuple

Flow Record Field	Value
Source IP address	192.168.10.1
Destination IP address	93.184.216.34
Source port	17238
Destination port	80
Protocol	TCP

Depending on the version of NetFlow, the router can also gather additional information, such as type of service (ToS) byte, differentiated services code point (DSCP), the device's input interface, TCP flags, byte counters, and start and end times.

Flexible NetFlow, Cisco's next-generation NetFlow, can track a wide range of Layer 2, IPv4, and IPv6 flow information, such as the following:

■ Source and destination MAC addresses

■ Source and destination IPv4 or IPv6 addresses

■ Source and destination ports

■ ToS

- DSCP
- Packet and byte counts
- Flow timestamps
- Input and output interface numbers
- TCP flags and encapsulated protocol (TCP/UDP) and individual TCP flags
- Sections of a packet for deep packet inspection
- All fields in an IPv4 header, including IP-ID and TTL
- All fields in an IPv6 header, including Flow Label and Option Header
- Routing information, such as next-hop address, source autonomous system number (ASN), destination ASN, source prefix mask, destination prefix mask, Border Gateway Protocol (BGP) next hop, and BGP policy accounting traffic index

NetFlow protocol data units (PDUs), also referred to as flow records, are generated and sent to a NetFlow collector after the flow concludes or expires (times out).

The NetFlow Cache

There are three types of NetFlow cache:

- **Normal cache:** This is the default cache type in many infrastructure devices enabled with NetFlow and Flexible NetFlow. The entries in the flow cache are removed (aged out) based on the configured timeout active seconds and timeout inactive seconds settings.
- **Immediate cache:**
  - Flow accounts for a single packet
  - Desirable for real-time traffic monitoring and distributed DoS (DDoS) detection
  - Used when only very small flows are expected (for example, sampling)

NOTE   The immediate cache may result in a large amount of export data.

- **Permanent cache:**
  - Used to track a set of flows without expiring the flows from the cache.
  - The entire cache is periodically exported (update timer).
  - The cache is a configurable value.
  - After the cache is full, new flows will not be monitored.
  - Uses update counters rather than delta counters.

Many people often confuse a flow with a session. All traffic in a flow is unidirectional; however, when the client establishes the HTTP connection (session) to the server and accesses a web page, this represents two separate flows. The first flow is the traffic from the client to the server, and the other is the return flow from the server to the client.

NetFlow Versions

There are several versions of NetFlow. Table 4-3 lists all versions of NetFlow and provides a brief description of the features supported.

Table 4-3 NetFlow Versions

NetFlow Version	Description
Version 1 (v1)	(Obsolete.) The first implementation of NetFlow. NetFlow v1 was limited to IPv4 without IP network masks and autonomous system numbers (ASNs).
Version 2 (v2)	Never released.
Version 3 (v3)	Never released.
Version 4 (v4)	Never released.
Version 5 (v5)	Popular NetFlow version on many routers from different vendors. Limited to IPv4 flows.
Version 6 (v6)	(Obsolete.) No longer supported by Cisco.
Version 7 (v7)	(Obsolete.) Like version 5, with a source router field.
Version 8 (v8)	(Obsolete.) Several aggregation forms, but only for information that is already present in v5 records.
Version 9 (v9)	Template based, available (as of 2009) on some recent routers. Mostly used to report flows such as IPv6, Multiprotocol Label Switching (MPLS), and even plain IPv4 with Border Gateway Protocol (BGP) next hop.
IPFIX	IPFIX is an IETF standard based on NetFlow v9 with several extensions.

Table 4-4 lists the NetFlow v1 flow header format, and Table 4-5 lists the attributes of the NetFlow v1 flow record format.

Table 4-4 NetFlow v1 Flow Header Format

Bytes	Contents	Description
0–1	version	NetFlow export format version number
2–3	count	Number of flows exported in this packet (1–24)
4–7	sys_uptime	Current time in milliseconds since the export device booted
8–11	unix_secs	Current count of seconds since 0000 UTC 1970
12–16	unix_nsecs	Residual nanoseconds since 0000 UTC 1970

Table 4-5   NetFlow v1 Flow Record Format

Bytes	Contents	Description
0–3	srcaddr	Source IP address
4–7	dstaddr	Destination IP address
8–11	nexthop	IP address of next-hop router
12–13	input	SNMP index of input interface
14–15	output	SNMP index of output interface
16–19	dPkts	Packets in the flow
20–23	dOctets	Total number of Layer 3 bytes in the packets of the flow
24–27	first	SysUptime at start of flow
28–31	last	SysUptime at the time the last packet of the flow was received
32–33	srcport	TCP/UDP source port number or equivalent
34–35	dstport	TCP/UDP destination port number or equivalent
36–37	pad1	Unused (0) bytes
38	prot	IP protocol type (for example, TCP = 6; UDP = 17)
39	tos	IP type of service (ToS)
40	flags	Cumulative OR of TCP flags
41-48	pad2	Unused (0) bytes

Table 4-6 lists the NetFlow v5 flow header format, and Table 4-7 lists the attributes of the NetFlow v5 flow record format.

Table 4-6   NetFlow v5 Flow Header Format

Bytes	Contents	Description
0–1	version	NetFlow export format version number.
2–3	count	Number of flows exported in this packet (1–30).
4–7	sys_uptime	Current time in milliseconds since the export device booted.
8–11	unix_secs	Current count of seconds since 0000 UTC 1970.
12–15	unix_nsecs	Residual nanoseconds since 0000 UTC 1970.
16-19	flow_sequence	Sequence counter of total flows seen.
20	engine_type	Type of flow-switching engine.
21	engine_id	Slot number of the flow-switching engine.
22–23	sampling_interval	First 2 bits hold the sampling mode; remaining 14 bits hold value of sampling interval.

Table 4-7 NetFlow v5 Flow Record Format

Bytes	Contents	Description
0–3	srcaddr	Source IP address
4–7	dstaddr	Destination IP address
8–11	nexthop	IP address of next-hop router
12–13	input	Simple Network Management Protocol (SNMP) index of input interface
14–15	output	SNMP index of output interface
16–19	dPkts	Packets in the flow
20–23	dOctets	Total number of Layer 3 bytes in the packets of the flow
24–27	first	SysUptime at start of flow
28–31	last	SysUptime at the time the last packet of the flow was received
32–33	srcport	TCP/UDP source port number or equivalent
34–35	dstport	TCP/UDP destination port number or equivalent
36	pad1	Unused (0) bytes
37	tcp_flags	Cumulative OR of TCP flags
38	prot	IP protocol type (for example, TCP = 6; UDP = 17)
39	tos	IP type of service (ToS)
40–41	src_as	Autonomous system number (ASN) of the source, either origin or peer
42–43	dst_as	ASN of the destination, either origin or peer
44	src_mask	Source address prefix mask bits
45	dst_mask	Destination address prefix mask bits
46–47	pad2	Unused (0) bytes

Table 4-8 lists the NetFlow v7 flow header format, and Table 4-9 lists the attributes of the NetFlow v7 flow record format.

Table 4-8 NetFlow v7 Flow Header Format

Bytes	Contents	Description
0–1	version	NetFlow export format version number
2–3	count	Number of flows exported in this packet (1–30)
4–7	sys_uptime	Current time in milliseconds since the export device booted
8–11	unix_secs	Current count of seconds since 0000 UTC 1970
12–15	unix_nsecs	Residual nanoseconds since 0000 UTC 1970

Bytes	Contents	Description
16–19	flow_sequence	Sequence counter of total flows seen
20–23	reserved	Unused (0) bytes

Table 4-9   NetFlow v7 Flow Record Format

Bytes	Contents	Description
0–3	srcaddr	Source IP address.
4–7	dstaddr	Destination IP address.
8–11	nexthop	IP address of next-hop router.
12–13	input	SNMP index of input interface.
14–15	output	SNMP index of output interface.
16–19	dPkts	Packets in the flow.
20–23	dOctets	Total number of Layer 3 bytes in the packets of the flow.
24–27	first	SysUptime at start of flow.
28–31	last	SysUptime at the time the last packet of the flow was received.
32–33	srcport	TCP/UDP source port number or equivalent.
34–35	dstport	TCP/UDP destination port number or equivalent.
36	pad1	Unused (0) bytes.
37	tcp_flags	Cumulative OR of TCP flags.
38	prot	IP protocol type (for example, TCP = 6; UDP = 17).
39	tos	IP type of service (ToS).
40–41	src_as	ASN of the source, either origin or peer.
42–43	dst_as	ASN of the destination, either origin or peer.
44	src_mask	Source address prefix mask bits.
45	dst_mask	Destination address prefix mask bits.
46–47	flags	Flags indicating, among other things, what flows are invalid.
48–51	router_sc	IP address of the router that is bypassed by the Catalyst 5000 series switch. (This is the same address the router uses when it sends NetFlow export packets. This IP address is propagated to all switches bypassing the router through the Fibre Channel Protocol [FCP].)

The most popular version of NetFlow is Version 9. The NetFlow v9 format is template based. Templates provide a flexible design to the record format. This feature allows for future enhancements to NetFlow services without requiring fundamental changes to the underlying flow record format.

The following are the benefits of using NetFlow templates:

■ They provide vendor-neutral support for companies that create applications that provide collector or analysis capabilities for NetFlow so that they are not required to reinvent their product each time a new NetFlow feature is added.

■ New features can be added to NetFlow more quickly, without breaking current implementations and with backward compatibility.

The NetFlow v9 record format consists of a packet header followed by at least one or more template or data FlowSets. A template FlowSet provides a description of the fields that will be present in future data FlowSets. These data FlowSets may occur later within the same export packet or in subsequent export packets. Figure 4-2 shows a basic illustration of the NetFlow v9 export packet.

Packet Header	Template FlowSet	Data FlowSet	Data FlowSet	....	Template FlowSet	Data FlowSet

Figure 4-2 *NetFlow v9 Export Packet*

Figure 4-3 shows a more detailed illustration of the NetFlow v9 export packet and the relationship between each field and its attributes.

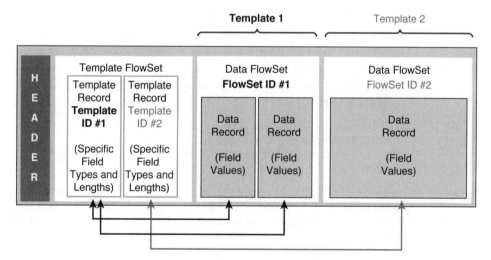

Figure 4-3 *NetFlow v9 Export Packet Details*

The format of the NetFlow v9 packet header is very similar to its predecessors and is illustrated in Figure 4-4.

0	1	2	3	4	5	6	7	8	9	10	11	12	13	14	15	16	17	18	19	20	21	22	23	24	25	26	27	28	29	30	31
Version																Count															
System Uptime																															
UNIX Seconds																															
Package Sequence																															
Source ID																															

Figure 4-4 *NetFlow v9 Packet Header Format*

Table 4-10 lists the NetFlow v9 packet header field descriptions.

Table 4-10   NetFlow v9 Packet Header Field Descriptions

Field Name	Value
Version	The version of NetFlow records exported in this packet. The hexadecimal value 0x0009 represents NetFlow v9.
Count	Number of FlowSet records (both template and data) contained within the export packet.
System Uptime	Time in milliseconds since the device started.
UNIX Seconds	Seconds since 0000 coordinated universal time (UTC) 1970.
Sequence Number	Incremental sequence counter of all export packets sent by this export device; this value is cumulative, and it can be used to identify whether any export packets have been missed. **Note:** This is a change from the NetFlow v5 and v8 headers, where this number represented "total flows."
Source ID	A 32-bit value that is used to ensure uniqueness for all flows exported from a particular NetFlow-enabled device. The Source ID field is the equivalent of the Engine Type and Engine ID fields found in the NetFlow v5 and v8 headers. The format of this field is vendor specific. In Cisco's implementation, the first 2 bytes are reserved for future expansion and will always be 0. Byte 3 provides uniqueness with respect to the routing engine on the exporting device. Byte 4 provides uniqueness with respect to the particular line card or Versatile Interface Processor on the exporting device. NetFlow collectors should use the combination of the source IP address plus the Source ID field to associate an incoming NetFlow export packet with a unique instance of NetFlow on a particular device.

As previously mentioned, templates are one of the main benefits of NetFlow v9 because they provide flexibility to allow a NetFlow collector or display application to process NetFlow data without necessarily knowing the format of the data in advance.

Figure 4-5 shows the format of the NetFlow v9 template FlowSet.

0	1	2	3	4	5	6	7	8	9	10	11	12	13	14	15
Flowset_Id = 0
Length
Template_Id
Field_Count
Field_1_Type
Field_1_Length
Field_2_Type
Field_2_Length
Field_3_Type
Field_3_Length
...
Field_N_Type
Field_N_Length
Template_Id
Field_Count
Field_1_Type
Field_1_Length
...
Field_N_Type
Field_N_Length

Figure 4-5 *NetFlow v9 Template FlowSet Format*

Table 4-11 lists the NetFlow v9 template FlowSet field descriptions.

Table 4-11 NetFlow v9 Template FlowSet Field Descriptions

Field	Description
flowset_id	The flowset_id field is used to distinguish template records from data records. A template record always has a flowset_id in the range of 0 to 255. Currently, the template record that describes flow fields has a flowset_id of 0, and the template record that describes option fields (described later) has a flowset_id of 1. A data record always has a nonzero flowset_id greater than 255.
length	Length refers to the total length of this FlowSet. Because an individual template FlowSet may contain multiple template IDs (as illustrated earlier), the length value should be used to determine the position of the next FlowSet record, which could be either a template or a data FlowSet.
	Length is expressed in type/length/value (TLV) format, meaning that the value includes the bytes used for the flowset_id and the length of bytes themselves, in addition to the combined lengths of all template records included in this FlowSet.

Field	Description
template_id	As a router generates different template FlowSets to match the type of NetFlow data it will be exporting, each template is given a unique ID. This uniqueness is local to the router that generated the template_id. Templates that define data record formats begin numbering at 256 because 0 through 255 are reserved for FlowSet IDs.
field_count	This field gives the number of fields in this template record. Because a template FlowSet may contain multiple template records, this field allows the parser to determine the end of the current template record and the start of the next.
field_type	This numeric value represents the type of the field. The possible values of the field type are vendor specific. Cisco-supplied values are consistent across all platforms that support NetFlow v9. At the time of the initial release of the NetFlow v9 code (and after any subsequent changes that could add new field-type definitions), Cisco provided a file that defines the known field types and their lengths. Table 4-12 details the currently defined field types.
field_length	This number gives the length of the field_type field, in bytes.

Table 4-12 lists the NetFlow v9 field type definitions.

Table 4-12   NetFlow v9 Field Type Definitions

Field Type	Value	Length (bytes)	Description
IN_BYTES	1	N (default is 4)	Incoming counter with length N × 8 bits for number of bytes associated with an IP flow.
IN_PKTS	2	N (default is 4)	Incoming counter with length N × 8 bits for the number of packets associated with an IP flow.
FLOWS	3	N	Number of flows that were aggregated; default for N is 4.
PROTOCOL	4	1	IP protocol byte.
SRC_TOS	5	1	Type of service byte setting when entering incoming interface.
TCP_FLAGS	6	1	Cumulative of all the TCP flags seen for this flow.
L4_SRC_PORT	7	2	TCP/UDP source port number (for example, FTP, Telnet, or equivalent).
IPV4_SRC_ADDR	8	4	IPv4 source address.

Field Type	Value	Length (bytes)	Description
SRC_MASK	9	1	The number of contiguous bits in the source address subnet mask (that is, the submask in slash notation).
INPUT_SNMP	10	N	Input interface index; default for N is 2, but higher values could be used.
L4_DST_PORT	11	2	TCP/UDP destination port number (for example, FTP, Telnet, or equivalent).
IPV4_DST_ADDR	12	4	IPv4 destination address.
DST_MASK	13	1	The number of contiguous bits in the destination address subnet mask (that is, the submask in slash notation).
OUTPUT_SNMP	14	N	Output interface index; default for N is 2, but higher values could be used.
IPV4_NEXT_HOP	15	4	IPv4 address of next-hop router.
SRC_AS	16	N (default is 2)	Source BGP ASN, where N could be 2 or 4.
DST_AS	17	N (default is 2)	Destination BGP ASN, where N could be 2 or 4.
BGP_IPV4_NEXT_HOP	18	4	Next-hop router's IP in the BGP domain.
MUL_DST_PKTS	19	N (default is 4)	IP multicast outgoing packet counter with length $N \times 8$ bits for packets associated with the IP flow.
MUL_DST_BYTES	20	N (default is 4)	IP multicast outgoing byte counter with length $N \times 8$ bits for bytes associated with the IP flow.
LAST_SWITCHED	21	4	System uptime at which the last packet of this flow was switched.
FIRST_SWITCHED	22	4	System uptime at which the first packet of this flow was switched.
OUT_BYTES	23	N (default is 4)	Outgoing counter with length $N \times 8$ bits for the number of bytes associated with an IP flow.
OUT_PKTS	24	N (default is 4)	Outgoing counter with length $N \times 8$ bits for the number of packets associated with an IP flow.
MIN_PKT_LNGTH	25	2	Minimum IP packet length on incoming packets of the flow.

4

Field Type	Value	Length (bytes)	Description
MAX_PKT_LNGTH	26	2	Maximum IP packet length on incoming packets of the flow.
IPV6_SRC_ADDR	27	16	IPv6 source address.
IPV6_DST_ADDR	28	16	IPv6 destination address.
IPV6_SRC_MASK	29	1	Length of the IPv6 source mask in contiguous bits.
IPV6_DST_MASK	30	1	Length of the IPv6 destination mask in contiguous bits.
IPV6_FLOW_LABEL	31	3	IPv6 flow label as per RFC 2460 definition.
ICMP_TYPE	32	2	Internet Control Message Protocol (ICMP) packet type; reported as ((ICMP Type * 256) + ICMP code).
MUL_IGMP_TYPE	33	1	Internet Group Management Protocol (IGMP) packet type.
SAMPLING_INTERVAL	34	4	When using sampled NetFlow, this is the rate at which packets are sampled. For example, a value of 100 indicates that 1 of every 100 packets is sampled.
SAMPLING_ALGORITHM	35	1	The type of algorithm used for sampled NetFlow: 0x01 = deterministic sampling, 0x02 = random sampling.
FLOW_ACTIVE_TIMEOUT	36	2	Timeout value (in seconds) for active flow entries in the NetFlow cache.
FLOW_INACTIVE_TIMEOUT	37	2	Timeout value (in seconds) for inactive flow entries in the NetFlow cache.
ENGINE_TYPE	38	1	Type of flow switching engine: RP = 0, VIP/Linecard = 1.
ENGINE_ID	39	1	ID number of the flow switching engine.
TOTAL_BYTES_EXP	40	N (default is 4)	Counter with length N × 8 bits for the number of bytes exported by the observation domain.
TOTAL_PKTS_EXP	41	N (default is 4)	Counter with length N × 8 bits for the number of packets exported by the observation domain.
TOTAL_FLOWS_EXP	42	N (default is 4)	Counter with length N × 8 bits for the number of flows exported by the observation domain.
Vendor proprietary	43	N/A	N/A

Field Type	Value	Length (bytes)	Description
IPV4_SRC_PREFIX	44	4	IPv4 source address prefix (specific for Catalyst architecture).
IPV4_DST_PREFIX	45	4	IPv4 destination address prefix (specific for Catalyst architecture).
MPLS_TOP_LABEL_TYPE	46	1	MPLS top label type: 0x00 = UNKNOWN, 0x01 = TE-MIDPT, 0x02 = ATOM, 0x03 = VPN, 0x04 = BGP, 0x05 = LDP.
MPLS_TOP_LABEL_IP_ADDR	47	4	Forwarding Equivalent Class corresponding to the MPLS top label.
FLOW_SAMPLER_ID	48	1	Identifier shown in show flow-sampler.
FLOW_SAMPLER_MODE	49	1	The type of algorithm used for sampling data: 0x02 = random sampling. Used in connection with FLOW_SAMPLER_MODE.
FLOW_SAMPLER_RANDOM_INTERVAL	50	4	Packet interval at which to sample. Used in connection with FLOW_SAMPLER_MODE.
Vendor proprietary	51	N/A	N/A
MIN_TTL	52	1	Minimum Time to Live (TTL) on incoming packets of the flow.
MAX_TTL	53	1	Maximum TTL on incoming packets of the flow.
IPV4_IDENT	54	2	The IP v4 identification field.
DST_TOS	55	1	Type of service byte setting when exiting outgoing interface.
IN_SRC_MAC	56	6	Incoming source MAC address.
OUT_DST_MAC	57	6	Outgoing destination MAC address.
SRC_VLAN	58	2	Virtual LAN identifier associated with ingress interface.
DST_VLAN	59	2	Virtual LAN identifier associated with egress interface.
IP_PROTOCOL_VERSION	60	1	Internet Protocol version set to 4 for IPv4, set to 6 for IPv6. If not present in the template, Version 4 is assumed.
DIRECTION	61	1	Flow direction: 0 = ingress flow, 1 = egress flow.
IPV6_NEXT_HOP	62	16	IPv6 address of the next-hop router.
BPG_IPV6_NEXT_HOP	63	16	Next-hop router in the BGP domain.

4

Field Type	Value	Length (bytes)	Description
IPV6_OPTION_HEADERS	64	4	Bit-encoded field identifying IPv6 option headers found in the flow.
Vendor proprietary	65	N/A	N/A
Vendor proprietary	66	N/A	N/A
Vendor proprietary	67	N/A	N/A
Vendor proprietary	68	N/A	N/A
Vendor proprietary	69	N/A	N/A
MPLS_LABEL_1	70	3	MPLS label at position 1 in the stack.
MPLS_LABEL_2	71	3	MPLS label at position 2 in the stack.
MPLS_LABEL_3	72	3	MPLS label at position 3 in the stack.
MPLS_LABEL_4	73	3	MPLS label at position 4 in the stack.
MPLS_LABEL_5	74	3	MPLS label at position 5 in the stack.
MPLS_LABEL_6	75	3	MPLS label at position 6 in the stack.
MPLS_LABEL_7	76	3	MPLS label at position 7 in the stack.
MPLS_LABEL_8	77	3	MPLS label at position 8 in the stack.
MPLS_LABEL_9	78	3	MPLS label at position 9 in the stack.
MPLS_LABEL_10	79	3	MPLS label at position 10 in the stack.
IN_DST_MAC	80	6	Incoming destination MAC address.
OUT_SRC_MAC	81	6	Outgoing source MAC address.
IF_NAME	82	N (default specified in template)	Shortened interface name (for example, FE1/0).
IF_DESC	83	N (default specified in template)	Full interface name (for example, FastEthernet 1/0).
SAMPLER_NAME	84	N (default specified in template)	Name of the flow sampler.
IN_PERMANENT_BYTES	85	N (default is 4)	Running byte counter for a permanent flow.
IN_PERMANENT_PKTS	86	N (default is 4)	Running packet counter for a permanent flow.
Vendor proprietary	87	N/A	N/A

Field Type	Value	Length (bytes)	Description
FRAGMENT_OFFSET	88	2	The fragment-offset value from fragmented IP packets.
FORWARDING STATUS	89	1	Forwarding status is encoded on 1 byte, with the 2 left bits giving the status and the 6 remaining bits giving the reason code.
MPLS PAL RD	90	8 (array)	MPLS PAL route distinguisher.
MPLS PREFIX LEN	91	1	Number of consecutive bits in the MPLS prefix length.
SRC TRAFFIC INDEX	92	4	BGP policy accounting source traffic index.
DST TRAFFIC INDEX	93	4	BGP policy accounting destination traffic index.
APPLICATION DESCRIPTION	94	N	Description of the application.
APPLICATION TAG	95	1+n	Eight bits of engine ID, followed by n bits of classification.
APPLICATION NAME	96	N	Application name associated with a classification.
Not used	97	N/A	N/A
postipDiffServCodePoint	98	1	The value of a differentiated services code point (DSCP) encoded in the Differentiated Services field, after modification.
replication factor	99	4	Multicast replication factor.
Deprecated	100	N	Deprecated.
Not used	101	N/A	N/A
layer2packetSectionOffset	102		Layer 2 packet section offset.
layer2packetSectionSize	103		Layer 2 packet section size.
layer2packetSectionData	104		Layer 2 packet section data.
Reserved for future use	105 thru 127	N/A	N/A

Figure 4-6 shows the NetFlow v9 template FlowSet format.

0	1	2	3	4	5	6	7	8	9	10	11	12	13	14	15
FlowSet ID = Template ID															
Length															
Record 1 - Field 1 Value															
Record 1 - Field 2 Value															
Record 1 - Field 3 Value															
Record 1 - Field 4 Value															
					.										
					.										
					.										
Record 1 - Field N Value															
Record 2 - Field 1 Value															
Record 2 - Field 2 Value															
Record 2 - Field 3 Value															
					.										
					.										
					.										
Record 2 - Field N Value															
					.										
					.										
					.										
Padding															

Figure 4-6 *NetFlow v9 Template FlowSet Format*

Table 4-13 lists the NetFlow v9 data FlowSet definitions.

Table 4-13 NetFlow v9 Data FlowSet Definitions

Field	Description
flowset_id	A FlowSet ID precedes each group of records within a NetFlow v9 data FlowSet. The FlowSet ID maps to a (previously received) template_id. The collector and display applications should use the flowset_id to map the appropriate type and length to any field values that follow.
length	This field gives the length of the data FlowSet. Length is expressed in TLV format, meaning that the value includes the bytes used for the flowset_id and the length bytes themselves, as well as the combined lengths of any included data records.
record_N through field_M	The remainder of the v9 data FlowSet is a collection of field values. The type and length of the fields have been previously defined in the template record referenced by the flowset_id/template_id.
padding	Padding should be inserted to align the end of the FlowSet on a 32-bit boundary. Pay attention that the length field will include those padding bits.

IPFIX is modeled after NetFlow v9. This is why many of these NetFlow v9 concepts and fields are very similar to IPFIX. Just like IPFIX, NetFlow v9 has the concept of options templates used to supply metadata about the NetFlow process itself. Figure 4-7 illustrates the format of the options template.

0	1	2	3	4	5	6	7	8	9	10	11	12	13	14	15
FlowSet_Id = 1															
Length															
Template_Id															
Option_Scope_Length															
Option_Length															
Scope_Field_1_Type															
Scope_Field_1_Length															
…															
Scope_Field_N_Length															
Option_Field_1_Type															
Option_Field_1_Length															
…															
Option_Field_N_Length															
Padding															

Figure 4-7   *NetFlow v9 Options Template Format*

Table 4-14 lists the NetFlow v9 data options template definitions.

Table 4-14   NetFlow v9 Data Options Template Definitions

Field	Description
flowset_id = 1	The flowset_id is used to distinguish template records from data records. A template record always has a flowset_id of 1. A data record always has a nonzero flowset_id that is greater than 255.
length	This field gives the total length of this FlowSet. Because an individual template FlowSet may contain multiple template IDs, the length value should be used to determine the position of the next FlowSet record, which could be either a template or a data FlowSet. Length is expressed in TLV format, meaning that the value includes the bytes used for the flowset_id and the length of bytes themselves, as well as the combined lengths of all template records included in this FlowSet.
template_id	As a router generates different template FlowSets to match the type of NetFlow data it will be exporting, each template is given a unique ID. This uniqueness is local to the router that generated the template_id. The template_id is greater than 255. Template IDs less than 255 are reserved.
option_scope_length	This field gives the length in bytes of any scope fields contained in this options template.
options_length	This field gives the length (in bytes) of any Options field definitions contained in this options template.

Field	Description
scope_field_N_type	This field gives the relevant portion of the NetFlow process to which the options record refers. Currently defined values follow: 0x0001 = system 0x0002 = interface 0x0003 = line card 0x0004 = NetFlow cache 0x0005 = template For instance, Random Sampled NetFlow can be implemented on a per-interface basis. So, if the options record were reporting on how sampling is configured, the scope for the report would be 0x0002 (interface).
scope_field_N_length	This field gives the length (in bytes) of the Scope field, as it would appear in an options record.
option_field_N_type	This numeric value represents the type of the field that appears in the options record. Possible values are detailed in template FlowSet format.
option_field_N_length	This number is the length (in bytes) of the field, as it would appear in an options record.
padding	Padding is inserted to align the end of the FlowSet on a 32-bit boundary.

Cisco Flexible NetFlow

Flexible NetFlow provides enhanced optimization of the network infrastructure, reduces costs, and improves capacity planning and security detection beyond other flow-based technologies available today. Flexible NetFlow supports IPv6 and Network-Based Application Recognition (NBAR) 2 for IPv6 starting in Cisco IOS Software Version 15.2(1)T. It also supports IPv6 transition techniques (IPv6 inside IPv4). Flexible NetFlow can detect the following tunneling technologies that give full IPv6 connectivity for IPv6-capable hosts that are on the IPv4 Internet but that have no direct native connection to an IPv6 network:

- Teredo
- Intra-Site Automatic Tunnel Addressing Protocol (ISATAP)
- 6to4
- 6rd

Flexible NetFlow classification inside Teredo, ISATAP, 6to4, and 6rd was introduced in Cisco IOS Software Version 15.2(2)T. Export over IPv6 was introduced in Cisco IOS Software Version 15.2(2)T, Cisco IOS XE 3.7.0S, and Cisco Nexus Software Version 4.2.1.

Flexible NetFlow tracks different applications simultaneously. For instance, security monitoring, traffic analysis, and billing can be tracked separately, and the information customized per application.

Flexible NetFlow allows the network administrator or security professional to create multiple flow caches or information databases to track. Conventionally, NetFlow has a single cache and all applications use the same cache information. Flexible NetFlow supports the collection of specific security information in one flow cache and traffic analysis in another. Subsequently, each NetFlow cache serves a different purpose. For instance, multicast and security information can be tracked separately and the results sent to two different collectors. Figure 4-8 shows the Flexible NetFlow model and how three different monitors are used. Monitor 1 exports Flexible NetFlow data to "Exporter 1." Monitor 2 exports Flexible NetFlow data to "Exporter 2," and Monitor 3 exports Flexible NetFlow data to "Exporter 1" and "Exporter 3."

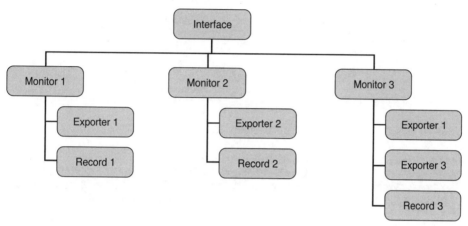

Figure 4-8   *The Flexible NetFlow Model*

The following are the Flexible NetFlow components:

- Records
- Flow monitors
- Flow exporters
- Flow samplers

In Flexible NetFlow, the administrator can specify what to track, resulting in fewer flows. This helps to scale in busy networks and use fewer resources that are already taxed by other features and services.

Flexible NetFlow Records

Flexible NetFlow records are a combination of key and non-key fields. In Flexible NetFlow, records are appointed to flow monitors to define the cache that is used for storing flow data. There are seven default attributes in the IP packet identity, or "key fields," for a flow and for a device to determine whether the packet information is unique or similar to other packets sent over the network. Fields such as TCP flags, subnet masks, packets, and number of bytes are "non-key fields." However, they are often collected and exported in NetFlow or in IPFIX.

Flexible NetFlow Key Fields

There are several Flexible NetFlow key fields in each packet that is forwarded within a NetFlow-enabled device. The device looks for a set of IP packet attributes for the flow and determines whether the packet information is unique or similar to other packets. In Flexible NetFlow, key fields are configurable, which enables the administrator to conduct a more granular traffic analysis.

Table 4-15 lists the key fields related to the actual flow, device interface, and Layer 2 services.

Table 4-15   Flexible NetFlow Key Fields Related to Flow, Interface, and Layer 2

	Flow	Interface	Layer 2
Fields	Sampler ID	Input	Source VLAN
	Direction	Output	Destination VLAN
	Class ID		Dot1q priority
			Source MAC address
			Destination MAC address

Table 4-16 lists the IPv4- and IPv6-related key fields.

Table 4-16   Flexible NetFlow IPv4 and IPv6 Key Fields

	IPv4	IPv6
Fields	IP (Source or Destination)	IP (Source or Destination)
	Prefix (Source or Destination)	Prefix (Source or Destination)
	Mask (Source or Destination)	Mask (Source or Destination)
	Minimum-Mask (Source or Destination)	Minimum-Mask (Source or Destination)
	Protocol	Protocol
	Fragmentation Flags	Traffic Class
	Fragmentation Offset	Flow Label
	Identification	Option Header
	Header Length	Header Length
	Total Length	Payload Length
	Payload Size	Payload Size
	Packet Section (Header)	Packet Section (Header)
	Packet Section (Payload)	Packet Section (Payload)
	Time to Live (TTL)	DSCP
	Options bitmap	Extension Headers
	Version	Hop-Limit
	Precedence	Length
	DSCP	Next-header
	TOS	Version

Table 4-17 lists the Layer 3 routing protocol–related key fields.

Table 4-17 Flexible NetFlow Layer 3 Routing Protocol Key Fields

	Routing
Fields	Source or Destination AS
	Peer AS
	Traffic Index
	Forwarding Status
	Input VRF Name
	IGP Next Hop
	BGP Next Hop

Table 4-18 lists the transport-related key fields.

Table 4-18 Flexible NetFlow Transport Key Fields

	Transport
Fields	Destination Port
	Source Port
	ICMP Code
	ICMP Type
	IGMP Type (IPv4 only)
	TCP ACK Number
	TCP Header Length
	TCP Sequence Number
	TCP Window-Size
	TCP Source Port
	TCP Destination Port
	TCP Urgent Pointer

Only the Application ID is a Layer 3 routing protocol key field.

Table 4-19 lists the multicast-related key fields.

Table 4-19   Flexible NetFlow Multicast Key Fields

	Multicast
Fields	Replication Factor (IPv4 only)
	RPF Check Drop (IPv4 only)
	Is-Multicast

Flexible NetFlow Non-Key Fields

There are several non-key Flexible NetFlow fields. Table 4-20 lists the non-key fields that are related to counters, such as byte counts, number of packets, and more. A network administrator can use non-key fields for different purposes. For instance, the number of packets and amount of data (bytes) can be used for capacity planning and also to identify denial-of-service (DoS) attacks as well as other anomalies in the network.

Table 4-20   Flexible NetFlow Counters Non-Key Fields

	Counters
Fields	Bytes
	Bytes Long
	Bytes Square Sum
	Bytes Square Sum Long
	Packets
	Packets Long
	Bytes Replicated
	Bytes Replicated Long
	Packets Replicated
	Packets Replicated Long

Table 4-21 lists the timestamp-related non-key fields.

Table 4-21   Flexible NetFlow Timestamp Non-Key Fields

	Timestamp
Fields	sysUpTime First Packet
	sysUpTime First Packet
	Absolute First Packet
	Absolute Last Packet

Table 4-22 lists the IPv4-only non-key fields.

Table 4-22   Flexible NetFlow IPv4-Only Non-Key Fields

	IPv4 Only
Fields	Total Length Minimum
	Total Length Maximum
	TTL Minimum
	TTL Maximum

Table 4-23 lists the IPv4 and IPv6 non-key fields.

Table 4-23   Flexible NetFlow IPv4 and IPv6 Non-Key Fields

	IPv4 and IPv6
Fields	Total Length Minimum
	Total Length Maximum

NetFlow Predefined Records

Flexible NetFlow includes several predefined records that can help an administrator and security professional start deploying NetFlow within their organization. Alternatively, they can create their own customized records for more granular analysis. As Cisco evolves Flexible NetFlow, many popular user-defined flow records could be made available as predefined records to make them easier to implement.

The predefined records guarantee backward compatibility with legacy NetFlow collectors. Predefined records have a unique blend of key and non-key fields that allows the network administrator and security professional to monitor different types of traffic in their environment without any customization.

NOTE   Flexible NetFlow predefined records that are based on the aggregation cache schemes in legacy NetFlow do not perform aggregation. Alternatively, the predefined records track each flow separately.

User-Defined Records

As the name indicates, Flexible NetFlow gives the network administrator and security professional the flexibility to create their own records (user-defined records) by specifying key and non-key fields to customize the data collection. The values in non-key fields are added to flows to provide additional information about the traffic in the flows. A change in the value of a non-key field does not create a new flow. In most cases, the values for non-key fields are taken from only the first packet in the flow. Flexible NetFlow enables you to capture counter values such as the number of bytes and packets in a flow as non-key fields.

Flexible NetFlow adds a new NetFlow v9 export format field type for the header and packet section types. A device configured for Flexible NetFlow communicates to the collector the configured section sizes in the corresponding NetFlow v9 export template fields.

Flow Monitors

In Flexible NetFlow, *flow monitors* are applied to the network device interfaces to perform network traffic monitoring. Flow data is collected from the network traffic and added to the flow monitor cache during the monitoring process based on the key and non-key fields in the flow record.

Flow Exporters

The entities that export the data in the flow monitor cache to a remote system are called *flow exporters*. Flow exporters are configured as separate entities and are assigned to flow monitors. An administrator can create several flow exporters and assign them to one or more flow monitors. A flow exporter includes the destination address of the reporting server, the type of transport (UDP or SCTP), and the export format corresponding of the NetFlow version or IPFIX.

> **NOTE**   You can configure up to eight flow exporters per flow monitor in Cisco IOS-XE software.

Flow Samplers

Flow samplers are created as separate components in a router's configuration. Flow samplers are used to reduce the load on the device that is running Flexible NetFlow by limiting the number of packets that are selected for analysis.

Flow sampling exchanges monitoring accuracy for router performance. When you apply a sampler to a flow monitor, the overhead load on the router due to running the flow monitor is reduced because the number of packets that the flow monitor must analyze is reduced. The reduction in the number of packets that are analyzed by the flow monitor causes a corresponding reduction in the accuracy of the information stored in the flow monitor's cache.

Flexible NetFlow Configuration

The following sections provide step-by-step configuration guidance on how to enable and configure Flexible NetFlow in a Cisco IOS device. Figure 4-9 shows the configuration steps in a sequential graphical representation.

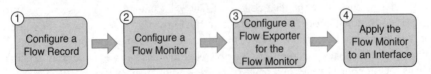

Figure 4-9   *Flexible NetFlow Configuration Steps*

The configuration steps, which are described in detail in the corresponding sections, are as follows:

Step 1.   Configure a flow record

Step 2.   Configure a flow monitor

Step 3.   Configure a flow exporter for the flow monitor

Step 4.   Apply the flow monitor to an interface

The topology shown in Figure 4-10 is used in the following examples.

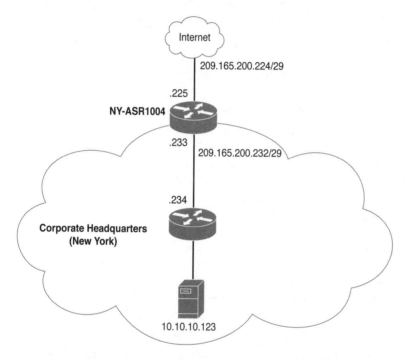

Figure 4-10 *Flexible NetFlow Configuration Example Topology*

This figure shows a Cisco ASR 1004 at the New York headquarters that is configured for Flexible NetFlow. The outside network is 209.165.200.224/29, and the inside network is 209.165.200.232/29.

Configure a Flow Record

The following are the steps required to configure a customized flow record.

NOTE   There are hundreds of possible ways to configure customized flow records. The following steps can be followed to create one of the possible variations. You can create a customized flow record depending on your organization's requirements.

Step 1.   Log in to your router and enter into enable mode with the **enable** command:

```
NY-ASR1004>enable
```

Step 2.   Enter into configuration mode with the **configure terminal** command:

```
NY-ASR1004#configure terminal
Enter configuration commands, one per line.  End with CNTL/Z.
```

Step 3.   Create a flow record with the **flow record** command. In this example, the record name is **NY-ASR-FLOW-RECORD-1**. After you've entered the **flow record** command, the router enters flow record configuration mode. You can also use the **flow record** command to edit an existing flow record:

```
NY-ASR1004(config)#flow record NY-ASR-FLOW-RECORD-1
```

Step 4.   (Optional.) Enter a description for the new flow record:

```
NY-ASR1004(config-flow-record)#description FLOW RECORD 1 for basic traf-
fic analysis
```

Step 5.   Configure a key field for the flow record using the **match** command. In this example, the IPv4 destination address is configured as a key field for the record:

```
NY-ASR1004(config-flow-record)#match ipv4 destination address
```

The output of the **match ?** command shows all the primary options for the key field categories that you learned earlier in this chapter:

```
NY-ASR1004(config-flow-record)#match ?
    application  Application fields
    flow         Flow identifying fields
    interface    Interface fields
    ipv4         IPv4 fields
    ipv6         IPv6 fields
    routing      Routing attributes
    transport    Transport layer fields
```

Step 6.   Configure a non-key field with the **collect** command. In this example, the input interface is configured as a non-key field for the record:

```
NY-ASR1004(config-flow-record)#collect interface input
```

The output of the **collect ?** command shows all the options for the non-key field categories that you learned earlier in this chapter:

```
NY-ASR1004(config-flow-record)#collect ?
    application  Application fields
    counter      Counter fields
    flow         Flow identifying fields
    interface    Interface fields
    ipv4         IPv4 fields
    ipv6         IPv6 fields
    routing      Routing attributes
    timestamp    Timestamp fields
    transport    Transport layer fields
```

Step 7.   Exit configuration mode with the **end** command and return to privileged EXEC mode:

```
NY-ASR1004(config-flow-record)#end
```

> **NOTE**   You can configure Flexible NetFlow to support Network-Based Application Recognition (NBAR) with the **match application name** command under Flexible NetFlow Flow Record configuration mode.

You can use the **show flow record** command to show the status and fields for the flow record. If multiple flow records are configured in the router, you can use the **show flow record** *name* command to show the output of a specific flow record, as shown in Example 4-1.

Example 4-1   *Output of the show flow record Command*

```
NY-ASR1004#show flow record NY-ASR-FLOW-RECORD-1
flow record NY-ASR-FLOW-RECORD-1:
  Description:       Used for basic traffic analysis
  No. of users:      0
  Total field space: 8 bytes
  Fields:
    match ipv4 destination address
    collect interface input
```

Use the **show running-config flow record** command to show the flow record configuration in the running configuration, as shown in Example 4-2.

Example 4-2   *Output of the show running-config flow record Command*

```
NY-ASR1004#show running-config flow record
Current configuration:
!
flow record NY-ASR-FLOW-RECORD-1
 description Used for basic traffic analysis
 match ipv4 destination address
 collect interface input
!
```

Configuring a Flow Monitor for IPv4 or IPv6

The following are the steps required to configure a flow monitor for IPv4 or IPv6 implementations. In the following examples, a flow monitor is configured for the previously configured flow record.

Step 1.   Log in to your router and enter into enable mode with the **enable** command:

```
NY-ASR1004>enable
```

Step 2.   Enter into configuration mode with the **configure terminal** command:

```
NY-ASR1004#configure terminal
Enter configuration commands, one per line.  End with CNTL/Z.
```

Step 3   Create a flow monitor with the **flow monitor** command. In this example, the flow monitor is called **NY-ASR-FLOW-MON-1**:

```
NY-ASR1004(config)#flow monitor NY-ASR-FLOW-MON-1
```

Step 4.   (Optional.) Enter a description for the new flow monitor:

```
NY-ASR1004(config-flow-monitor)#description monitor for IPv4 traffic in
NY
```

Step 5.   Identify the record for the flow monitor:

```
NY-ASR1004(config-flow-monitor)#record netflow NY-ASR-FLOW-RECORD-1
```

In the following example, the **record ?** command is used to see all the flow monitor record options:

```
NY-ASR1004(config-flow-monitor)#record ?
  NY-ASR-FLOW-RECORD-1  Used for basic traffic analysis
  netflow               Traditional NetFlow collection schemes
  netflow-original      Traditional IPv4 input NetFlow with origin ASs
```

Step 6.   Exit configuration mode with the **end** command and return to privileged EXEC mode:

```
NY-ASR1004(config-flow-record)#end
```

You can use the **show flow monitor** command to show the status and configured parameters for the flow monitor, as shown in Example 4-3.

Example 4-3   *Output of the show flow monitor Command*

```
NY-ASR1004#show flow monitor
Flow Monitor NY-ASR-FLOW-MON-1:
  Description:       monitor for IPv4 traffic in NY
  Flow Record:       NY-ASR-FLOW-RECORD-1
  Cache:
    Type:            normal (Platform cache)
    Status:          not allocated
    Size:            200000 entries
    Inactive Timeout: 15 secs
    Active Timeout:  1800 secs
    Update Timeout:  1800 secs
```

Use the **show running-config flow monitor** command to display the flow monitor configuration in the running configuration, as shown in Example 4-4.

Example 4-4   *Output of the show running-config flow monitor Command*

```
NY-ASR1004#show running-config flow monitor
Current configuration:
!
flow monitor NY-ASR-FLOW-MON-1
 description monitor for IPv4 traffic in NY
 record NY-ASR-FLOW-RECORD-1
 cache entries 200000
```

Configuring a Flow Exporter for the Flow Monitor

Complete the following steps to configure a flow exporter for the flow monitor in order to export the data that is collected by NetFlow to a remote system for further analysis and storage. This is an optional step. IPv4 and IPv6 are supported for flow exporters.

> **NOTE**   Flow exporters use UDP as the transport protocol and use the NetFlow v9 export format. Each flow exporter supports only one destination. If you want to export the data to multiple destinations, you must configure multiple flow exporters and assign them to the flow monitor.

Step 1.   Log in to the router and enter into enable and configuration modes, as you learned in previous steps.

Step 2.   Create a flow exporter with the **flow exporter** command. In this example, the exporter name is **NY-EXPORTER-1**:

```
NY-ASR1004(config)#flow exporter NY-EXPORTER-1
```

Step 3.   (Optional.) Enter a description for the exporter:

```
NY-ASR1004(config-flow-exporter)#description exports to New York
Collector
```

Step 4.   Configure the export protocol using the **export-protocol** command. In this example, NetFlow v9 is used. You can also configure legacy NetFlow v5 with the **netflow-v5** keyword or IPFIX with the **ipfix** keyword. IPFIX support was added in Cisco IOS Software Release 15.2(4)M and Cisco IOS XE Release 3.7S:

```
NY-ASR1004(config-flow-exporter)#export-protocol netflow-v9
```

Step 5.   Enter the IP address of the destination host with the **destination** command. In this example, the destination host is 10.10.10.123:

```
NY-ASR1004(config-flow-exporter)#destination 10.10.10.123
```

Step 6.   You can configure the UDP port used by the flow exporter with the **transport udp** command. The default is UDP port 9995.

Step 7.   Exit the Flexible NetFlow flow monitor configuration mode with the **exit** command and specify the name of the exporter in the flow monitor:

```
NY-ASR1004(config)#flow monitor NY-ASR-FLOW-MON-1
NY-ASR1004(config-flow-monitor)#exporter NY-EXPORTER-1
```

You can use the **show flow exporter** command to view the configured options for the Flexible NetFlow exporter, as demonstrated in Example 4-5.

Example 4-5   *Output of the show flow exporter Command*

```
NY-ASR1004#show flow exporter
Flow Exporter NY-EXPORTER-1:
  Description:              exports to New York Collector
  Export protocol:         NetFlow Version 9
  Transport Configuration:
    Destination IP address: 10.10.10.123
    Source IP address:      209.165.200.225
    Transport Protocol:     UDP
    Destination Port:       9995
    Source Port:            55939
    DSCP:                   0x0
    TTL:                    255
    Output Features:        Used
```

You can use the **show running-config flow exporter** command to view the flow exporter configuration in the command line interface (CLI), as demonstrated in Example 4-6.

Example 4-6   *Output of the show running-config flow exporter Command*

```
NY-ASR1004# show running-config flow exporter
Current configuration:
!
flow exporter NY-EXPORTER-1
 description exports to New York Collector
 destination 10.10.10.123
```

You can use the **show flow monitor name NY-ASR-FLOW-MON-1 cache format record** command to display the status and flow data in the NetFlow cache for the flow monitor, as demonstrated in Example 4-7.

Example 4-7   *Output of the show flow monitor name NY-ASR-FLOW-MON-1 cache format record Command*

```
NY-ASR1004#show flow monitor name NY-ASR-FLOW-MON-1 cache format record
  Cache type:                       Normal (Platform cache)
  Cache size:                       200000
  Current entries:                       4
  High Watermark:                        4
  Flows added:                         132
  Flows aged:                           42
    - Active timeout   ( 3600 secs)      3
    - Inactive timeout (   15 secs)     94
    - Event aged                         0
```

```
    - Watermark aged                  0
    - Emergency aged                  0
IPV4 DESTINATION ADDRESS:   10.10.20.5
ipv4 source address:        10.10.10.42
trns source port:           25
trns destination port:      25
counter bytes:              34320
counter packets:            1112
IPV4 DESTINATION ADDRESS:   10.10.1.2
ipv4 source address:        10.10.10.2
trns source port:           20
trns destination port:      20
counter bytes:              3914221
counter packets:            5124
IPV4 DESTINATION ADDRESS:   10.10.10.200
ipv4 source address:        10.20.10.6
trns source port:           32
trns destination port:      3073
counter bytes:              82723
counter packets:            8232
```

Applying a Flow Monitor to an Interface

A flow monitor must be applied to at least one interface. To apply the flow monitor to an interface, use the **ip flow monitor** *name* **input** command in interface configuration mode, as demonstrated in Example 4-8.

Example 4-8   *Applying the Flow Monitor to an Interface*

```
NY-ASR1004(config)#interface FastEthernet0/1/1
NY-ASR1004(config-if)#ip flow monitor NY-ASR-FLOW-MON-1 input
```

In Example 4-8, the flow monitor **NY-ASR-FLOW-MON-1** is applied to interface FastEthernet0/1/1. Example 4-9 shows the complete configuration.

Example 4-9   *Flexible NetFlow Configuration*

```
flow record NY-ASR-FLOW-RECORD-1
 description used for basic traffic analysis
 match ipv4 destination address
 collect interface input
!
!
flow exporter NY-EXPORTER-1
 description exports to New York Collector
 destination 10.10.10.123
!
```

```
!
flow monitor NY-ASR-FLOW-MON-1
 description monitor for IPv4 traffic in NY
 record NY-ASR-FLOW-RECORD-1
 exporter NY-EXPORTER-1
 cache entries 200000
!
interface FastEthernet0/1/1
 ip address 209.165.200.233 255.255.255.248
 ip flow monitor NY-ASR-FLOW-MON-1 input
```

IPFIX

Key Topic

The Internet Protocol Flow Information Export (IPFIX) is a network flow standard led by the Internet Engineering Task Force (IETF). IPFIX was created to develop a common, universal standard of export for flow information from routers, switches, firewalls, and other infrastructure devices. IPFIX defines how flow information should be formatted and transferred from an exporter to a collector. IPFIX is documented in RFC 7011 through RFC 7015 as well as RFC 5103. Cisco NetFlow Version 9 is the basis and main point of reference for IPFIX. IPFIX changes some of the terminologies of NetFlow, but in essence they are the same principles of NetFlow v9.

> **NOTE**   The different NetFlow versions, as well as each of the components, packet types, and other detailed information, are covered in Chapter 2, "Forensics."

IPFIX defines different elements that are placed into 12 groups according to their applicability:

1. Identifiers
2. Metering and exporting process configuration
3. Metering and exporting process statistics
4. IP header fields
5. Transport header fields
6. Sub-IP header fields
7. Derived packet properties
8. Min/Max flow properties
9. Flow timestamps
10. Per-flow counters
11. Miscellaneous flow properties
12. Padding

IPFIX is considered to be a push protocol. Each IPFIX-enabled device regularly sends IPFIX messages to configured collectors (receivers) without any interaction by the receiver. The sender controls most of the orchestration of the IPFIX data messages. IPFIX introduces the concept of templates, which make up these flow data messages to the receiver. IPFIX also allows the sender to use user-defined data types in its messages. IPFIX prefers the Stream Control Transmission Protocol (SCTP) as its transport layer protocol; however, it also supports the use of the Transmission Control Protocol (TCP) or User Datagram Protocol (UDP) messages.

Traditional Cisco NetFlow records are usually exported via UDP messages. The IP address of the NetFlow collector and the destination UDP port must be configured on the sending device. The NetFlow standard (RFC 3954) does not specify a specific NetFlow listening port. The standard or most common UDP port used by NetFlow is UDP port 2055, but other ports, such as 9555, 9995, 9025, and 9026, can also be used. UDP port 4739 is the default port used by IPFIX.

IPFIX Architecture

IPFIX uses the following architecture terminology:

- **Metering process (MP):** Generates flow records from packets at an observation point. It timestamps, samples, and classifies flows. The MP also maintains flows in an internal data structure and passes complete flow information to an exporting process (EP).
- **Exporting process (EP):** Sends flow records via IPFIX from one or more MPs to one or more collecting processes (CPs).
- **Collecting process (CP):** Receives records via IPFIX from one or more EPs.

IPFIX Mediators

IPFIX introduces the concept of mediators. Mediators collect, transform, and re-export IPFIX streams to one or more collectors. Their main purpose is to allow federation of IPFIX messages. Mediators include an intermediate process (ImP) that allows for the following:

- For NetFlow data to be kept anonymously
- For NetFlow data to be aggregated
- Filtering of NetFlow data
- Proxying of web traffic
- IP translation

IPFIX Templates

An IPFIX template describes the structure of flow data records within a dataset. Templates are identified by a template ID, which corresponds to set ID in the set header of the dataset. Templates are composed of "information element (IE) and length" pairs. IEs provide field type information for each template.

A standard information model covers nearly all common flow collection use cases, such as the following:

- The traditional 5-tuple (source IP address, destination IP address, source port, destination port, and IP protocol)

- Packet treatment such as IP next-hop IPv4 addresses, BGP destination ASN, and others
- Timestamps to nanosecond resolution
- IPv4, IPv6, ICMP, UDP, and TCP header fields
- Sub-IP header fields such as source MAC address and wireless local area network (WLAN) service set identifier (SSID)
- Various counters (packet delta counts, total connection counts, top talkers, and so on)
- Flow metadata information such as ingress and egress interfaces, flow direction, and virtual routing and forwarding (VRF) information

NOTE   There are numerous others defined at the Internet Assigned Numbers Authority (IANA) website: http://www.iana.org/assignments/ipfix/ipfix.xhtml.

Option Templates

Option templates are a different type of IPFIX template used to define records referred to as "options" that are associated with a specified scope. A scope may define an entity in the IPFIX architecture, including the exporting process, other templates, or a property of a collection of flows. Flow records describe flows, and option records define things other than flows, such as the following:

- Information about the collection infrastructure
- Metadata about flows or a set of flows
- Other properties of a set of flows

Introduction to the Stream Control Transmission Protocol (SCTP)

IPFIX uses SCTP, which provides a packet transport service designed to support several features beyond TCP or UDP capabilities. These features include the following:

- Packet streams
- Partial reliability (PR) extension
- Unordered delivery of packets or records
- Transport layer multihoming

Many refer to SCTP as a simpler state machine (compared to the features provided by TCP) with an "a la carte" selection of features. PR-SCTP provides a reliable transport with a mechanism to skip packet retransmissions. It allows for multiple applications with different reliability requirements to run on the same flow association. In other words, it combines the best effort reliability of UDP while still providing TCP-like congestion control. SCTP ensures that IPFIX templates are sent reliably by improving end-to-end delay. RFC 6526 introduces additional features such as per-template drop counting with partial reliability and fast template reuse.

NetFlow and IPFIX Comparison

IPFIX was derived from NetFlow v9. The IPFIX standard specifications (RFC 5101 and RFC 5102) were co-authored by Benoit Clais, who also co-authored the NetFlow v9 RFC (RFC 3954).

IPFIX introduces several extensions, the most popular of which are the *Information Element identifiers*. These identifiers are compatible with the *field types* used by NetFlow v9 that you learned about in the previous sections of this chapter.

There are several similar concepts between NetFlow v9 and IPFIX. The first identifier in NetFlow v9 is called **IN_BYTES**, and in IPFIX is called **octetDeltaCount**.

As you learned earlier in this chapter, NetFlow v9 has 127 field types. IPFIX defines 238, many of which are the same as the ones defined in NetFlow v9. IPFIX allows a vendor ID to be specified, whereby the vendor can stick proprietary information into NetFlow.

The Cisco Flexible NetFlow IPFIX Export Format feature allows a NetFlow-enabled device to export packets using the IPFIX export protocol.

NetFlow for Cybersecurity and Incident Response

NetFlow is a tremendous security tool. It provides anomaly detection and investigative capabilities that can be helpful in incident response. The Cisco Cyber Threat Defense (CTD) solution uses NetFlow as the primary security visibility tool. Complete visibility is one of the key requirements when identifying and classifying security threats.

The first step in the process of preparing your network and staff to successfully identify security threats is achieving complete network visibility. You cannot protect against or miti-gate what you cannot view/detect. You can achieve this level of network visibility through existing features on network devices you already have and on devices whose potential you do not even realize. In addition, you should create strategic network diagrams to clearly illustrate your packet flows as well as where, within the network, you may enable security mechanisms to identify, classify, and mitigate the threat. Remember that network security is a constant war. When defending against the enemy, you must know your own territory and implement defense mechanisms in place. Your goal should be to eliminate any network blind spots.

NetFlow as an Anomaly Detection Tool

You can use NetFlow as an anomaly detection tool. Anomaly-based analysis keeps track of network traffic that diverges from "normal" behavioral patterns. You must define what is considered to be normal behavior. You can use anomaly-based detection to mitigate DDoS attacks and zero-day outbreaks. DDoS attacks are often used maliciously to consume the resources of your hosts and network that would otherwise be used to serve legitimate users. The goal with these types of attacks is to overwhelm the victim network resources, or a sys-tem's resources such as CPU and memory. In most cases, this is done by sending numerous IP packets or forged requests.

Particularly dangerous is when an attacker builds up a more powerful attack with a more sophisticated and effective method of compromising multiple hosts and installing small attack daemons. This is what many call zombies, or bot hosts/nets. Subsequently, an attacker can launch a coordinated attack from thousands of zombies onto a single victim. This daemon typically contains both the code for sourcing a variety of attacks and some basic communications infrastructure to allow for remote control.

Typically, an anomaly-detection system monitors network traffic and alerts and then reacts to any sudden increase in traffic and any other anomalies.

NetFlow, along with other mechanisms such as syslog and SNMP, can be enabled within your infrastructure to provide the necessary data used for identifying and classifying threats and anomalies. Before implementing these anomaly-detection capabilities, you should perform traffic analysis to gain an understanding of general traffic rates and patterns. In anomaly detection, learning is generally performed over a significant interval, including both the peaks and valleys of network activity.

Incident Response and Network Security Forensics

NetFlow is often compared to a phone bill. When police want to investigate criminals, for instance, they often collect and investigate their phone records. NetFlow provides information about all network activity that can be very useful for incident response and network forensics. This information can help you discover indicators of compromise (IOC).

The following six-step methodology on security incident handling has been adopted by many organizations, including service providers, enterprises, and government organizations:

Step 1.   Preparation

Step 2.   Identification

Step 3.   Containment

Step 4.   Eradication

Step 5.   Recovery

Step 6.   Lessons learned

NetFlow plays a crucial role in the preparation and identification phases. Information collected in NetFlow records can be used as part of identifying, categorizing, and scoping suspected incidents as part of the identification. NetFlow data also provides great benefits for attack traceback and attribution. In addition, NetFlow provides visibility into what is getting into your network and what information is being exfiltrated out of your network.

Figure 4-11 shows an example of how a botnet is performing a DDoS attack against the corporate network, while at the same time communicating with an internal host in the call center. NetFlow in this case can be used as an anomaly-detection tool for the DDoS attack and also as a forensics tool to potentially find other IOCs of more sophisticated attacks that may be carried out incognito.

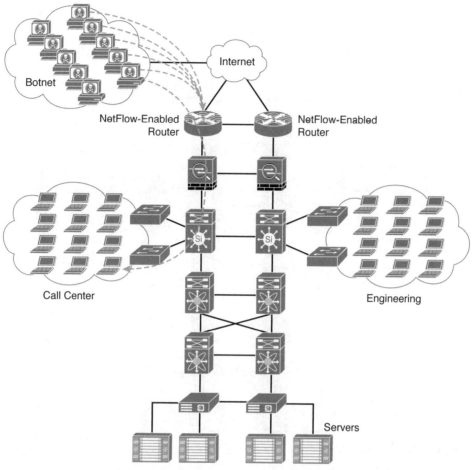

Figure 4-11 *Detecting What Is Getting Into Your Network*

Figure 4-12 shows how a "stepping-stone" attack is carried out in the corporate network. A compromised host in the engineering department is extraditing large amounts of sensitive data to an attacker in the Internet from a server in the data center.

You can also use NetFlow in combination with DNS records to help you detect suspicious and malicious traffic, such as the following:

- Suspicious requests to .gov, .mil, and .edu sites when you do not even do business with any of those entities

- Large amounts of traffic leaving the organization late at night to suspicious sites

- Traffic to embargoed countries that should not have any business partners or transactions

- Suspicious virtual private network (VPN) requests and VPN traffic

- Requests and transactions to sites without any content

- Pornography sites or any other sites that violate corporate policy

- Illegal file-sharing sites

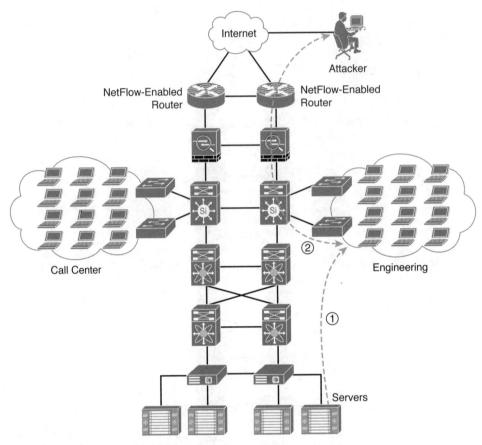

Figure 4-12 *Detecting What Is Getting Out of Your Network*

Syslog and packet captures are also often used in network forensics; however, an area where these traditional network forensics tools fall short is in coverage. For instance, it is very difficult to deploy hundreds of sniffers (packet-capture devices) in the network of large organizations. In addition, the cost will be extremely high. When a security incident or breach is detected, the incident responders need answers fast! They do not have time to go over terabytes of packet captures, and they can definitely not analyze every computer on the network to find the root cause, miscreant, and source of the breach. You can use NetFlow to obtain a high-level view of what is happening in the network, and then the incident responder can perform a deep-dive investigation with packet captures and other tools later in the investigation. Sniffers then can be deployed as needed in key locations where suspicious activity is suspected. The beauty of NetFlow is that you can deploy it anywhere you have a supported router, switch, or Cisco ASA; alternatively, you can use Cisco NetFlow Generation Appliance (NGA). After the Lancope acquisition, Cisco also sells the StealthWatch FlowSensor product, which is a physical or virtual appliance that can generate NetFlow data when legacy Cisco network infrastructure components are not capable of producing line-rate, unsampled NetFlow data.

NetFlow can fill in some of the gaps and challenges regarding the collection of packet captures everywhere in the network. It is easier to store large amounts of NetFlow data because
it is only a transactional record. Therefore, administrators can keep a longer history of events
that occurred on their networks. Historical records can prove very valuable when investigating a breach. Network transactions can show you where an initial infection came from, what
command-and-control channel was initiated by the malware, what other computers on the
internal network were accessed by that infected host, and whether other hosts in the network reached out to the same attacker or command-and-control system.

The logging facility on Cisco IOS routers, switches, Cisco ASA, and other infrastructure
devices allows you to save syslog messages locally or to a remote host. By default, routers send logging messages to a logging process. The logging process controls the delivery
of logging messages to various destinations, such as the logging buffer, terminal lines, a
syslog server, or a monitoring event correlation system such as Cisco Prime Infrastructure
or Splunk. You can set the severity level of the messages to control the type of messages
displayed, in addition to a timestamp to successfully track the reported information. Every
security professional and incident responder knows how important it is to have good logs.
There is no better way to find out what was happening in a router, switch, or firewall at the
time an attack occurred. However, like all things, syslog has limitations. You have to enable
the collection of logs from each endpoint; so in many environments, syslog coverage is
incomplete, and after a computer has been compromised, it is not possible to trust the logs
coming from that device anymore. Syslog is extremely important, but it cannot tell you
everything. Many network telemetry sources can also be correlated with NetFlow while
responding to security incidents and performing network forensics, including the following:

- Dynamic Host Configuration Protocol (DHCP) logs
- VPN logs
- Network address translation (NAT) information
- 802.1x authentication logs
- Server logs (syslog)
- Web proxy logs
- Spam filters from email security appliances such as the Cisco Email Security
  Appliance (ESA)
- DNS server logs
- Active directory logs

Table 4-24 lists the different event types, their source, and their respective events that can
be combined with NetFlow while you're responding to security incidents and performing
network forensics.

Table 4-24 Network Telemetry Type, Sources, and Events

Event Type	Source	Events
Attribution	DHCP server	IP assignments to machine MAC addresses
	VPN server	IP assignments to users VPN source addresses
	NAT gateway	NAT/PAT logs
	802.1x authentication logs DNS logs	IP assignment to user MAC addresses Known malware domains
System activity	Syslog server	Authentication and authorization events Services starting and stopping Configuration changes Security events
Web proxy logs	Web proxies, such as Cisco Web Security (CWS) and Web Security Appliance (WSA)	Web malware downloads Command-and-control check-ins
Spam filter logs	Spam filter, such as Cisco Email Security Appliance (ESA)	Malicious URLs Malicious attachments
Firewall logs	Network firewall, such as Cisco ASA	Accepted/denied connections
Web server logs	Web servers	Access logs Error logs

TIP It is extremely important that your syslog and other messages are timestamped with the correct date and time. This is why the use of Network Time Protocol (NTP) is strongly recommended.

Network forensics can be an intimidating topic for many security professionals. Everyone knows that forensic investigation may entail many other sources of information from end hosts, servers, and any affected systems. Each forensics team needs to have awareness of many different areas, such as the following:

■ Having thorough knowledge of assets, risks, impact, and likelihood of events.

■ Practicing incident response policies and procedures in mock events and collecting NetFlow on a regular basis to analyze what is happening in the network.

■ Awareness of current vulnerabilities and threats.

- Understanding evidence handling and chain of custody. (Even NetFlow events can be used as evidence.)

- Enacting mitigation based on evidence collected.

- Knowing the documentation requirements for evidence, depending on your country and local laws.

- Understanding the analysis process during and after the incident.

- Having a framework for communications, both within the team and external to the team.

Using NetFlow for Data Leak Detection and Prevention

Many network administrators, security professionals, and business leaders struggle in the effort to prevent data loss within their organizations. The ability to identify anomalous behavior in data flows is crucial to detect and prevent data loss. The application of analytics to data collected via NetFlow can aid security professionals in detecting anomalous amounts of data leaving the organization and abnormal traffic patterns inside of the organization.

Using NetFlow along with identity management systems, you can detect who initiated the data transfer, the hosts (IP addresses) involved, the amount of data transferred, and the services used. In addition, you can measure how long the communications lasted as well as the frequency of the same connection attempts.

> **TIP**   Often, tuning is necessary because certain traffic behavior could cause false positives. For instance, your organization may be legitimately sharing large amounts of data or streaming training videos to business partners and customers. In addition, analytics software that examines baseline behavior may be able to detect typical file transfers and incorporate them into existing baselines.

In the following scenario, a large retail organization is the victim of a major breach where attackers stole more than 100,000 credit card numbers. The retailer headquarters is in New York, NY and has two large secondary offices in Raleigh, North Carolina, and San Juan, Puerto Rico. This retailer also has more than 1000 stores in the United States and Canada. Figure 4-13 illustrates these offices and stores.

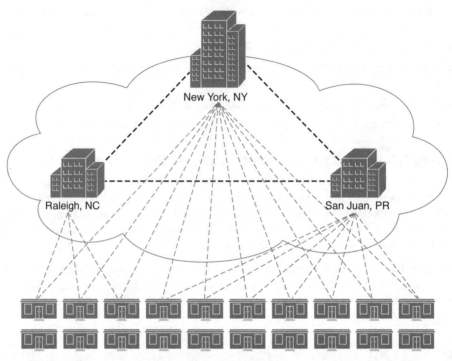

Figure 4-13 *Retailer High-Level Network Topology*

The breach was not detected for several months after the attackers had already penetrated the network. The retailer had firewalls and intrusion prevention devices, but those were not enough to detect or mitigate the attack. The attack was thought to be an inside job, because the malware that was extracting the credit card numbers was very sophisticated and tailored to such an organization. The breach was detected only because law enforcement contacted the victimized retailer, telling them that thousands of fraudulent credit card transactions had been detected on credit cards that were last legitimately used at their stores.

After the organization started their incident response and forensics investigation, they decided to deploy NetFlow in routers at the edge of the data center. The topology in Figure 4-14 illustrates the network at the New York headquarters and the two routers that were configured with NetFlow.

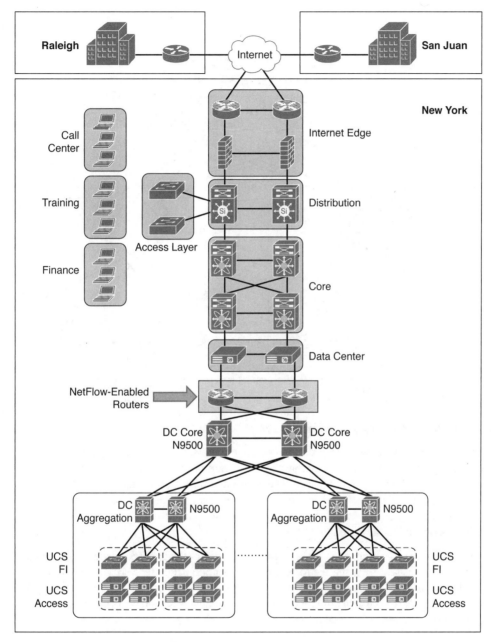

Figure 4-14   *New York Headquarters NetFlow Routers*

The data center has numerous servers that are dedicated for credit card processing applications (software), as illustrated in Figure 4-15.

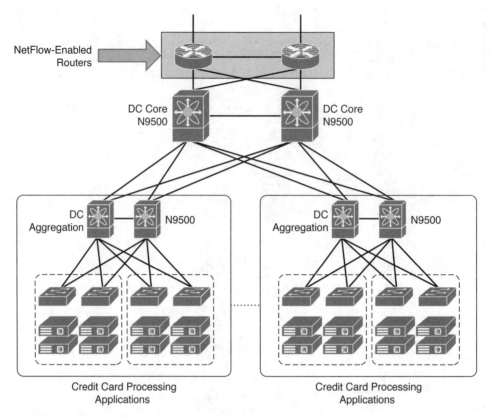

Figure 4-15 *Credit Card Processing Servers*

After deploying NetFlow in their data center edge routers, the retailer observed that numerous DNS requests were being sent from the credit card processing servers to DNS servers outside of the country (United States). The most interesting fact was that such DNS servers were in embargoed countries where the retailer previously had never transacted any business. In addition, most of these DNS requests were being sent during off-hours (mostly around 2:00 to 4:00 a.m. local time).

The retailer was able to inspect NetFlow traffic and detect the country where the credit card information was sent by using the MaxMind Geolocation database. MaxMind provides IP intelligence to thousands of companies to locate their Internet visitors and perform analytics. MaxMind has a service called minFraud, which helps businesses prevent fraudulent online transactions and reduce manual review.

NOTE   You can obtain more information about MaxMind at https://www.maxmind.com. You can also get access to their database files and open source utilities at https://github. com/maxmind.

The attackers were sending stolen credit card data over DNS using tunneling. DNS is a protocol that enables systems to resolve domain names (for example, example.com) into IP addresses (for example, 93.184.216.34). DNS is not intended for a command channel or even tunneling. However, attackers have developed software that enables tunneling over DNS. Because traditionally DNS it is not designed for data transfer, it is less inspected in terms of security monitoring. Undetected DNS tunneling (otherwise known as *DNS exfiltration*) represents a significant risk to any organization.

In this case, the credit cards were base64 encoded and sent over DNS requests (tunneling) to cybercriminals abroad. Attackers nowadays use different DNS record types and encoding methods to exfiltrate data from victims' systems and networks. The following are some examples of encoding methods:

- Base64 encoding
- Binary (8-bit) encoding
- NetBIOS encoding
- Hex encoding

Several utilities have been created to perform DNS tunneling (for the good and also the bad). The following are a few examples:

- **DeNiSe:** A Python tool for tunneling TCP over DNS.
- **dns2tcp:** Written by Olivier Dembour and Nicolas Collignon in C, dns2tcp supports KEY and TXT request types.
- **DNScapy:** Created by Pierre Bienaime, this Python-based Scapy tool for packet generation even supports SSH tunneling over DNS, including a SOCKS proxy.
- **DNScat or DNScat-P:** This Java-based tool created by Tadeusz Pietraszek supports bidirectional communication through DNS.
- **DNScat (DNScat-B):** Written by Ron Bowes, this tool runs on Linux, Mac OS X, and Windows. DNScat encodes DNS requests in NetBIOS or hex encoding.
- **Heyoka:** This tool, written in C, supports bidirectional tunneling for data exfiltration.
- **Iodine:** Written by Bjorn Andersson and Erik Ekman in C, Iodine runs on Linux, Mac OS X, and Windows, and can even be ported to Android.
- **Nameserver Transfer Protocol (NSTX):** Creates IP tunnels using DNS.
- **OzymanDNS:** Written in Perl by Dan Kaminsky, this tool is used to set up an SSH tunnel over DNS or for file transfer. The requests are base32 encoded, and responses are base64-encoded TXT records.
- **psudp:** Developed by Kenton Born, this tool injects data into existing DNS requests by modifying the IP/UDP lengths.
- **Feederbot and Moto:** This malware using DNS has been used by attackers to steal sensitive information from many organizations.

NOTE Some of these tools were not created with the intent to steal data, but cybercriminals have used them for their own purposes.

The retailer's network security personnel were able to perform detailed analysis of the techniques used by the attackers to steal this information and discovered the types of malware and vulnerabilities being exploited in systems in the data center. Network telemetry tools such as NetFlow are invaluable when trying to understand what is happening (good and bad) in the network, and it is a crucial tool for incident response and network forensics.

Retailers or any organizations that process credit cards or electronic payments are often under regulation from the Payment Card Industry Data Security Standard (PCI DSS). PCI DSS was created to encourage and maintain cardholder data security and expedite the consistent use of data security methodologies. This standard enforces a baseline of technical and operational requirements. PCI DSS applies to the following:

- Banks
- "Brick-and-mortar" retailers and online retailers
- Merchants
- Processors
- Acquirers
- Issuers
- Service providers or any other organizations that store, process, or transmit cardholder data (CHD) and/or sensitive authentication data (SAD)

The PCI DSS defines general requirements for the following:

- Building and maintaining secure networks
- Protecting cardholder data
- Enforcing vulnerability management and patching programs
- Implementing adequate access control measures
- Consistently monitoring networks and their systems
- Guaranteeing the maintenance of information security policies

As you can see from this list, adequate monitoring of systems is an underlying and fundamental requirement. NetFlow, intrusion prevention systems, and others are often used to maintain this required visibility into what is happening in the network. Additional details about PCI DSS are covered in Chapter 7, "Compliance Frameworks."

Many threat actors are seeking to steal intellectual property from many organizations and individuals. According to the *Merriam-Webster* dictionary, intellectual property is "something (such as an idea, invention, or process) that derives from the work of the mind or intellect; an application, right, or registration relating to this." Intellectual property (and other forms of expression) is often protected by patent, trademark, and copyright (in addition to state and federal laws). In today's world, espionage (both cyber and corporate) is a huge business. Many types of attackers (for example, corporations, cybercriminals, and nation states) are after information with independent economic value, such as the following:

- Blueprints
- Chemical formulas

- Research and development documents
- Marketing strategies
- Manufacturing processes
- Source code
- Songs
- Books
- Documentation guides

In 1996, to maintain the health and competitiveness of the U.S. economy, the United States Congress passed the Economic Espionage Act to protect trade secrets from bad actors.

NetFlow Analysis Tools

There are many different commercial and open source NetFlow analysis tools in the industry. The following two sections cover several examples of commercial and open source NetFlow analysis tools.

Commercial NetFlow Analysis Tools

Table 4-25 lists the most popular commercial NetFlow monitoring and analysis software packages in the industry today.

Table 4-25   Examples of Commercial NetFlow Monitoring and Analysis Software

Commercial Software	Description	Website
ManageEngine NetFlow Analyzer	A web-based bandwidth monitoring tool.	http://manageengine.adventnet.com/products/netflow
NetUsage	Tool for network traffic monitoring, capacity planning, business justification, and cost control.	http://www.netusage.net
Caligare	Traffic monitoring and network anomalies detection.	http://www.caligare.com/
Evident Software Evident Analyze	Tool for billing and traffic analysis.	http://www.evidentsoftware.com/products/anlz_functions.aspx
Fluke Networks	Traffic analysis, NetFlow collection, and low-cost Windows-based NetFlow product.	http://www.flukenetworks.com/
Hewlett Packard NetFlow Insight	Traffic analysis and NetFlow collection using HP Insight Network Performance Monitoring.	http://www.openview.hp.com/products/ovpi_net/

Commercial Software	Description	Website
IBM NetFlow Aurora	NetFlow traffic profiling tool commercially available as Tivoli Netcool Performance Flow Analyzer (TNPFA).	http://www.zurich.ibm.com/aurora
IdeaData NetFlow Auditor	Tool used for network troubleshooting, security monitoring, and baseline trending.	http://www.netflowauditor.com
InfoVista 5View NetFlow	NetFlow monitoring tool.	http://www.infovista.com/products/NetFlow-Monitoring-Network-Traffic-Analysis
Cisco Lancope StealthWatch	Traffic analysis, NetFlow collection, and security monitoring tool suite part of Cisco's Cyber Threat Defense Solution.	http://lancope.com
Paessler PRTG	Network monitoring tool suite.	http://www.paessler.com
Plixer International Scrutinizer	Plixer offers free and commercial NetFlow reporting software. Scrutinizer is an incident response and network monitoring suite of tools.	http://www.plixer.com
SolarWinds NetFlow Traffic Analyzer	NetFlow traffic analyzer and performance management tool.	http://www.solarwinds.com/netflow-traffic-analyzer.aspx

Two of the most popular commercial products are Lancope's StealthWatch solution and Plixer Scrutinizer, as described in greater detail in the sections that follow.

Cisco's Lancope StealthWatch Solution

Cisco acquired Lancope, a company who produced the StealthWatch solution, which is a key component of the Cisco Cyber Threat Defense (CTD) solution. One of the key benefits of Lancope's StealthWatch is its capability to scale in large enterprises. It also provides integration with the Cisco Identity Services Engine (ISE) for user identity information. Cisco ISE is a security policy management and control system that you can use for access control and security compliance for wired, wireless, and virtual private network (VPN) connections.

One other major benefit of Lancope's StealthWatch is its graphical interface, which includes great visualizations of network traffic, customized summary reports, and integrated security and network intelligence for drill-down analysis.

Figure 4-16 shows a screenshot of Lancope's StealthWatch Management Console (SMC).

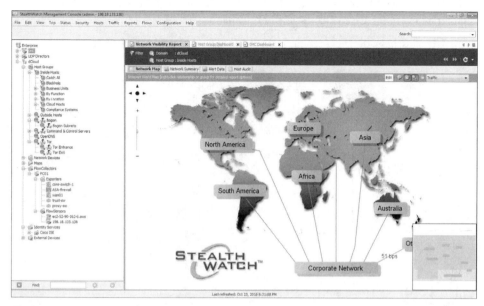

Figure 4-16 *SMC Web Management Application*

Figure 4-17 shows a report of the top applications observed in the network. You can drill down into each application and host to get more detailed information about what is happening in the network.

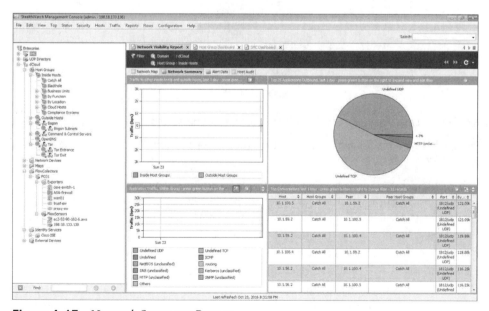

Figure 4-17 *Network Summary Report*

Lancope used to have a security research initiative that tracked emerging threat information from around the world, called the StealthWatch Labs Intelligence Center (SLIC). Nowadays, it's integrated with the Cisco Talos security research team.

Figure 4-18 illustrates the major components of Lancope's StealthWatch solution.

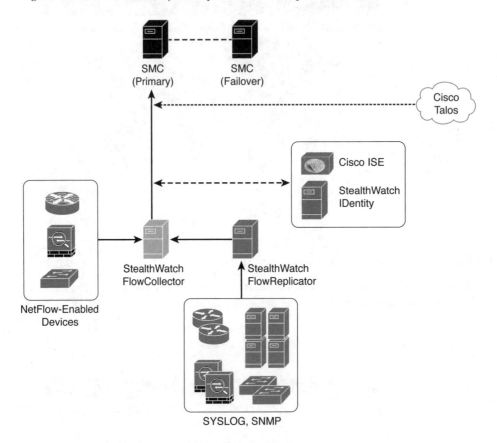

Figure 4-18   *The Lancope's StealthWatch Solution Components*

The following are the primary components of the Lancope StealthWatch solution shown in Figure 4-18:

- **StealthWatch Management Console:** Provides centralized management, configuration, and reporting of the other StealthWatch components. It can be deployed in a physical server or a virtual machine (VM). The StealthWatch Management Console provides high-availability features (failover), as shown in Figure 4-18.

- **FlowCollector:** A physical or virtual appliance that collects NetFlow data from infrastructure devices.

- **FlowSensor:** A physical or virtual appliance that can generate NetFlow data when legacy Cisco network infrastructure components are not capable of producing line-rate, unsampled NetFlow data. Alternatively, the Cisco NetFlow Generator Appliance (NGA) can be used.

- **FlowReplicator:** A physical appliance used to forward NetFlow data as a single data stream to other devices.

- **StealthWatch IDentity:** Provides user identity monitoring capabilities. Administrators can search on usernames to obtain a specific user network activity. Identity data can be obtained from the StealthWatch IDentity appliance or through integration with the Cisco ISE.

> **NOTE**   Lancope StealthWatch also supports usernames within NetFlow records from Cisco ASA appliances.

Lancope's StealthWatch solution supports a feature called *network address translation (NAT) stitching*. NAT stitching uses data from network devices to combine NAT information from inside a firewall (or a NAT device) with information from outside the firewall (or a NAT device) to identify which IP addresses and users are part of a specific flow. A great feature of the StealthWatch solution is its ability to perform "NetFlow deduplication." This feature allows you to deploy several NetFlow collectors within your organization without worrying about double or triple counting the traffic.

Plixer's Scrutinizer

Plixer's Scrutinizer is another commercial NetFlow monitoring and analysis software package that has gone through interoperability tests by Cisco. Scrutinizer is used for incident response and network monitoring. Just like several components of Lancope's StealthWatch solution, Scrutinizer is available as a physical or virtual appliance. Plixer also sells two other products that provide additional network visibility: FlowPro and Flow Replicator.

FlowPro is an appliance that can be deployed in a specific area of the corporate network to perform deep packet inspection (DPI) by combining NetFlow/IPFIX data. Plixer's Flow Replicator allows several sources of network device and server log data to be replicated to different destinations. Flow Replicator can also be configured as a syslog-to-IPFIX gateway. It converts syslog messages and forwards them on inside IPFIX datagrams.

Open Source NetFlow Monitoring and Analysis Software Packages

The number of open source NetFlow monitoring and analysis software packages is on the rise. You can use these open source tools to successfully identify security threats within your network.

Table 4-26 lists the most popular open source NetFlow monitoring and analysis software packages.

Table 4-26   Examples of Open Source NetFlow Monitoring and Analysis Software

Open Source Software	Description	Website
cflowd	Traffic flow analysis tool provided by the Center for Applied Internet Data Analysis.	http://www.caida.org/tools/measurement/cflowd
flowtools	Tool set created by Mark Fullmer for collecting and working with NetFlow data.	http://www.splintered.net/sw/flow-tools
flowviewer	FlowViewer is a web-based interface to flow tools and SiLK.	http://sourceforge.net/projects/flowviewer
flowd	Small-packaged NetFlow collector.	http://www.mindrot.org/projects/flowd
IPFlow	NetFlow collector developed by Christophe Fillot of the University of Technology of Compiegne, France.	http://www.ipflow.utc.fr
NFdump	NetFlow analysis toolkit under the BSD license.	http://nfdump.sourceforge.net
NfSen	Web interface for NFdump.	http://sourceforge.net/projects/nfsen
Stager	Provides visualizations for NFdump.	https://trac.uninett.no/stager
Panoptis	NetFlow tool for detecting denial-of-service attacks. Development is fairly limited.	http://panoptis.sourceforge.net
Plixer's Scrutinizer NetFlow Analyzer	Scrutinizer NetFlow Analyzer is a free version of Plixer's Scrutinizer.	http://www.plixer.com/Support/free-tools.html
SiLK	System for Internet-Level Knowledge (SiLK) is a NetFlow collector and analysis tool developed by the Carnegie Mellon University's CERT Network Situational Awareness Team (CERT NetSA).	https://tools.netsa.cert.org/silk
iSiLK	iSiLK is a graphical front end for the SiLK toolkit.	http://tools.netsa.cert.org/isilk
Elasticsearch, Logstash, and Kibana (ELK)	A distributed, scalable, open source, Big Data analytics platform.	https://www.elastic.co
Graylog	A scalable open source log visualization solution.	https://www.graylog.org

NFdump

NFdump is a set of Linux-based tools that support NetFlow Versions 5, 7, and 9. You can download NFdump from http://nfdump.sourceforge.net and install it from source. Alternatively, you can easily install NFdump in multiple Linux distributions such as Ubuntu using **sudo apt-get install nfdump**.

Table 4-27 lists all the components of the NFdump toolkit.

Table 4-27 NFdump Components

Component	Description
nfcapd	The NetFlow capture daemon. A separate **nfcapd** process needs to be launched for each NetFlow stream.
nfdump	Reads the NetFlow data from the files stored by **nfcapd**. The output and syntax are very similar to the Linux-based packet-capture tool **tcpdump**.
nfprofile	Filters the NetFlow data recorded by **nfcapd** and stores the filtered data into files for later use. The filters are referred to as **profiles**.
nfreplay	Replays NetFlow data.
nfclean.pl	Pearl sample script to clean up historical NetFlow data.
ft2nfdump	Converts flow tools data from files or from standard input into **nfdump** format.

The command to capture the NetFlow data is **nfcapd**. All processed NetFlow records are stored in one or more binary files. These binary files are read by **nfdump** and can be displayed in plaintext to standard output (stdout) or written to another file. Example 4-10 demonstrates how the **nfcapd** command is used to capture and store NetFlow data in a directory called netflow. The server is configured to listen to port 9996 for NetFlow communication.

Example 4-10   *Using the nfcapd Command*

```
omar@server1:~$ nfcapd -w -D -l netflow -p 9996
omar@server1:~$ cd netflow
omar@server1:~/netflow$ ls -l
total 544
-rw-r--r-- 1 omar omar  20772 Jun 18 00:45 nfcapd.201506180040
-rw-r--r-- 1 omar omar  94916 Jun 18 00:50 nfcapd.201506180045
-rw-r--r-- 1 omar omar  84108 Jun 18 00:55 nfcapd.201506180050
-rw-r--r-- 1 omar omar  78564 Jun 18 01:00 nfcapd.201506180055
-rw-r--r-- 1 omar omar 106732 Jun 18 01:05 nfcapd.201506180100
-rw-r--r-- 1 omar omar  73692 Jun 18 01:10 nfcapd.201506180105
-rw-r--r-- 1 omar omar  76996 Jun 18 01:15 nfcapd.201506180110
-rw-r--r-- 1 omar omar    276 Jun 18 01:15 nfcapd.current
```

Flows are read either from a single file or from a sequence of files. In Example 4-10, a series of files were created by the **nfcapd** daemon. Example 4-11 shows the command options of the **nfcapd** daemon command.

Example 4-11 *nfcapd Daemon Command Options*

```
omar@ server1:~$ nfcapd   -h
usage nfcapd [options]
-h              this text you see right here
-u userid       Change user to username
-g groupid      Change group to groupname
-w              Sync file rotation with next 5min (default) interval
-t interval     set the interval to rotate nfcapd files
-b host         bind socket to host/IP addr
-j mcastgroup   Join multicast group <mcastgroup>
-p portnum      listen on port portnum
-l basdir       set the output directory. (no default)
-S subdir       Sub directory format. see nfcapd(1) for format
-I Ident        set the ident string for stat file. (default 'none')
-H              Add port histogram data to flow file.(default 'no')
-n Ident,IP,logdir  Add this flow source - multiple streams
-P pidfile      set the PID file
-R IP[/port]    Repeat incoming packets to IP address/port
-s rate         set default sampling rate (default 1)
-x process      launch process after a new file becomes available
-z              Compress flows in output file.
-B bufflen      Set socket buffer to bufflen bytes
-e              Expire data at each cycle.
-D              Fork to background
-E              Print extended format of netflow data. for debugging purpose only.
-T              Include extension tags in records.
-4              Listen on IPv4 (default).
-6              Listen on IPv6.
-V              Print version and exit.
```

Example 4-12 demonstrates how to use the **nfdump** command to process and analyze all files that were created by **nfcapd** in the netflow directory.

Example 4-12 *Processing and Displaying the nfcapd Files with nfdump*

```
omar@server1::~$ nfdump -R netflow -o extended -s srcip -s ip/flows
Top 10 Src IP Addr ordered by flows:
Date first seen         Duration Proto      Src IP Addr    Flows(%)    Packets(%)
Bytes(%)        pps     bps   bpp
2017-01-2222:35:10.805     2.353 any      192.168.1.140   1582(19.5)      0(-nan)
0(-nan)         0       0     0
2017-01-2222:35:10.829     2.380 any      192.168.1.130    875(10.8)      0(-nan)
0(-nan)         0       0     0
```

```
2017-01-2222:35:10.805      2.404 any      192.168.1.168     807( 9.9)      0(-nan)
0(-nan)          0           0    0
2017-01-2222:35:11.219      1.839 any      192.168.1.142     679( 8.4)      0(-nan)
0(-nan)          0           0    0
2017-01-2222:35:10.805      2.258 any      192.168.1.156     665( 8.2)      0(-nan)
0(-nan)          0           0    0
2017-01-2222:35:10.805      2.297 any      192.168.1.205     562( 6.9)      0(-nan)
0(-nan)          0           0    0
2017-01-2222:35:10.805      2.404 any       192.168.1.89     450( 5.5)      0(-nan)
0(-nan)          0           0    0
2017-01-2222:35:11.050      1.989 any      10.248.91.231     248( 3.1)      0(-nan)
0(-nan)          0           0    0
2017-01-2222:35:11.633      1.342 any      192.168.1.149     234( 2.9)      0(-nan)
0(-nan)          0           0    0.
2017-01-2222:35:11.040      2.118 any      192.168.1.157     213( 2.6)      0(-nan)
0(-nan)          0           0    0


Top 10 IP Addr ordered by flows:
Date first seen         Duration Proto         IP Addr   Flows(%)      Packets(%)
Bytes(%)        pps      bps   bpp
2017-01-2222:35:10.805      2.353 any      192.168.1.140    1582(19.5)      0(-nan)
0(-nan)          0           0    0
2017-01-2222:35:10.805      2.353 any            10.8.8.8    1188(14.6)
0(-nan)          0(-nan)     0          0    0
2017-01-2222:35:10.805      2.297 any        192.168.1.1    1041(12.8)      0(-nan)
0(-nan)          0           0    0
2017-01-2222:35:10.829      2.380 any      192.168.1.130     875(10.8)      0(-nan)
0(-nan)          0           0    0
2017-01-2222:35:10.805      2.404 any      192.168.1.168     807( 9.9)      0(-nan)
0(-nan)          0           0    0
2017-01-2222:35:11.219      1.839 any      192.168.1.142     679( 8.4)      0(-nan)
0(-nan)          0           0    0
2017-01-2222:35:10.805      2.258 any      192.168.1.156     665( 8.2)      0(-nan)
0(-nan)          0           0    0
2017-01-2222:35:10.805      2.297 any      192.168.1.205     562( 6.9)      0(-nan)
0(-nan)          0           0    0
2017-01-2222:35:10.825      2.277 any       10.190.38.99     467( 5.8)      0(-nan)
0(-nan)          0           0    0
2017-01-2222:35:10.805      2.404 any       192.168.1.89     450( 5.5)      0(-nan)
0(-nan)          0           0    0


Summary: total flows: 8115, total bytes: 0, total packets: 0, avg bps: 0, avg pps: 0,
avg bpp: 0
Time window: 2017-01-2222:35:10 - 2017-01-2222:35:13
Total flows processed: 8115, Blocks skipped: 0, Bytes read: 457128
Sys: 0.009s flows/second: 829924.3   Wall: 0.008s flows/second: 967222.9
```

In Example 4-12, you can see the top talkers (top hosts that are sending the most traffic in the network). You can refer to the **nfdump** man pages for details about usage of the **nfdump** command (using the **man nfdump** command). Example 4-13 shows an excerpt of the output of the **nfdump** man pages showing several examples of the **nfdump** command usage.

Example 4-13   *nfdump Man Pages Excerpt*

```
EXAMPLES
        nfdump -r /and/dir/nfcapd.201107110845 -c 100 'proto tcp and ( src ip
172.16.17.18 or
dst ip 172.16.17.19 )' Dumps the first 100 netflow records which match the given fil-
ter:
        nfdump -r /and/dir/nfcapd.201107110845 -B Map matching flows as bin-directional
single flow.
        nfdump -R /and/dir/nfcapd.201107110845:nfcapd.200407110945 'host 192.168.1.2'
Dumps all netflow records of host 192.168.1.2 from July 11 08:45 - 09:45
        nfdump -M /to/and/dir1:dir2 -R nfcapd.200407110845:nfcapd.200407110945 -s
record -n 20 Generates the Top 20 statistics from 08:45 to 09:45 from 3 sources
        nfdump -r /and/dir/nfcapd.201107110845 -s record -n 20 -o extended Generates
the Top 20 statistics, extended output format
        nfdump -r /and/dir/nfcapd.201107110845 -s record -n 20 'in if 5 and bps > 10k'
Generates the Top 20 statistics from flows coming from interface 5
        nfdump -r /and/dir/nfcapd.201107110845 'inet6 and proto tcp and ( src port >
1024
and dst port 80 ) Dumps all port 80 IPv6 connections to any web server.


NOTES
        Generating the statistics for data files of a few hundred MB is no problem.
However be careful if you want to create statistics of several GB of data. This may
consume a lot of memory and can take a while. Flow anonymization has moved into
nfanon.


SEE ALSO
        nfcapd(1), nfanon(1), nfprofile(1), nfreplay(1)
```

NfSen

NfSen is the graphical web-based frontend for NFdump. You can download and obtain more information about NFSen at http://nfsen.sourceforge.net.

SiLK

The SiLK analysis suite is a very popular open source command-line "Swiss army knife" developed by the Computer Emergency Response Team (CERT) at Carnegie Mellon University. Administrators and security professionals combine these tools in various ways to perform detailed NetFlow analysis. SiLK includes numerous tools and plug-ins.

The SiLK packing system includes several applications (daemons) that collect NetFlow data and translate them into a more space-efficient format. SiLK stores these records into service-specific binary flat files for use by the analysis suite. Files are organized in a time-based directory hierarchy.

Elasticsearch, Logstash, and Kibana Stack

Elasticsearch ELK stack is a very powerful open source analytics platform. ELK stands for Elasticsearch, Logstash, and Kibana.

Elasticsearch is the name of a distributed search and analytics engine, but it is also the name of the company founded by the folks behind Elasticsearch and Apache Lucene. Elasticsearch is built on top of Apache Lucene, which is a high-performance search and information retrieval library written in Java. Elasticsearch is a schema-free, full-text search engine with multilanguage support. It provides support for geolocation, suggestive search, auto-completion, and search snippets.

Logstash offers centralized log aggregation of many types, such as network infrastructure device logs, server logs, and also Netflow. Logstash is written in JRuby and runs in a Java virtual machine (JVM). It has a very simple message-based architecture. Logstash has a single agent that is configured to perform different functions in combination with the other ELK components. The following are the four major components in the Logstash ecosystem:

■ **The shipper:** Sends events to Logstash. Typically, remote agents will only run this component.

■ **The broker and indexer:** Receive and index the events.

■ **The search and storage:** Allow you to search and store events.

■ **The web interface:** A web-based interface called Kibana.

Logstash is very scalable because servers running Logstash can run one or more of these aforementioned components independently.

Kibana is an analytics and visualization platform architected for Elasticsearch. It provides real-time summary and charting of streaming data, with the ability to share and embed dashboards.

Marvel and Shield are two additional components that can be integrated with ELK:

■ **Marvel:** Provides monitoring of an Elasticsearch deployment. It uses Kibana to visualize the data. It provides a detailed explanation of things that are happening within the ELK deployment that are very useful for troubleshooting and additional analysis. You can obtain information about Marvel at http://www.elasticsearch.org/overview/marvel.

■ **Shield:** Provides security features to ELK such as role-based access control, authentication, IP filtering, encryption of ELK data, and audit logging. Shield is not free, and it requires a license. You can obtain more information about Shield at http://www.elasticsearch.org/overview/shield.

Elasticsearch also provides integration with Big Data platforms such as Hadoop.

NOTE   Refer to the Elasticsearch documentation at https://www.elastic.co/guide/index.html for more information.

TIP   You can review examples and provide your own at Omar's NetFlow GitHub repository at https://github.com/santosomar/netflow.

Exam Preparation Tasks

Review All Key Topics

Review the most important topics in the chapter, noted with the Key Topic icon in the outer margin of the page. Table 4-28 lists these key topics and the page numbers on which each is found.

Table 4-28   Key Topics

Key Topic Element	Description	Page
Summary	What is a flow?	78
List	NetFlow versions	81
List	NetFlow fields	87
Summary	What is IPFIX?	110
Summary	Comparing NetFlow and IPFIX	113
Summary	How can NetFlow be used for anomaly detection?	113
Summary	How can NetFlow be used for incident response?	114
Summary	Using NetFlow for Data Leak Detection and Prevention	119
List	Commercial NetFlow analysis tools	125
List	Open source NetFlow analysis tools	129

Print a copy of Appendix B, "Memory Tables," (found on the book website), or at least the section for this chapter, and complete the tables and lists from memory. Appendix C, "Memory Tables Answer Key," also on the website, includes completed tables and lists to check your work.

Define Key Terms

Define the following key terms from this chapter and check your answers in the glossary:

IPFIX, flow collector, Stream Control Transmission Protocol (SCTP)

Q&A

The answers to these questions appear in Appendix A, "Answers to the 'Do I Know This Already' Quizzes and Q&A." For more practice with exam format questions, use the exam engine on the website.

1. Using NetFlow along with identity management systems, an administrator can detect which of the following? (Select all that apply.)

   a. Who initiated the data transfer

   b. The hosts (IP addresses) involved

   c. Who configured NetFlow

   d. Which RADIUS server has an active NetFlow connection

2. Network forensics can be an intimidating topic for many security professionals. Everyone knows that forensic investigation may entail many other sources of information, including end hosts, servers, and any affected systems. Each forensics team needs to have awareness of many different areas, such as which of the following? (Select all that apply.)

   a. Assets, risks, impacts, and the likelihood of events

   b. Incident response policies and procedures in mock events as well as NetFlow to analyze what is happening in the network

   c. The current budget

   d. Evidence handling and chain of custody (even NetFlow events can be used as evidence)

3. What are some telemetry sources that are good for attribution? (Select all that apply.)

   a. DHCP server logs

   b. VPN server logs

   c. 802.1x authentication logs

   d. IP route table

4. What are some of the necessary steps in order to configure Flexible NetFlow in a Cisco IOS or Cisco IOS-XE device? (Select all that apply.)

   a. Configure a flow record.

   b. Configure a flow monitor.

   c. Configure a neighbor.

   d. Apply a crypto map to an interface.

5. It is extremely important that your syslog and other messages are timestamped with the correct date and time. The use of which of the following protocols is strongly recommended?

   a. SNMP

   b. BGP

   c. TNP

   d. NTP

6. Which of the following is *not* an example of a Flexible NetFlow component?

   a. Flow records

   b. Flow monitors

   c. Flow NTP

   d. Flow samplers

7. Which of the following is *not* a component of the 5-tuple of a flow in NetFlow?

    a. Source IP address

    b. Destination IP address

    c. Gateway

    d. Source port

    e. Destination port

8. Which of the following is *not* true about the NetFlow immediate cache?

    a. It is the default cache used in many NetFlow implementations.

    b. The flow accounts for a single packet.

    c. It is desirable for real-time traffic monitoring and DDoS detection.

    d. It is used when only very small flows are expected (NetFlow sampling).

9. Flexible NetFlow can track a wide range of Layer 2, IPv4, and IPv6 flow information, except which of the following?

    a. Source and destination MAC addresses

    b. ToS

    c. DSCP

    d. Encryption security association serial numbers

10. Which of the following statements is true about Flexible NetFlow?

    a. It is supported in IPv6 and IPv4, but only when IPv6 tunnels are used.

    b. It supports IPv4, but not IPv6.

    c. It supports encryption of NetFlow data to a collector.

    d. It uses the concept of templates.

This chapter covers the following topics:

- Introduction to incident response
- The incident response plan
- The incident response process
- Information sharing and coordination
- Incident response team structure

CHAPTER 5

Introduction to Incident Response and the Incident Handling Process

This chapter starts with an introduction to incident response and the different guidelines provided by the National Institute of Standards and Technology (NIST). In this chapter, you will learn the details about how to create an incident response plan and a good incident response process. You will also learn details about information sharing and coordination and the different incident response team structures.

"Do I Know This Already?" Quiz

The "Do I Know This Already?" quiz helps you identify your strengths and deficiencies in this chapter's topics. The 10-question quiz, derived from the major sections in the "Foundation Topics" portion of the chapter, helps you determine how to spend your limited study time. Table 5-1 outlines the major topics discussed in this chapter and the "Do I Know This Already?" quiz questions that correspond to those topics.

Table 5-1 "Do I Know This Already?" Foundation Topics Section-to-Question Mapping

Foundation Topics Section	Questions Covered in This Section
Introduction to Incident Response	1
The Incident Response Plan	2–3
The Incident Response Process	4–6
Information Sharing and Coordination	7–8
Incident Response Team Structure	9–10

1. What NIST special publication covers the incident response process?

    a. Special Publication 800-61

    b. Judiciary, private, and individual investigations

    c. Public, private, and corporate investigations

    d. Government, corporate, and private investigations

2. Which of the following is not part of the policy elements described in NIST's Special Publication 800-61?

    a. Statement of management commitment

    b. Purpose and objectives of the incident response policy

    c. The scope of the incident response policy

    d. Definition of QoS policies in network infrastructure devices

3. Which of the following is NIST's definition of standard operating procedures (SOPs)?

    a. A delineation of the specific IPS signatures to be deployed in the network

    b. A delineation of the specific technical processes, techniques, checklists, and forms used by the incident response team

    c. A delineation of the specific firewall rules to be deployed in the network

    d. A suspect-led approach that's mostly used in private investigations

4. Which of the following is not a phase of the incident response process?

    a. Preparation

    b. Containment, eradication, and recovery

    c. Post-incident activity

    d. Network monitoring phase

5. Incident prioritization is part of which phase of the incident response process?

    a. Preparation

    b. Containment, eradication, and recovery

    c. Post-incident activity

    d. Detection and analysis

6. Which of the following is not part of the post-incident activity phase?

    a. Lessons learned

    b. Identifying the attacking hosts

    c. Using collected incident data

    d. Evidence retention

7. Which of the following is a good example of an information-sharing community?

    a. The National Institute of Security and Technology (NIST)

    b. The National Institute of Standards and Technology (NIST)

    c. The Cyber Services Information Sharing and Analysis Center (CS-ISAC)

    d. The Financial Services Information Sharing and Analysis Center (FS-ISAC)

8. During the investigation and resolution of a security incident, you may also need to communicate with outside parties regarding the incident. Which of the following are examples of those external entities?

    a. Law enforcement

    b. Internet service providers (ISPs)

    c. The vendor of your hardware and software products

    d. Coordination centers

9. Which of the following is not an example of a type of incident response team?

   a. Product Security Incident Response Team (PSIRT)

   b. National CSIRT and Computer Emergency Response Team (CERT)

   c. Incident response team of a security vendor and managed security service provider (MSSP)

   d. Penetration testing team

10. Which of the following is not an example of the most common incident response team structures?

   a. Product Security Incident Response Team (PSIRT)

   b. Centralized incident response team

   c. Distributed incident response team

   d. Coordinating team

5

Foundation Topics

This chapter starts with an introduction to incident response. Then it describes, in detail, the incident response plan and incident response process, as defined in National Institute of Standards and Technology (NIST) Special Publication 800-61. This chapter also touches on how to share information and coordinate with external parties during the investigation of security incidents. You will also learn the different incident response team structures.

Introduction to Incident Response

Computer security incident response is a critical component of information technology (IT) programs. The incident response process and incident handling activities can be very complex. In order for you to establish a successful incident response program, you must dedicate substantial planning and resources. Several industry resources were created to help organizations establish a computer security incident response program and learn how to handle cybersecurity incidents efficiently and effectively. One of the best resources available is NIST Special Publication 800-61, which can be obtained from the following URL:

http://nvlpubs.nist.gov/nistpubs/SpecialPublications/NIST.SP.800-61r2.pdf

NIST developed Special Publication 800-61 due to statutory responsibilities under the Federal Information Security Management Act (FISMA) of 2002, Public Law 107-347.

You will learn the basics of the guidelines provided in NIST Special Publication 800-61 in this chapter, as required for the CCNA Cyber Ops SECOPS exam, but you should also read it and become familiar with all the topics discussed in that publication.

What Are Events and Incidents?

Before you learn the details about how to create a good incident response program within your organization, you must understand the difference between security "events" and security "incidents." The following is from NIST Special Publication 800-61:

> "An event is any observable occurrence in a system or network. Events include a user connecting to a file share, a server receiving a request for a web page, a user sending email, and a firewall blocking a connection attempt. Adverse events are events with a negative consequence, such as system crashes, packet floods, unauthorized use of system privileges, unauthorized access to sensitive data, and execution of malware that destroys data."

According to the same document, "a computer security incident is a violation or imminent threat of violation of computer security policies, acceptable use policies, or standard security practices."

> **NOTE**   In Chapter 3, "Fundamentals of Intrusion Analysis," you learned that some security events can also be false positives or true positives.

Figure 5-1 lists a few examples of security incidents.

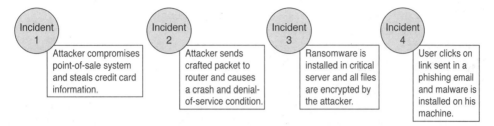

Figure 5-1 *Sample Security Events*

The Incident Response Plan

Having a good incident response plan and incident response process will help you minimize loss or theft of information and disruption of services caused by incidents. It will also help you enhance your incident response program by using lessons learned and information obtained during the security incident.

Section 2.3 of NIST Special Publication 800-61 goes over the incident response policies, plans, and procedures, including information on how to coordinate incidents and interact with outside parties. The policy elements described in NIST Special Publication 800-61 include the following:

- Statement of management commitment
- Purpose and objectives of the incident response policy
- The scope of the incident response policy
- Definition of computer security incidents and related terms
- Organizational structure and definition of roles, responsibilities, and levels of authority
- Prioritization or severity ratings of incidents
- Performance measures
- Reporting and contact forms

NIST's incident response plan elements include the following:

- Incident response plan's mission
- Strategies and goals of the incident response plan
- Senior management approval of the incident response plan
- Organizational approach to incident response
- How the incident response team will communicate with the rest of the organization and with other organizations
- Metrics for measuring the incident response capability and its effectiveness
- Roadmap for maturing the incident response capability
- How the program fits into the overall organization

NIST also defines standard operating procedures (SOPs) as "a delineation of the specific technical processes, techniques, checklists, and forms used by the incident response team. SOPs should be reasonably comprehensive and detailed to ensure that the priorities of the organization are reflected in response operations."

The Incident Response Process

NIST Special Publication 800-61 goes over the major phases of the incident response process in detail. You should become familiar with that publication, as it provides additional information that will help you succeed in your security operations center (SOC). The important key points are summarized here.

NIST defines the major phases of the incident response process as illustrated in Figure 5-2.

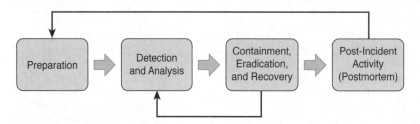

Figure 5-2 *The Major Phases of the Incident Response Process*

The Preparation Phase

The preparation phase includes creating and training the incident response team, as well as deploying the necessary tools and resources to successfully investigate and resolve cybersecurity incidents. In this phase, the incident response team creates a set of controls based on the results of risk assessments. The preparation phase also includes the following tasks:

■ Creating processes for incident handler communications and the facilities that will host the security operation center (SOC) and incident response team

■ Making sure that the organization has appropriate incident analysis hardware and software as well as incident mitigation software

■ Creating risk assessment capabilities within the organization

■ Making sure the organization has appropriately deployed host security, network security, and malware prevention solutions

■ Developing user awareness training

The Detection and Analysis Phase

The detection and analysis phase is one of the most challenging phases. While some incidents are easy to detect (for example, a denial-of-service attack), many breaches and attacks are left undetected for weeks or even months. This is why detection may be the most difficult task in incident response. The typical network is full of "blind spots" where anomalous traffic goes undetected. Implementing analytics and correlation tools is critical to eliminating these network blind spots. As a result, the incident response team must react quickly to analyze and validate each incident. This is done by following a predefined process while documenting each step the analyst takes. NIST provides several recommendations for making incident analysis easier and more effective:

- Profile networks and systems
- Understand normal behaviors
- Create a log retention policy
- Perform event correlation
- Maintain and use a knowledge base of information
- Use Internet search engines for research
- Run packet sniffers to collect additional data
- Filter the data
- Seek assistance from others
- Keep all host clocks synchronized
- Know the different types of attacks and attack vectors
- Develop processes and procedures to recognize the signs of an incident
- Understand the sources of precursors and indicators
- Create appropriate incident documentation capabilities and processes
- Create processes to effectively prioritize security incidents
- Create processes to effectively communicate incident information (internal and external communications)

Containment, Eradication, and Recovery

The containment, eradication, and recovery phase includes the following activities:

- Evidence gathering and handling
- Identifying the attacking hosts
- Choosing a containment strategy to effectively contain and eradicate the attack, as well as to successfully recover from it

NIST Special Publication 800-61 also defines the following criteria for determining the appropriate containment, eradication, and recovery strategy:

- The potential damage to and theft of resources
- The need for evidence preservation
- Service availability (for example, network connectivity as well as services provided to external parties)
- Time and resources needed to implement the strategy
- Effectiveness of the strategy (for example, partial containment or full containment)
- Duration of the solution (for example, emergency workaround to be removed in four hours, temporary workaround to be removed in two weeks, or permanent solution)

Post-Incident Activity (Postmortem)

The post-incident activity phase includes lessons learned, how to use collected incident data, and evidence retention. NIST Special Publication 800-61 includes several questions that can be used as guidelines during the lessons learned meeting(s):

- Exactly what happened, and at what times?
- How well did the staff and management perform while dealing with the incident?
- Were the documented procedures followed? Were they adequate?
- What information was needed sooner?
- Were any steps or actions taken that might have inhibited the recovery?
- What would the staff and management do differently the next time a similar incident occurs?
- How could information sharing with other organizations be improved?
- What corrective actions can prevent similar incidents in the future?
- What precursors or indicators should be watched for in the future to detect similar incidents?
- What additional tools or resources are needed to detect, analyze, and mitigate future incidents?

Information Sharing and Coordination

During the investigation and resolution of a security incident, you may also need to communicate with outside parties regarding the incident. Examples include, but are not limited to, contacting law enforcement, fielding media inquiries, seeking external expertise, and working with Internet service providers (ISPs), the vendor of your hardware and software products, threat intelligence vendor feeds, coordination centers, and members of other incident response teams. You can also share relevant incident indicator of compromise (IoC) information and other observables with industry peers. A good example of information-sharing communities includes the Financial Services Information Sharing and Analysis Center (FS-ISAC).

Your incident response plan should account for these types of interactions with outside entities. It should also include information about how to interact with your organization's public relations (PR) department, legal department, and upper management. You should also get their buy-in when sharing information with outside parties to minimize the risk of information leakage. In other words, avoid leaking sensitive information regarding security incidents with unauthorized parties. These actions could potentially lead to additional disruption and financial loss. You should also maintain a list of all the contacts at those external entities, including a detailed list of all external communications for liability and evidentiary purposes.

Incident Response Team Structure

In Chapter 6, "Incident Response Teams," you will learn all the details about incident response teams. There are different incident response teams. The most popular is the

Computer Incident Response Team (CSIRT) within your organization. Others include the following:

- Product Security Incident Response Team (PSIRT)
- National CSIRTs and Computer Emergency Response Team (CERT)
- Coordination center
- Incident response teams of security vendors and managed security service providers (MSSP)

The following are the most common incident response team structures:

- Centralized incident response team
- Distributed incident response team
- Coordinating team

The following are the most common incident response team staffing models:

- Employees
- Partially outsourced
- Fully outsourced

The Vocabulary for Event Recording and Incident Sharing (VERIS)

The Vocabulary for Event Recording and Incident Sharing (VERIS) is a collection of schemas and a common language for describing security incidents in a standard way. VERIS was first created by a team of cybersecurity professionals from Verizon and other industry peers. It has now been adopted by many security teams in the industry.

The VERIS documentation can be found at: http://veriscommunity.net/index.html

> **TIP**   You will learn all the elements of the VERIS schema in this chapter, but it is recommended that you review and become familiar with the VERIS documentation at the VERIS website (http://veriscommunity.net). You can also access several tools that the community has created at their GitHub repository at: https://github.com/vz-risk.

The VERIS schema and examples can be accessed at the VERIS GitHub repository at: https://github.com/vz-risk/veris.

The VERIS schema is divided into the following five main sections:

- Incident Tracking
- Victim Demographics
- Incident Description
- Discovery & Response
- Impact Assessment

Figure 5-3 includes a mind-map that illustrates these five sections and their related elements.

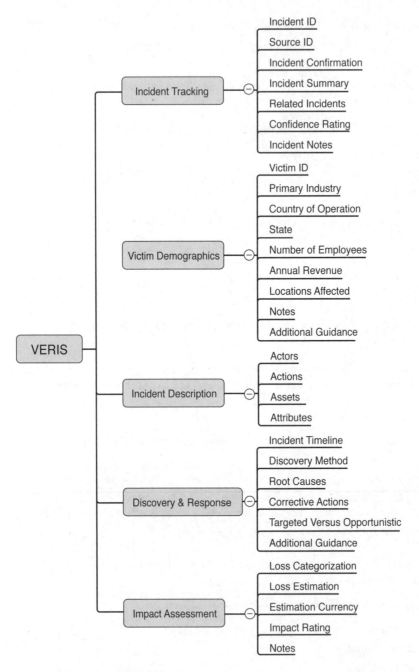

Figure 5-3 *The VERIS Schema*

As you can see in Figure 5-3, the Incident Tracking section contains the following elements:

- Incident ID—an identifier for the incident.
- Source ID—the source or handler ID of the incident.
- Incident Confirmation—whether the security incident has been confirmed or not confirmed.
- Incident Summary—the summary of the incident.
- Related Incidents—any other related incidents.
- Confidence Rating—an enumerated list that describes how certain you are that the information pertaining to this incident is complete.
- Incident Notes—any additional notes that may be relevant to the incident description.

The Victim Demographics section contains the following elements:

- Victim ID—an identifier of the victim.
- Primary Industry—the victim's primary industry (for example, healthcare, manufacturing, banking, IT, and so on).
- Country of Operation—the country the victim operates in
- State—the state or region of operation.
- Number of Employees—the number of employees of the victim organization.
- Annual Revenue—the annual revenue of the victim organization.
- Locations Affected—the locations affected by the incident.
- Notes—any additional notes about the victim.
- Additional Guidance—any additional guidance you may want to provide about the victim and incident.

The Incident Description section contains the following elements:

- Actors—the known threat actors.
- Actions—the actions taken by the threat actor(s).
- Assets—the assets that were compromised.
- Attributes—any additional attributes related to the CIA triad.

The Discovery & Response section contains the following elements:

- Incident Timeline—the incident timeline.
- Discovery Method—the methodology used to discover the incident.
- Root Causes—the incident root cause(s).
- Corrective Actions—any corrective actions to mitigate and remediate the incident.
- Targeted vs. Opportunistic—to describe if the incident was targeted or opportunistic.
- Additional Guidance—any additional guidance about the incident.

The Impact Assessment section contains the following elements:

■ Loss Categorization—describes the different types of losses experienced as a result of the incident (direct or indirect losses).

■ Loss Estimation—an estimate of all the losses experienced because of the incident.

■ Estimation Currency—the currency used in the loss estimation (for example, US dollar, EURO, and so on)

■ Impact Rating—a rating used to describe the overall impact of the incident.

■ Notes—any additional notes about the impact and losses.

One of the main purposes of VERIS is to categorize incident data so that it can be used as lessons learned and shared among security professionals and many organizations. VERIS created an open source database of incident information called the VERIS Community Database (VCDB). This database can be accessed at the following GitHub repository: https://github.com/vz-risk/VCDB.

There is also a useful tool that can get you started adopting VERIS called the VERIS Incident Recording Tool and it can be accessed at: https://incident.veriscommunity.net/s3/example You can play with this tool to become familiar with all the different fields, the VERIS schema, and how to apply VERIS to your incident handling process.

Exam Preparation Tasks

Review All Key Topics

Review the most important topics in the chapter, noted with the Key Topic icon in the outer margin of the page. Table 5-2 lists these key topics and the page numbers on which each is found.

Table 5-2 Key Topics

Key Topic Element	Description	Page
Paragraph	What is incident response?	144
Summary	What are security events and incidents?	144
Summary	Understanding the incident response plan.	145
Summary	Understanding the incident response process.	146
Summary	Understanding information sharing and coordination.	148
Summary	Applying VERIS to the incident response and incident handling process.	149

Complete Tables and Lists from Memory

Print a copy of Appendix B, "Memory Tables," (found on the book website), or at least the section for this chapter, and complete the tables and lists from memory. Appendix C, "Memory Tables Answer Key," also on the website, includes completed tables and lists to check your work.

Define Key Terms

Define the following key terms from this chapter, and check your answers in the glossary:

security event, security incident, standard operating procedure

Q&A

The answers to these questions appear in Appendix A, "Answers to the 'Do I Know This Already' Quizzes and Q&A." For more practice with exam format questions, use the exam engine on the website.

1. What is a violation or imminent threat of violation of computer security policies, acceptable use policies, or standard security practices?

    a. Exploit

    b. Vulnerability

    c. Threat

    d. Computer security incident

2. What is a delineation of the specific technical processes, techniques, checklists, and forms used by the incident response team?

    a. CSIRT team plan

    b. Standard operating procedure (SOP)

    c. Standard incident plan (SIP)

    d. Operation and incident plan (OIP)

3. What is any observable occurrence in a system or network?

    a. Security event

    b. Security incident

    c. Security vulnerability

    d. An exploit

4. Which of the following is not an example of the most common incident response team staffing models?

    a. Employees

    b. Partially outsourced

    c. Fully outsourced

    d. PSIRT

5. The containment, eradication, and recovery phase includes which of the following? (Choose two.)

    a. Choosing a firewall to be able to block traffic proactively or during an attack

    b. Choosing an intrusion prevention system to be able to block traffic proactively or during an attack

    c. Choosing a containment strategy to effectively contain and eradicate the attack, as well as to be able to successfully recover from it

    d. Evidence gathering and handling

6. Which phase in the incident response process includes lessons learned, how to use collected incident data, and evidence retention?

    a. Post-incident activity (postmortem)

    b. Containment, eradication, and recovery

    c. The detection and analysis phase

    d. The preparation phase

7. Which phase in the incident response process includes creating processes for incident handler communications and the facilities that will host the security operation center (SOC) and incident response team?

    a. The preparation phase

    b. The detection and analysis phase

    c. Containment, eradication, and recovery

    d. Post-incident activity (postmortem)

8. Which of following are examples of the most common incident response team structures? (Choose two.)

    a. Centralized incident response team

    b. Partially outsourced

    c. Fully outsourced

    d. Distributed incident response team

9. Which of following is not an example of the VERIS main schema categories?

    a. Incident Tracking

    b. Victim Demographics

    c. Incident Description

    d. Incident Forensics ID

10. Which of following is not an example of an element in the Incident Description section of the VERIS schema?

    a. Actors

    b. Actions

    c. Victims and Losses

    d. Attributes

5

This chapter covers the following topics:

- Computer Security Incident Response Teams (CSIRTs)

- Product Security Incident Response Teams (PSIRTs)

- National CSIRTs and Computer Emergency Response Teams (CERTs)

- Coordination Centers

- Incident response providers and managed security service providers (MSSPs)

CHAPTER 6

Incident Response Teams

In this chapter, you will learn the different types of incident response teams and their responsibilities. You already learned about Computer Security Incident Response Teams (CSIRTs), and in this chapter you will learn details of Product Security Incident Response Teams (PSIRTs), National CSIRTs and Computer Emergency Response Teams (CERTs), Coordination Centers, and incident response teams of Managed Security Service Providers (MSSPs).

"Do I Know This Already?" Quiz

The "Do I Know This Already?" quiz helps you identify your strengths and deficiencies in this chapter's topics. The seven-question quiz, derived from the major sections in the "Foundation Topics" portion of the chapter, helps you determine how to spend your limited study time. Table 6-1 outlines the major topics discussed in this chapter and the "Do I Know This Already?" quiz questions that correspond to those topics.

Table 6-1 "Do I Know This Already?" Foundation Topics Section-to-Question Mapping

Foundation Topics Section	Questions Covered in This Section
Computer Security Incident Response Teams (CSIRTs)	1–2
Product Security Incident Response Teams (PSIRTs)	3–4
National CSIRTs and Computer Emergency Response Teams (CERTs)	5
Coordination Centers	6
Incident Response Providers and Managed Security Service Providers (MSSP)	7

1. Which of the following are examples of some of the responsibilities of a corporate CSIRT and the policies it helps create? (Select all that apply.)

   a. Scanning vendor customer networks

   b. Incident classification and handling

   c. Information classification and protection

   d. Information dissemination

   e. Record retentions and destruction

2. Which of the following is one of the main goals of the CSIRT?

   a. To configure the organization's firewalls

   b. To monitor the organization's IPS devices

   c. To minimize and control the damage associated with incidents, provide guidance for mitigation, and work to prevent future incidents

   d. To hire security professionals who will be part of the InfoSec team of the organization.

3. Which of the following are the three metrics, or "scores," of the Common Vulnerability Scoring System (CVSS)? (Select all that apply.)

   a. Baseline score

   b. Base score

   c. Environmental score

   d. Temporal score

4. Which of the following is typically a responsibility of a PSIRT?

   a. Configure the organization's firewall

   b. Monitor security logs

   c. Investigate security incidents in a security operations center (SOC)

   d. Disclose vulnerabilities in the organization's products and services

5. Which of the following are core responsibilities of a national CSIRT and CERT?

   a. Provide solutions for bug bounties

   b. Protect their citizens by providing security vulnerability information, security awareness training, best practices, and other information

   c. Provide vulnerability brokering to vendors within a country

   d. Create regulations around cybersecurity within the country

6. Which of the following is an example of a coordination center?

   a. Cisco PSIRT

   b. Microsoft MSRC

   c. CERT division of the Software Engineering Institute (SEI)

   d. FIRST

7. Which of the following is an example of a managed security offering where incident response experts monitor and respond to security alerts in a security operations center (SOC)?

   a. Cisco CloudLock

   b. Cisco's Active Threat Analytics (ATA)

   c. Cisco Managed Firepower Service

   d. Cisco Jasper

Foundation Topics

Computer Security Incident Response Teams (CSIRTs)

There are different incident response teams. The most popular is the Computer Security Incident Response Team (CSIRT). Others include the following:

- Product Security Incident Response Team (PSIRT)
- National CSIRT and Computer Emergency Response Team (CERT)
- Coordination center
- The incident response team of a security vendor and Managed Security Service Provider (MSSP)

In this section, you will learn about CSIRTs. The rest of the incident response team types will be covered in the subsequent sections in this chapter.

The CSIRT is typically the team that works hand-in-hand with the information security teams (often called InfoSec). In smaller organizations, InfoSec and CSIRT functions may be combined and provided by the same team. In large organizations, the CSIRT focuses on the investigation of computer security incidents while the InfoSec team is tasked with the implementation of security configurations, monitoring, and policies within the organization.

Establishing a CSIRT involves the following steps:

Step 1.   Defining the CSIRT constituency.

Step 2.   Ensuring management and executive support.

Step 3.   Making sure that the proper budget is allocated.

Step 4.   Deciding where the CSIRT will reside within the organization's hierarchy.

Step 5.   Determining whether the team will be central, distributed, or virtual.

Step 6.   Developing the process and policies for the CSIRT.

It is important to recognize that every organization is different, and these steps can be accomplished in parallel or in sequence. However, defining the constituency of a CSIRT is certainly one of the first steps in the process. When defining the constituency of a CSIRT, one should answer the following questions:

- Who will be the "customer" of the CSIRT?
- What is the scope? Will the CSIRT cover only the organization or also entities external to the organization? For example, at Cisco, all internal infrastructure and Cisco's websites and tools (that is, Cisco.com) are a responsibility of the Cisco CSIRT, and any incident or vulnerability concerning a Cisco product or service is the responsibility of the Cisco PSIRT.

- Will the CSIRT provide support for the complete organization or only for a specific area or segment? For example, an organization may have a CSIRT for traditional infrastructure and IT capabilities and a separate one dedicated to cloud security.

- Will the CSIRT be responsible for part of the organization or all of it? If external entities will be included, how will they be selected?

Determining the value of a CSIRT can be challenging. One of the main questions that executives will ask is, what is the return on investment for having a CSIRT? The main goals of the CSIRT are to minimize risk, contain cyber damage, and save money by preventing incidents from happening—and when they do occur, to mitigate them efficiently. For example, the smaller the scope of the damage, the less money you need to spend to recover from a compromise (including brand reputation). Many studies in the past have covered the cost of security incidents and the cost of breaches. Also, the Ponemon Institute periodically publishes reports covering these costs. It is a good practice to review and calculate the "value add" of the CSIRT. This calculation can be used to determine when to invest more, not only in a CSIRT, but also in operational best practices. In some cases, an organization might even outsource some of the cybersecurity functions to a managed service provider, if the organization cannot afford or retain security talent.

In Chapter 5, "Introduction to Incident Response and the Incident Handling Process," you learned that any incident response team must have several basic policies and procedures in place to operate satisfactorily, including the following:

- Incident classification and handling
- Information classification and protection
- Information dissemination
- Record retention and destruction
- Acceptable usage of encryption
- Engaging and cooperating with external groups (other IRTs, law enforcement, and so on)

Also, some additional policies or procedures can be defined, such as the following:

- Hiring policy
- Using an outsourcing organization to handle incidents
- Working across multiple legal jurisdictions

Even more policies can be defined depending on the team's circumstances. The important thing to remember is that not all policies need to be defined on the first day.

The following are great sources of information from the International Organization for Standardization/International Electrotechnical Commission (ISO/IEC) that you can leverage when you are conscripting your policy and procedure documents:

- ISO/IEC 27001:2005: Information technology – Security techniques – Information security management systems – Requirements
- ISO/IEC 27002:2005: Information technology – Security techniques – Code of practice for information security management

- ISO/IEC 27005:2008: Information technology – Security techniques – Information security risk management

- ISO/PAS 22399:2007: Societal Security – Guidelines for Incident Preparedness and Operational Continuity Management

- ISO/IEC 27033: Information technology – Security techniques – Information security incident management

> **TIP**   CERT provides a good overview of the goals and responsibilities of a CSIRT at the following site: https://www.cert.org/incident-management/csirt-development/csirt-faq.cfm.

Product Security Incident Response Teams (PSIRTs)

Software and hardware vendors may have separate teams that handle the investigation, resolution, and disclosure of security vulnerabilities in their products and services. Typically, these teams are called Product Security Incident Response Teams (PSIRTs). Before you can understand how a PSIRT operates, you must understand what constitutes security vulnerability.

The U.S. National Institute of Standards and Technology (NIST) defines a security vulnerability as follows:

> "A flaw or weakness in system security procedures, design, implementation, or internal controls that could be exercised (accidentally triggered or intentionally exploited) and result in a security breach or a violation of the system's security policy."

> **NOTE**   There are many more definitions, but they tend to be variations on the one from the NIST.

Security Vulnerabilities and Their Severity

Why are product security vulnerabilities a concern? Because each vulnerability represents a potential risk that threat actors can use to compromise your systems and your network. Each vulnerability carries an associated amount of risk with it. One of the most widely adopted standards to calculate the severity of a given vulnerability is the Common Vulnerability Scoring System (CVSS), which has three components: base, temporal, and environmental scores. Each component is presented as a score on a scale from 0 to 10. You learned all about CVSS in the SECFND exam, so this might be a refresher.

 CVSS is an industry standard maintained by FIRST that is used by many PSIRTs to convey information about the severity of vulnerabilities they disclose to their customers.

In CVSS, a vulnerability is evaluated under three aspects and a score is assigned to each of them:

- The *base* group represents the intrinsic characteristics of a vulnerability that are constant over time and do not depend on a user-specific environment. This is the most important information and the only one that's mandatory to obtain a vulnerability score.

- The *temporal* group assesses the vulnerability as it changes over time.

- The *environmental* group represents the characteristics of a vulnerability, taking into account the organizational environment.

The score for the base group is between 0 and 10, where 0 is the least severe and 10 is assigned to highly critical vulnerabilities. For example, a highly critical vulnerability could allow an attacker to remotely compromise a system and get full control. Additionally, the score comes in the form of a vector string that identifies each of the components used to make up the score.

The formula used to obtain the score takes into account various characteristics of the vulnerability and how the attacker is able to leverage these characteristics.

CVSSv3 defines several characteristics for the base, temporal, and environmental groups.

The base group defines Exploitability metrics that measure how the vulnerability can be exploited, as well as Impact metrics that measure the impact on confidentiality, integrity, and availability. In addition to these two metrics, a metric called Scope Change (S) is used to convey impact on systems that are impacted by the vulnerability but do not contain vulnerable code.

The Exploitability metrics include the following:

- **Attack Vector (AV)** represents the level of access an attacker needs to have to exploit a vulnerability. It can assume four values:
  - Network (N)
  - Adjacent (A)
  - Local (L)
  - Physical (P)
- **Attack Complexity (AC)** represents the conditions beyond the attacker's control that must exist in order to exploit the vulnerability. The values can be the following:
  - Low (L)
  - High (H)
- **Privileges Required (PR)** represents the level of privileges an attacker must have to exploit the vulnerability. The values are as follows:
  - None (N)
  - Low (L)
  - High (H)
- **User Interaction (UI)** captures whether a user interaction is needed to perform an attack. The values are as follows:
  - None (N)
  - Required (R)

- **Scope (S)** captures the impact on systems other than the system being scored. The values are as follows:
    - Unchanged (U)
    - Changed (C)

The Impact metrics include the following:

- **Confidentiality (C)** measures the degree of impact to the confidentiality of the system. It can assume the following values:
    - Low (L)
    - Medium (M)
    - High (H)
- **Integrity (I)** measures the degree of impact to the integrity of the system. It can assume the following values:
    - Low (L)
    - Medium (M)
    - High (H)
- **Availability (A)** measures the degree of impact to the availability of the system. It can assume the following values:
    - Low (L)
    - Medium (M)
    - High (H)

The temporal group includes three metrics:

- **Exploit Code Maturity (E),** which measures whether or not public exploit is available
- **Remediation Level (RL),** which indicates whether a fix or workaround is available
- **Report Confidence (RC),** which indicates the degree of confidence in the existence of the vulnerability

The environmental group includes two main metrics:

- **Security Requirements (CR, IR, AR),** which indicate the importance of confidentiality, integrity, and availability requirements for the system
- **Modified Base Metrics (MAV, MAC, MAPR, MUI, MS, MC, MI, MA),** which allow the organization to tweak the base metrics based on specific characteristic of the environment

For example, a vulnerability that might allow a remote attacker to crash the system by sending crafted IP packets would have the following values for the base metrics:

- Access Vector (AV) would be Network because the attacker can be anywhere and can send packets remotely.
- Attack Complexity (AC) would be Low because it is trivial to generate malformed IP packets (for example, via the Scapy tool).

- Privilege Required (PR) would be None because there are no privileges required by the attacker on the target system.

- User Interaction (UI) would also be None because the attacker does not need to interact with any user of the system in order to carry out the attack.

- Scope (S) would be Unchanged if the attack does not cause other systems to fail.

- Confidentiality Impact (C) would be None because the primary impact is on the availability of the system.

- Integrity Impact (I) would be None because the primary impact is on the availability of the system.

- Availability Impact (A) would be High because the device could become completely unavailable while crashing and reloading.

Additional examples of CVSSv3 scoring are available at the FIRST website (https://www.first.org/cvss).

Vulnerability Chaining Role in Fixing Prioritization

In numerous instances, security vulnerabilities are not exploited in isolation. Threat actors exploit more than one vulnerability "in a chain" to carry out their attack and compromise their victims. By leveraging different vulnerabilities in a chain, attackers can infiltrate progressively further into the system or network and gain more control over it. This is something that PSIRT teams must be aware of. Developers, security professionals, and users must be aware of this because chaining can change the order in which a vulnerability needs to be fixed or patched in the affected system. For instance, multiple low-severity vulnerabilities can become a severe one if they are combined.

Performing vulnerability chaining analysis is not a trivial task. Although several commercial companies claim that they can easily perform chaining analysis, in reality the methods and procedures that can be included as part of a chain vulnerability analysis are pretty much endless. PSIRT teams should utilize an approach that works for them to achieve the best end result.

Fixing Theoretical Vulnerabilities

Exploits cannot exist without a vulnerability. However, there isn't always an exploit for a given vulnerability. From your preparation for the SECFND test, you already know the difference between a vulnerability and an exploit. Also, earlier in this chapter you were reminded of the definition of a vulnerability. As another reminder, an exploit is not a vulnerability. An exploit is a concrete manifestation, either a piece of software or a collection of reproducible steps, that leverage a given vulnerability to compromise an affected system.

In some cases, users call vulnerabilities without exploits "theoretical vulnerabilities." One of the biggest challenges with "theoretical vulnerabilities" is that there are many smart people out there capable of exploiting them. If you do not know how to exploit a vulnerability today, it does not mean that someone else will not find a way in the future. In fact, someone else may already have found a way to exploit the vulnerability and perhaps is even selling the exploit of the vulnerability in underground markets without public knowledge.

PSIRT personnel should understand there is no such thing as an "entirely theoretical" vulnerability. Sure, having a working exploit can ease the reproducible steps and help to verify whether that same vulnerability is present in different systems. However, because an exploit may not come as part of a vulnerability, you should not completely deprioritize it.

Internally Versus Externally Found Vulnerabilities

A PSIRT can learn about a vulnerability in a product or service during internal testing or during the development phase. However, vulnerabilities can also be reported by external entities, such as security researchers, customers, and other vendors.

The dream of any vendor is to be able to find and patch all security vulnerabilities during the design and development phases. However, that is close to impossible. On the other hand, that is why a secure development lifecycle (SDL) is extremely important for any organization that produces software and hardware. Cisco has an SDL program that is documented at the following URL:

http://www.cisco.com/c/en/us/about/security-center/security-programs/secure-development-lifecycle.html

Cisco defines its SDL as "a repeatable and measurable process we've designed to increase the resiliency and trustworthiness of our products." Cisco's SDL is part of Cisco Product Development Methodology (PDM) and ISO9000 compliance requirements. It includes, but is not limited to, the following:

- Base product security requirements
- Third-party software (TPS) security
- Secure design
- Secure coding
- Secure analysis
- Vulnerability testing

The goal of the SDL is to provide tools and processes that are designed to accelerate the product development methodology, by developing secure, resilient, and trustworthy systems. TPS security is one of the most important tasks for any organization. Most of today's organizations use open source and third-party libraries. This approach creates two requirements for the product security team. The first is to know what TPS libraries are used, reused, and where. The second is to patch any vulnerabilities that affect such library or TPS components. For example, if a new vulnerability in OpenSSL is disclosed, what do you have to do? Can you quickly assess the impact of such a vulnerability in all your products?

If you include commercial TPS, is the vendor of such software transparently disclosing all the security vulnerabilities, including in their software? Nowadays, many organizations are including security vulnerability disclosure SLAs in their contracts with third-party vendors. This is very important because many TPS vulnerabilities (both commercial and open source) go unpatched for many months—or even years.

TPS software security is a monumental task for any company of any size. To get a feeling of the scale of TPS code usage, visit the third-party security bulletins published by Cisco at https://tools.cisco.com/security/center/publicationListing.x?product=NonCisco#~ Vulnerabilities. Another good resource is CVE Details (www.cvedetails.com).

Many tools are available on the market today to enumerate all open source components used in a product. These tools either interrogate the product source code or scan binaries for the presence of TPS. The following are a few examples:

- **BlackDuck Software:** https://www.blackducksoftware.com
- **AppCheck:** http://www.codenomicon.com/products/appcheck
- **Palamida:** http://www.palamida.com
- **Lexumo:** https://www.lexumo.com
- **SRC:CLR:** https://www.sourceclear.com

National CSIRTs and Computer Emergency Response Teams (CERTs)

Numerous countries have their own Computer Emergency Response (or Readiness) Teams. Examples include the US-CERT (https://www.us-cert.gov), Indian Computer Emergency Response Team (http://www.cert-in.org.in), CERT Australia (https://cert.gov.au), and the Australian Computer Emergency Response Team (https://www.auscert.org.au/). The Forum of Incident Response and Security Teams (FIRST) website includes a list of all the national CERTS and other incident response teams at https://www.first.org/members/teams.

These national CERTS and CSIRTs aim to protect their citizens by providing security vulnerability information, security awareness training, best practices, and other information. For example, the following is the US-CERT mission posted at https://www.us-cert.gov/about-us:

"US-CERT's critical mission activities include:

- Providing cybersecurity protection to Federal civilian executive branch agencies through intrusion detection and prevention capabilities.

- Developing timely and actionable information for distribution to federal departments and agencies; state, local, tribal and territorial (SLTT) governments; critical infrastructure owners and operators; private industry; and international organizations.

- Responding to incidents and analyzing data about emerging cyber threats.

- Collaborating with foreign governments and international entities to enhance the nation's cybersecurity posture."

Coordination Centers

Several organizations around the world also help with the coordination of security vulnerability disclosures to vendors, hardware and software providers, and security researchers.

One of the best examples is the CERT Division of the Software Engineering Institute (SEI). Their website can be accessed at cert.org, and their "About Us" page summarizes well their role and the role of many coordination centers alike:

"CERT Division of the Software Engineering Institute (SEI), we study and solve problems with widespread cybersecurity implications, research security vulnerabilities in software products, contribute to long-term changes in networked systems, and develop cutting-edge information and training to help improve cybersecurity.

We are more than a research organization. Working with software vendors, we help resolve software vulnerabilities. We develop tools, products, and methods to help organizations conduct forensic examinations, analyze vulnerabilities, and monitor large-scale networks. We help organizations determine how effective their security-related practices are. And we share our work at conferences; in blogs, webinars, and podcasts; and through our many articles, technical reports, and white papers. We collaborate with high-level government organizations, such as the U.S. Department of Defense and the Department of Homeland Security (DHS); law enforcement, including the FBI; the intelligence community; and many industry organizations.

Working together, DHS and the CERT Division meet mutually set goals in areas such as data collection and mining, statistics and trend analysis, computer and network security, incident management, insider threat, software assurance, and more. The results of this work include exercises, courses, and systems that were designed, implemented, and delivered to DHS and its customers as part of the SEI's mission to transition SEI capabilities to the public and private sectors and improve the practice of cybersecurity."

 ## Incident Response Providers and Managed Security Service Providers (MSSPs)

Cisco, along with several other vendors, provides incident response and managed security services to its customers. These incident response teams and outsourced CSIRTs operate a bit different because their task is to provide support to their customers. However, they practice the tasks outlined earlier in this chapter for incident response and CSIRTs.

The following are examples of these teams and their services:

- **Cisco's Incident Response Service:** Provides Cisco customers with readiness or proactive services and post-breach support. The proactive services include infrastructure breach preparedness assessments, security operations readiness assessments, breach communications assessment, and security operations and incident response training. The post-breach (or reactive) services include the evaluation and investigation of the attack, countermeasure development and deployment, as well as the validation of the countermeasure effectiveness. You can obtain more information about Cisco's Incident Response Service at http://www.cisco.com/c/dam/en/us/services/collateral/se/at-a-glance-c45-734212.pdf.

- **Cisco's Active Threat Analytics (ATA) managed security service:** The Cisco ATA service offers customers 24-hour continuous monitoring and advanced-analytics capabilities, combined with threat intelligence as well as security analysts and investigators to detect security threats in customer networks. More information about Cisco ATA can be obtained at https://www.cisco.com/c/en/us/products/security/managed-services.html.

Exam Preparation Tasks

Review All Key Topics

Review the most important topics in the chapter, noted with the Key Topic icon in the outer margin of the page. Table 6-2 lists these key topics and the page numbers on which each is found.

Table 6-2   Key Topics for Chapter 6

Key Topic Element	Description	Page
Summary	What is a CSIRT?	159
Summary	What is a PSIRT?	161
Summary	What is CVSS?	161
Summary	What is a national CSIRT or CERT?	166
Summary	What are vulnerability coordination centers?	166
Summary	Understanding Incident Response Providers and Managed Security Service Providers (MSSPs)	167

Define Key Terms

Define the following key terms from this chapter, and check your answers in the glossary:

CSIRT, PSIRT, CVSS, national CSIRT and CERTs

Q&A

The answers to these questions appear in Appendix A, "Answers to the 'Do I Know This Already' Quizzes and Q&A." For more practice with exam format questions, use the exam engine on the website.

1. Which of the following aim to protect their citizens by providing security vulnerability information, security awareness training, best practices, and other information?

   a. National CERTs

   b. PSIRT

   c. ATA

   d. Global CERTs

2. Which of the following is the team that handles the investigation, resolution, and disclosure of security vulnerabilities in vendor products and services?

   a. CSIRT

   b. ICASI

   c. USIRP

   d. PSIRT

3. Which of the following is an example of a coordination center?

   a. PSIRT

   b. FIRST

   c. The CERT/CC division of the Software Engineering Institute (SEI)

   d. USIRP from ICASI

4. Which of the following is the most widely adopted standard to calculate the severity of a given security vulnerability?

   a. VSS

   b. CVSS

   c. VCSS

   d. CVSC

5. The CVSS base score defines Exploitability metrics that measure how a vulnerability can be exploited as well as Impact metrics that measure the impact on which of the following? (Choose three.)

   a. Repudiation

   b. Non-repudiation

   c. Confidentiality

   d. Integrity

   e. Availability

6

This chapter covers the following topics:

- Payment Card Industry Data Security Standard (PCI DSS)

- Health Insurance Portability and Accountability Act (HIPAA)

- Sarbanes-Oxley Act of 2002 (SOX)

CHAPTER 7

Compliance Frameworks

Compliance may seem like a tedious effort designed to punish people who are responsible for security. The reality is these requirements are extremely critical to how an organization and its customers are protected against cyber attacks. Think about how often you've had to get a new credit card due to unauthorized charges being seen against that account. When I speak to large audiences about security in the United States, I ask the question, "How many people have had to replace a credit card due to unauthorized charges?" I always find more than half of the attendees have had their credit card stolen. Typically in other countries that have adopted smart chip technology, the number is very low. This brings up an interesting question. Are the citizens of the United States all doing something wrong when their credit card data is stolen? I say this because I've had my own credit card data stolen numerous times while living in the States. The answer is, probably not. Most likely, a business we spent money with failed at meeting compliance standards to secure our financial transaction, and the cost was our data being stolen. This failure happens all the time with large retailers as well as smaller restaurants. Think about how many privately owned restaurants probably have an old laptop that hasn't been properly secured, yet it's designated as the point-of-sale terminal. This is the reality we live in, and failures in compliance impact more than just the organization responsible for being compliant. I pointed out the smart chip enabled countries as the exception to this example since that technology dramatically reduces this attack vector.

The CCNA Cyber Ops SECOPS exam includes a focus on some of the most important compliance frameworks. This does not mean other frameworks do not matter. However, due to the limited scope in this program, the following frameworks are what you should expect to see when attempting the exam. The first framework covered, known as Payment Card Industry Data Security Standard (PCI DSS), focuses on any organization involved with financial transactions. It should be obvious why this framework was selected, as the majority of organizations are responsible for being PCI compliant.

The second framework you should expect on the CCNA Cyber Ops SECOPS exam is known as the Health Insurance Portability and Accountability Act (HIPAA). Simply put, HIPAA focuses on security for health care data. This is extremely important because the loss of this data could lead to identity fraud, leakage of unwanted private health conditions, as well as other negative outcomes. HIPAA targets health care providers. However, anybody with health care data, such as the human resources department of any organization, must comply with securing HIPAA-related data.

The last framework we will cover is known as Sarbanes-Oxley (SOX). SOX compliance states all publicly held companies are required to establish internal controls and procedures for financial reporting. The goal for SOX is to reduce the risk of corporate fraud.

It is important to know that in the real world, an organization hiring for security operation skillsets will most likely not care if you know the details of specific compliance standards—meaning they don't expect you to quote line by line from a compliance manual. Most managers will train you on what compliance they must adhere to while on the job; however, they probably will expect that you are aware of the importance of compliance as well as have a basic understanding of the main compliance standards that apply to most organizations. For this reason, you should not expect the questions around compliance on the SECOPS exam to go into gory detail.

"Do I Know This Already?" Quiz

The "Do I Know This Already?" quiz allows you to assess whether you should read this entire chapter thoroughly or jump to the "Exam Preparation Tasks" section. If you are in doubt about your answers to these questions or your own assessment of your knowledge of the topics, read the entire chapter. Table 7-1 lists the major headings in this chapter and their corresponding "Do I Know This Already?" quiz questions. You can find the answers in Appendix A, "Answers to the 'Do I Know This Already?' Quizzes and Q&A."

Table 7-1   "Do I Know This Already?" Section-to-Question Mapping

Foundation Topics Section	Questions
Payment Card Industry Data Security Standard (PCI DSS)	1–5
Health Insurance Portability and Accountability Act (HIPAA)	6–8
Sarbanes-Oxley (SOX)	9–10

1. PCI DSS is designed to ensure which of the following?

    a. Protect electronic health care information

    b. Protect financial data such as the PAN, account data on a magnetic strip, and data on embedded chips

    c. Prevent data loss

    d. Prevent corporate fraud

2. What is the best answer for defining who must be compliant for PCI DSS?

    a. Any financial transactions

    b. Any merchant, processor, acquirer, issuer, or service provider that handles payment card processing, outsourced and third parties involved with payment card processing, and the home networks for the contractors responsible for maintaining PCI compliance

    c. Any merchant, processor, acquirer, issuer, or service provider that handles payment card processing

    d. Any merchant, processor, acquirer, issuer, or service provider that handles payment card processing along with outsourced or third parties involved with payment card processing

3. Which of the following PCI data must be protected?

   a. Geographic location of a user

   b. The payment amount

   c. The full account number

   d. A related health condition

4. Which of the following is not a high-level PCI DSS 3.2 requirement?

   a. Encryption on all PCI-related servers

   b. Implementing strong access control measures

   c. Regularly monitoring and testing networks

   d. Maintaining a vulnerability management program

5. Which is the best answer for addressing what must be PCI compliant?

   a. Any device associated with financial transactions must be PCI compliant.

   b. Any device and the network it connects to must be PCI compliant.

   c. The system, version of software installed, environment, and contracted resources must be PCI approved.

   d. The system, version of software installed, and environment of software must be PCI approved.

6. HIPAA is designed to protect which of the following?

   a. PHI

   b. e-PHI

   c. PHI and e-PHI

   d. PHI, ePHI, and PCI

7. What does PHI stand for?

   a. Personal health information

   b. Protected health insurance

   c. Personal health insurance

   d. Protected health information

8. Which of the following is protected by HIPAA?

   a. The full account number in a financial transaction

   b. Geolocation of a user

   c. Health conditions

   d. Full name of the patient

9. SOX does not apply to which of the following?

   a. All publicly held American companies

   b. Accounting firms involved with financial services

   c. International organizations that have registered equity or debt securities within the U.S. Security Exchange Commission

   d. Third-party service providers involved with companies responsible for SOX within in the U.S.

10. Which of the following is not a security framework based on what PCOAB publishes?

   a. COBIT

   b. OWASP

   c. ITGI

   d. COSO

Foundation Topics

Payment Card Industry Data Security Standard (PCI DSS)

Being PCI compliant is mandatory for any merchant, processor, acquirer, issuer, or service provider that handles payment card processing. This includes any entities that store, process, or transmit cardholder or authentication data. In addition, PCI compliance is required for payment operations that are outsourced and for third parties involved with payment card processing. The goal of the PCI Data Security Standard (PCI DSS) program is to protect the customer cardholder data when it's processed, stored, or transmitted. Failure to meet PCI could include large fines and have legal ramifications.

My personal feeling is PCI DSS needs to be better enforced. That way, in the future when I ask an audience about credit card theft, not so many people will raise their hands, showing that more people have avoided becoming victims due to a failure in a payment transaction. It is very possible that either the current standards are not being enforced properly across all organization types or there is a gap between what PCI DSS requires to be secure versus what is actually needed to secure PCI-related data.

PCI DSS Data

The data being protected by PCI DSS includes the primary account number (*PAN*), the account data on the *magnetic strip*, and the data on the *embedded chip*. This protection is required during the entire sales process, including the vendor or service provider's obligation to release the data upon completing the transaction. Releasing the data is a good thing because attackers can't access stored sensitive data that should no longer be needed after the sales transaction.

Account data defined by PCI DSS 3.2 is shown in the following lists:

- Cardholder data includes the following:
    - Primary account number (PAN)
    - Cardholder name
    - Expiration date
    - Service code
- Sensitive authentication data includes the following:
    - Full track data (magnetic-strip data or equivalent on a chip)
    - CAV2/CVC2/CVV2/CID
    - PINs/PIN blocks

PCI DSS is very specific about what type of data is and is not permitted to be stored. This includes data that is encrypted, meaning data encryption doesn't give you a reason not to follow PCI DSS standards. It is recommended that you contact the individual payment brand directly to fully understand what data is and is not permitted to be stored. Examples of payment brands are Visa, MasterCard, and American Express.

Table 7-2 illustrates examples of data storage regulations. Note that you most likely won't have to memorize this level of detail for the SECOPS exam. However, that doesn't mean it isn't useful to have a decent understanding of PCI DSS.

Note the requirements referenced will be covered later in this chapter, as we review the 12 PCI DSS requirements.

Table 7-2   Account Data

		Data Element	Storage Permitted	Render Stored Data Unreadable per Requirement 3.2
Account Data	Cardholder data	Primary account number (PAN)	Yes	Yes
		Cardholder name	Yes	No
		Service code	Yes	No
		Expiration date	Yes	No
	Sensitive authentication data	Full track data	No	Cannot store per Requirement 3.2
		CAV2/CVC2/CVV2/CID	No	Cannot store per Requirement 3.2
		PIN/PIN block	No	Cannot store per Requirement 3.2

PCI DSS Compliance

The PCI DSS compliance standard is administered by the PCI Security Standards Council, which established and released the 1.0 version of PCI on December 15, 2004. Since then, the PCI Security Standards Council has been releasing updates, with 3.2 being the latest version at time of this writing. It is recommended that you reference the PCI Security Standards Council website for the latest release information; however, you should also verify which version to expect on the Cyber Ops SECOPS exam. Most likely having an understanding of a fairly recent release of the PCI security standards will be sufficient for passing the Cyber Ops SECOPS exam. The PCI DSS release history is shown in Table 7-3. Most likely you won't be tested on the history of PCI releases; however, it doesn't hurt to be aware of this timeline for your personal studies.

Table 7-3   PCI DSS Release History

Month	Year	Release	Notes
December	2004	PCI 1.0	First release.
September	2006	PCI 1.1	Provided minor revisions.
October	2008	PCI 1.2	Updated based on new risks and threats.
August	2009	PCI 1.2.1	Provided minor revisions.

Month	Year	Release	Notes
October	2010	PCI 2.0	Major release.
November	2013	PCI 3.0	Major release.
April	2015	PCI 3.1	Minor release. Was retired October 31, 2016.
April	2016	PCI 3.2	Latest release.

Our focus will be on PCI Data Security Standard 3.2 (PCI DSS 3.2) being that it is the most current release. The major goals and aligned requirements are shown in Table 7-4, which reflects the latest standard. Once again, the SECOPS exam will most likely not dive into this level of detail around PCI DSS 3.2; however, it doesn't hurt to be aware for your personal studies.

NOTE: Understand that there are many checks that make up a major goal, which we will touch on later in this chapter.

Table 7-4   PCI Data Security Standard—High-Level Overview

Goals	PCI DSS Requirements
Build and maintain a secure network and systems	1. Install and maintain a firewall configuration to protect cardholder data. 2. Do not use vendor-supplied defaults for system passwords and other security parameters.
Protect cardholder data	3. Protect stored cardholder data. 4. Encrypt transmission of cardholder data across open, public networks.
Maintain a vulnerability management program	5. Protect all systems against malware and regularly update antivirus software or programs. 6. Develop and maintain secure systems and applications.
Implement strong access control measures	7. Restrict access to cardholder data by business need to know. 8. Identify and authenticate access to system components. 9. Restrict physical access to cardholder data.
Regularly monitor and test networks	10. Tack and monitor all access to network resources and cardholder data. 11. Regularly test security systems and processes.
Maintain an information security policy	12. Maintain a policy that addresses information security for all personnel.

7

Testing for PCI DSS 3.2 follows 12 requirements and corresponding testing procedures to validate compliance. There may be other legislation and regulatory requirements requiring additional protection of personal information or other data elements based on laws, government regulations, and so on. It is important to be aware that PCI DSS does not supersede any legal requirements. Also be aware there are legal obligations to be PCI compliant.

It is important to be aware that using a Payment Application Data Security Standard (PA DSS) compliant application by itself does not make the entity PCI compliant. PCI DSS requires that the PA-DSS–compliant application be implemented in a PCI DSS environment according to the guide provided by the PA-DSS-application vendor. For example, we have seen security products that require specific features to be enabled or disabled before they are considered PCI compliant. Failing to follow those guidelines stated by the vendor violates the PCI DSS compliancy. The same problem could happen if a PA-DSS-compliant application resides on a network that isn't following PCI DSS requirements, meaning that data leaving that application could be vulnerable. It is recommended that you validate with every vendor how its solution meets the current PCI DSS standards, including the *approved version of software* and the *required configurations and controls*. You can learn more about determining if a PA DSS applies to a payment application by reviewing the PA DSS program guide found at www.pcisecuritystandards.org. Trust us—we have seen the mistake of believing one is compliant with PCI DSS and later failing a PCI audit due to errors in deploying systems with PCI data.

In our experience, we find many PCI violations occur when an administrator sets up systems containing PCI data to auto-upgrade that could install a non-PCI-DSS-approved operating system. The downside of having PCI-approved software means there could be times the administrator is sacrificing more secure software due to that software not being "PCI tested and approved." This is just one of the many situations where being compliant could potentially reduce the quality of security, hence why we continue to recommend that you use security standards that exceed PCI requirements whenever possible.

Let's summarize the concepts in this section: You can't just isolate a specific device or application when evaluating its PCI-DSS-compliance status. You must consider everything about it, including what is installed, where it's installed, and what data it comes in contact with. A failure in any area of that system's lifecycle or environment is a failure to be PCI DSS compliant.

NOTE   It is important to understand that PCI DSS is a baseline of technical and operational requirements, meaning the minimal effort that should be enforced. PCI DSS also targets protecting personal data versus securing credit cards. Best practice is to implement security beyond these requirements, because advanced threats will require security controls that are more current than what is defined in PCI DSS and other compliance standards.

We recommend that you design your network to have higher security standards than what is required by PCI DSS. This would include proper network segmentation of sensitive systems holding PCI-related data from the rest of the network as well as monitoring sensitive systems using a layered approach of defenses.

PCI DSS 3.2 Overview

Let's look at a breakdown of the security controls and processes that make up the requirements for the PCI DSS 3.2 standard. Remember the security controls are how an organization is evaluated for each of the 12 PCI requirements. This applies to all system components included and connected to the *cardholder data environment (CDE)*. The CDE can be defined as the people, processes, and technologies that store, process, or transmit cardholder data or authentication data. Technologies could include but are not limited to physical and virtual network devices, servers, computing devices, and applications. Basically this list includes anything in contact with payment card data.

NOTE The SECOPS exam may not go into the level of detail of enumerating the different requirements for PCI DSS 3.2 or specifics on how it's listed in the official documentation. However, it is good to be aware of the latest version of PCI DSS 3.2 for your personal study.

- **Requirement 1: Build and maintain a secure network and systems.** The purpose of the following requirements is to enable security to reduce the risk of having a network containing PCI-related data compromised by a virtual attacker. For example, an attacker could breach a company's network security and remotely take credit card data or other sensitive information. One would hope many of these security practices are enforced in order to avoid a breach.

NOTE The following is a summary of the PCI DSS 3.2 requirements. See https://www.pcisecuritystandards.org for the complete and most current listing.

7

- 1.1. Establish and implement firewall and router configuration standards. Document and diagram cardholder data flows across systems and networks.

- 1.2. Build firewall and router configurations that restrict connections between untrusted networks and any system components in the cardholder data environment.

- 1.3. Prohibit direct public access between the Internet and any system component in the cardholder data environment.

- 1.4. Install personal firewall software or equivalent functionality on any portable computing devices that connect to the Internet when outside the network.

- 1.5. Ensure that security policies and operational procedures for managing firewalls are documented, in use, and known to all affected parties.

- **Requirement 2: Do not use vendor-supplied defaults for system passwords and other security parameters.** This requirement enforces the general best practice of never leaving the default passwords on systems. This should be common practice and include more advanced authentication programs such as multifactor authentication and the use of passphrases versus passwords. You would be surprised how many times we have found default passwords on core network systems during penetration testing exercises!

  - 2.1. Always change vendor-supplied defaults and remove or disable unnecessary default accounts before installing a system on the network.

- 2.2. Develop configuration standards for all system components. Ensure that these standards address all known security vulnerabilities and are consistent with industry-accepted system-hardening standards.

- 2.3. Encrypt all non-console administrative access using strong cryptography.

- 2.4. Maintain an inventory of system components that are in scope for PCI DSS.

- 2.5. Ensure that security policies and operational procedures for managing vendor defaults and other security parameters are documented, in use, and known to all affected parties.

- 2.6. Shared hosting providers must protect each entity's hosted environment and cardholder data.

- **Requirement 3: Protect stored cardholder data.** The focus of this requirement targets protecting the primary account number (PAN). Requirements include how PAN data is stored and practices to keep the area of storage protected from unwanted parties.

  - 3.1. Keep cardholder data storage to a minimum by implementing data retention and disposal policies, procedures, and processes. Purge unnecessary stored data at least quarterly.

  - 3.2. Do not store sensitive authentication data after authorization (even if encrypted). If sensitive authentication data is received, render all data unrecoverable upon completion of the authorization process.

  - 3.3. Mask PANs when displayed such that only personnel with a legitimate business need can see more than the first six/last four digits of the PAN.

  - 3.4. Render PAN unreadable anywhere it is stored (including on portable digital media, backup media, and in logs).

  - 3.5. Document and implement procedures to protect keys used to secure stored cardholder data against disclosure and misuse.

  - 3.6. Fully document and implement all key-management processes and procedures for cryptographic keys used for encryption of cardholder data.

  - 3.7. Ensure that security policies and operational procedures for protecting stored cardholder data are documented, in use, and known to all affected parties.

- **Requirement 4: Encrypt transmission of cardholder data across open, public networks.** This requirement protects card data while it's being sent over a network. The goal is to prevent man-in-the-middle compromises of the data, meaning attackers trying to capture the PAN data while it's sent between parties such as a point-of-sale system to the credit card operations center. Requirements also limit the approved methods of communicating with PCI DSS data to tools that include the proper level of security. Tools such as social media and SMS are big no-no's.

  - 4.1. Use strong cryptography and security protocols to safeguard sensitive cardholder data during transmission over open, public networks.

  - 4.2. Never send unprotected PANs by end-user messaging technologies (email, instant messaging, SMS, chat, and so on).

- 4.3. Ensure that security policies and operational procedures for encrypting transmissions of cardholder data are documented, in use, and known to all affected parties.

- **Requirement 5: Protect all systems against malware and regularly update antivirus software or programs.** This requirement is focused on best practices for defending against malware. The target is host system antivirus and antimalware software, meaning this type of protection must always be updated and running to reduce the risk of this threat vector.

  - 5.1. Deploy antivirus software on all systems commonly affected by malicious software.

  - 5.2. Ensure that all antivirus mechanisms are maintained.

  - 5.3. Ensure that antivirus mechanisms are actively running and cannot be disabled or altered by users, unless specifically authorized by management on a case-by-case basis for a limited time period.

  - 5.4. Ensure that security policies and operational procedures for protecting systems against malware are documented, in use, and known to all affected parties.

- **Requirement 6: Develop and maintain secure systems and applications.** Requirement 6 establishes rules around how systems should be continuously evaluated for vulnerabilities as well as the process to reduce the risk of those vulnerabilities when identified. This one is important because everybody has vulnerabilities, so best practice is to continuously audit your network for weaknesses before a malicious party finds it and exploits it. The key is not only continuously enforcing this but how quickly you take action on vulnerabilities found to be potentially devastating to your environment. Hopefully anybody hosting PCI DSS data is following this best practice.

  - 6.1. Establish a process to identify security vulnerabilities, using reputable outside sources for security vulnerability information, and assign a risk ranking to newly discovered security vulnerabilities.

  - 6.2. Ensure that all system components and software are protected from known vulnerabilities by installing applicable vendor-supplied security patches. Install critical security patches within one month of release.

  - 6.3. Develop internal and external software applications (including web-based administrative access to applications) securely.

  - 6.4. Follow change control processes and procedures for all changes to system components.

  - 6.5. Address common coding vulnerabilities in software-development processes.

  - 6.6. For public-facing web applications, address new threats and vulnerabilities on an ongoing basis and ensure these applications are protected against known attacks.

  - 6.7. Ensure that security policies and operational procedures for developing and maintaining secure systems and applications are documented, in use, and known to all affected parties.

- **Requirement 7: Restrict access to cardholder data by business need to know.** This requirement is a summary of the least privilege concept, meaning only providing access to what you need to do your job. This is ideal to reduce the risk of exposing sensitive data to unauthorized parties because access is limited to only those who would actually need access to the data.

    - 7.1. Limit access to system components and cardholder data to only those individuals whose job requires such access.

    - 7.2. Establish an access control system for system components that restricts access based on a user's need to know and is set to "deny all" unless specifically allowed.

    - 7.3. Ensure that security policies and operational procedures for restricting access to cardholder data are documented, in use, and known to all affected parties.

- **Requirement 8: Identify and authenticate access to system components.** This requirement complements Requirement 7 by enforcing proper identity and authentication practices to sensitive systems. Combining need to know and access control dramatically reduces the risk of exposing sensitive data.

    - 8.1. Define and implement policies and procedures to ensure proper user identification management for non-consumer users and administrators on all system components.

    - 8.2. In addition to assigning a unique ID, ensure proper user-authentication management for non-consumer users and administrators on all system components.

    - 8.3. Secure all individual non-console administrative access and all remote access to the CDE using multifactor authentication.

    - 8.4. Document and communicate authentication policies and procedures to all users.

    - 8.5. Do not use group, shared, or generic IDs, passwords, or other authentication methods.

    - 8.6. Where other authentication mechanisms are used (physical or logical security tokens, smart cards, certificates, and so on), use of these mechanisms must be assigned.

    - 8.7. All access to any database containing cardholder data (including access by applications, administrators, and all other users) is restricted.

    - 8.8. Ensure that security policies and operational procedures for identification and authentication are documented, in use, and known to all affected parties.

- **Requirement 9: Restrict physical access to cardholder data.** This requirement looks at how physical security measures should be implemented to protect access to systems storing PCI DSS data. This complements the previous requirements that focus on digital access control practices.

    - 9.1. Use appropriate facility entry controls to limit and monitor physical access to systems in the cardholder data environment.

    - 9.2. Develop procedures to easily distinguish between onsite personnel and visitors.

    - 9.3. Control physical access for onsite personnel to sensitive areas.

    - 9.4. Implement procedures to identify and authorize visitors.

    - 9.5. Physically secure all media.

    - 9.6. Maintain strict control over the internal or external distribution of any kind of media.

- 9.7. Maintain strict control over the storage and accessibility of media.

- 9.8. Destroy media when it is no longer needed for business or legal reasons.

- 9.9. Protect devices that capture payment card data via direct physical interaction with the card from tampering and substitution.

- 9.10. Ensure that security policies and operational procedures for restricting physical access to cardholder data are documented, in use, and known to all affected parties.

- **Requirement 10: Track and monitor all access to network resources and cardholder data.** Requirement 10 focuses on tracking who and what are accessing systems with PCI-DSS-related data. This is important for enforcing Requirement 7, meaning knowing that least privilege access level is being used by all systems.

  - 10.1. Implement audit trails to link all access to system components to each individual user.

  - 10.2. Implement automated audit trails for all system components to reconstruct security events.

  - 10.3. Record audit trail entries for all system components for each event based on PCI DSS best practices.

  - 10.4. Using time-synchronization technology, synchronize all critical system clocks and times and ensure that best practices are implemented for acquiring, distributing, and storing time.

  - 10.5. Secure audit trails so they cannot be altered.

  - 10.6. Review logs and security events for all system components to identify anomalies or suspicious activity.

  - 10.7. Retain audit trail history for at least one year, with a minimum of three months immediately available for analysis.

  - 10.8. **Additional requirement for service providers only:** Implement a process for the timely detection and reporting of failures of critical security control systems.

  - 10.9. Ensure that security policies and operational procedures for monitoring all access to network resources and cardholder data are documented, in use, and known to all affected parties.

- **Requirement 11: Regularly test security systems and processes.** Requirement 11 speaks to processes for regularly testing the capabilities and effectiveness of existing security systems. This complements Requirement 6 by not only testing security applications but also testing all forms of existing security. This truly is a best practice because attackers will evaluate any path to get to the data, making your weakest area of security the most probable place you will be hit.

  - 11.1. Implement processes to test for the presence of wireless access points (802.11), and detect and identify all authorized and unauthorized wireless access points on a quarterly basis.

  - 11.2. Run internal and external network vulnerability scans at least quarterly and after any significant change in the network.

  - 11.3. Implement a methodology for penetration testing.

- 11.4. Use intrusion-detection and/or intrusion-prevention techniques to detect and/or prevent intrusions into the network. Monitor all traffic at the perimeter of the cardholder data environment as well as at critical points in the cardholder data environment, and alert personnel to suspected compromises.

- 11.5. Deploy a change-detection mechanism (for example, file to alert personnel to unauthorized modification of critical system files, configuration files, or content files) and configure the software to perform critical file comparisons at least weekly.

- 11.6. Ensure that security policies and operational procedures for security monitoring and testing are documented, in use, and known to all affected parties.

- **Requirement 12: Maintain a policy that addresses information security for all personnel.** This requirement targets properly developing and managing a security policy. This includes training, the mission behind the organization's security program, and the actual program used to enforce the previous requirements.

  - 12.1. Establish, publish, maintain, and disseminate a security policy.

  - 12.2. Implement a risk-assessment process.

  - 12.3. Develop usage policies for critical technologies and define proper use of these technologies.

  - 12.4. Ensure that the security policy and procedures clearly define information security responsibilities for all personnel.

  - 12.5. Assign to an individual or team the information security management responsibilities.

  - 12.6. Implement a formal security awareness program to make all personnel aware of the cardholder data security policy and procedures.

  - 12.7. Screen potential personnel prior to hire to minimize the risk of attacks from internal sources.

  - 12.8. Maintain and implement policies and procedures to manage service providers with whom cardholder data is shared, or that could affect the security of cardholder data.

  - 12.9. **Additional requirement for service providers only**: Service providers should acknowledge in writing to customers that they are responsible for the security of cardholder data the service provider possesses or otherwise stores, processes, or transmits on behalf of the customer, as well as the extent to which they could impact the security of the customer's cardholder data environment.

  - 12.10. Implement an incident response plan. Be prepared to respond immediately to a system breach.

  - 12.11. **Additional requirement for service providers only**: Perform reviews at least quarterly to confirm personnel are following security policies and operational procedures.

The list that follows highlights the key PCI DSS concepts:

■ PCI DSS protects financial data, meaning the primary account number (PAN), account data on the magnetic strip, and data on the embedded chip. Most PCI SECOPS exam questions will test you on this.

■ PCI DSS compliance is mandatory for any merchant, processor, acquirer, issuer, or service provider that handles payment card processing as well as any outsourced or third parties involved with payment card processing.

■ PCI DSS 3.2 is very specific about what it means to be compliant. You must consider the system, version of software installed, and environment it resides in, regardless of how secure the system may appear to be even with data encryption or the latest version of software installed. That software must also be PCI approved.

■ PCI DSS does not supersede laws; however, there are legal and finical ramifications if compliance is not met.

■ PCI DSS 3.2 requirements, at a high level, are as follows:

   ■ Building and maintaining a secure network and systems

   ■ Protecting cardholder data

   ■ Maintaining a vulnerability management program

   ■ Implementing strong access control measures

   ■ Regularly monitoring and testing networks

   ■ Maintaining an information security policy

Next, we will review the health-care-focused compliance requirement known as HIPAA.

Health Insurance Portability and Accountability Act (HIPAA)

Securing health care data is more than a privacy concern. Leaked, sensitive health-related data could be used for blackmail, expose health risks that could end careers, be used for identity fraud, and so much more. For these reasons, the Health Insurance Portability and Accountability Act of 1996 (HIPAA) was created, with the secretary of the U.S. Department of Health and Human Services (HHS) developing regulations to protect health-related information.

From a high level, HIPAA is made up of the following goals:

■ To provide the ability to transfer and continue health insurance coverage for millions of American workers and their families when they change or lose their jobs

■ To reduce health care fraud and abuse

■ To mandate industry-wide standards for health care information on electronic billing and other processes

■ To require the protection and confidential handling of protected health information

HHS developed the HIPAA *privacy rule* as a standard to protect certain health care information. This is why when you call a hospital and ask for health-care-related information on a person, they may say they can't provide it due to HIPAA regulations. This privacy rule is also known as the Standards for Privacy of Individually Identifiable Health Information and is designed for *protected health information (PHI)*. The privacy rule is the basis of another HIPAA rule focused on digital data, known as the *security rule*.

HIPAA Security Rule

The **security rule** was developed with a goal similar to the HIPAA privacy rule; however, its focus is on health-care-related data being transferred in digital form, called *electronic pro-tected health information*, or *e-PHI*. It should be obvious that the security rule is the focus of the Cyber Ops SECOPS exam because it is information technology related. The security rule is also known as the Security Standards for the Protection of Electronic Protected Health Information.

The HIPAA security rule applies to all health plans, health care clearinghouses, and any health care provider involved with transmitting health information in electronic form. Basically any-body who offers any health-related treatment, payment, or operations must be HIPAA compli-ant. It is probably obvious this impacts hospitals; however, it also impacts other organizations such as a business that does business with a health care provider, meaning I can't access the health care records of my coworkers at Cisco based on HIPAA compliance.

The HIPAA security rule can be broken down into the following requirements:

1. Ensure the confidentiality, integrity, and availability of all e-PHI the organization cre-ates, receives, maintains, or transmits.

2. Identify and protect against reasonably anticipated threats to the security or integrity of the information.

3. Protect against reasonably anticipated, impermissible uses or disclosures.

4. Ensure compliance by the organization's workforce.

Rule 1 should be familiar to anybody who has studied for the CISSP exam. *Confidentiality* means information should not be disclosed to unauthorized people or systems. *Integrity* means the data should not be altered or destroyed in an unauthorized manner (in other words, the data must stay authentic). *Availability* means authorized people or systems should have access to the data.

Rule 2 and **Rule 3** speak about due diligence, meaning being responsible to provide the proper security in order to protect health care data. This means if you know you have HIPAA-related data, you must provide the right level of effort in hardware and manpower to secure that data. For example, if you are breached and are found to only have a basic firewall as your security strategy, you most likely will be in violation of Rule 2 and Rule 3, meaning you should have invested more money and manpower into securing HIPAA-related data.

> **NOTE**   Some organizations will mitigate the risk of being compromised using insurance. Insurance companies are also enforcing due diligence, meaning they might not provide the contracted protection if they find your organization is not enforcing proper security. Insurance companies may also pay the insurance amount owed however fine your organiza-tion for being insecure. An example of this is the *Cottage Healthcare System case*, where Columbia Casualty Company took Cottage Healthcare to court after a data breach claiming Cottage's computers were "hopelessly insecure."

Rule 4 makes it mandatory for the entire workforce to be HIPAA compliant. For example, I do not work for human resources; however, I have the same responsibility as any employee within Cisco to protect HIPAA-related data. In summary, security is *everybody's* responsibly. This is a very good rule.

The security rule requires an organization with HIPAA-related data to provide a *risk analysis*. The goal of this exercise is to do the following:

NOTE   This should be a regularly occurring practice rather than a one-time evaluation.

1. Evaluate the likelihood and impact of potential risks to e-PHI.
2. Implement appropriate security measures to address the risks identified in the risk analysis.
3. Document the chosen security measures and, where required, the rationale for adopting those measures.
4. Maintain continuous, reasonable, and appropriate security protections.

NOTE   Like with PCI, you should consider HIPAA compliance a baseline for security rather than considering its requirements a method for protecting you from real-world cyber threats. The HIPAA security rule is challenged with balancing protection versus encouraging adoption of new technologies that handle health-care-related data. This means that sometimes the latest, more secure platforms will not be available due to not being validated as "HIPAA compliant," thus reducing the quality of security for the system.

HIPAA Safeguards

Buying a product or set of products will not make you HIPAA compliant. HIPAA is a series of policies and procedures that must be implemented to protect HIPAA-related information (PHI and e-PHI). Products must be implemented by HIPAA-defined policies and in HIPAA-compliant environments. Therefore, just buying a HIPAA-approved product or enabling a specific HIPAA-approved function doesn't make the organization HIPAA compliant. Like with PCI DSS, compliance considers the system and application, what software is installed, and its environment.

The HIPAA security rule has specific *safeguards* that are used to evaluate whether an entity is compliant. Entities must maintain reasonable and appropriate administrative, technical, and physical safeguards for protecting e-PHI.

Let's review each of the HIPAA security rule safeguards.

NOTE   The SECOPS exam might not require you to know the specifics of each HIPAA safeguard; however, it is good to be aware of these safeguards for your personal studies.

Administrative Safeguards

This subset of the security rule targets internal organizations, policies, procedures, and maintenance of security measures used to protect PHI and e-PHI. Specific areas of concern are the following:

- **Security management process:** How to identify and analyze potential risks to PHI and e-PHI as well as what security measures are used to reduce risks and vulnerabilities.

- **Security personnel:** There must be a designated security official responsible for developing and implementing security policies and procedures.

- **Information access management:** The idea of least privilege must be enforced, which means limiting users and disclosures of PHI and e-PHI to the "minimum necessary" based on what is required for the user or recipient's role.

- **Workforce training and management:** There must be the appropriate authorization and supervision of anybody in contact with e-PHI. The entire workforce must be trained in security policies and procedures. If a violation occurs, the appropriate sanctions must be implemented.

- **Evaluation:** Periodic assessments must be performed to evaluate how the entity is meeting the HIPAA security rule requirements.

Physical Safeguards

This subset of the security rule focuses on environmental risks, such as environmental hazards and unauthorized access, and includes the following physical measures, policies, and procedures:

- **Facility access control:** Ensuring only authorized access to the physical environment is permitted.

- **Workstation and device security:** Implementing policies and procedures to enforce proper use of and access to workstations and electronic media with e-PHI data. This covers how e-PHI and the related system are transferred, removed, disposed of, and reused.

- **Device and media controls:** Hardware and electronic media need to be tracked in and out of a facility and inventoried while within the facility.

Technical Safeguards

This subset of the security rule includes policies and procedures to govern who has access to e-PHI. Technical safeguards are made up of the following:

- **Access control:** Technical policies and procedures to only permit authorized persons to have access to e-PHI.

- **Audit controls:** Hardware, software, and procedural mechanisms that can record and evaluate access and other activity within systems that contain e-PHI.

- **Integrity:** Policies must be enforced to ensure e-PHI isn't improperly altered or destroyed. Electronic measures must also confirm the integrity of the e-PHI.

- **Transmission security:** Security measures to protect e-PHI in transit over an electronic network.

- **Person or entity authentication**: Authentication ensures the person or entity is in fact who they claim to be.

Cisco has many resources and technical documents dedicated to helping organizations meet HIPAA requirements. You can learn more about how to meet HIPAA safeguards from Cisco by visiting the following website:

http://www.cisco.com/c/en/us/td/docs/solutions/Enterprise/Compliance/HIPAA/default.html

The list that follows highlights the key HIPAA concepts:

- HIPAA is designed to protect protected health information (PHI) and electronic PHI (e-PHI). For the SECOPS exam, make sure you know what PHI stands for.

- HIPAA applies to all health plans, health care clearinghouses and any health care provider involved with transmitting health information in electronic form.

- The security rule focuses on e-PHI and is made up of **safeguards**.

- There are administrative, physical, and technical safeguards under the security rule.

- Key safeguard areas to consider are proper management and security personnel and policies, access controls, audit controls, integrity controls, transmission security, facility controls, and system controls.

The last compliance requirement we will review, known as Sarbanes-Oxley (SOX), is related to corporate fraud.

Sarbanes-Oxley (SOX)

The Sarbanes-Oxley Act of 2002 was created as a result of corporate financial scandals involving WorldCom, Enron, and Global Crossing. The purpose of SOX is forcing any publicly held company to have internal controls and procedures for financial reporting to avoid future corporate fraud. Organizations must demonstrate compliance in the event of an audit or else they will receive various forms of criminal and civil penalties, such as fines, being removed from listings on the public stock exchange, and invalidation of insurance policies.

SOX applies to all publicly held American companies as well as any international organizations that have registered equity or debt securities within the U.S. Securities Exchange Commission. SOX also applies to any accounting firm or third-party service provider involved with financial services to the previously stated companies responsible for SOX.

Administrators responsible for SOX in information technology typically focus on a few sections of SOX-compliance regulations. The sections of interest are **Section 302, Section 404, and Section 409**. Let's review each of these sections in more detail.

> **NOTE** The SECOPS exam might not ask you for details on each section of SOX compliance; however, it is good to be aware of these details for self-study purposes.

Section 302

The section requires a company's CEO and CFO to personally certify that all financial reporting records are complete and accurate. This means these C-level members are personally responsible for the data security internal controls. This puts the C-level executives on the hot seat for information security.

Section 302 requires the following to be in an annual report:

- That signing officers have reviewed the report
- That reports don't contain untrue material or omissions in material
- That financial statements and related information are current
- That signing officers are responsible and have evaluated controls within the previous 90 days of the report's findings
- That any deficiencies in the controls as well as information on fraud are disclosed
- That any significant changes in controls that could have negative impact on internal controls are listed

Section 404

This section complements Section 302 by requiring an annual audit of the security controls by an outside auditor. The findings must be published and list any concerns about the scope and adequacy of internal control structures and procedures for financial reporting as well as the effectiveness of such internal controls and procedures.

Section 409

This section states that organizations must disclose to the public, on an urgent basis, information on material changes in their financial condition or operations. This information must be delivered in a way that is easy to understand. This means an organization must have tools in place to not only enforce SOX compliance, but also to be able to demonstrate critical information, such as changes stated in Section 409, in a way people can understand. Think of this as a reason to have great reporting and logging.

In regard of SOX audits, a SOX auditor will review the organization's controls, policies, and procedures during a Section 404 audit. Typically an audit leverages a control framework such as COBIT. Organizations must be prepared to share collected logs to establish a proven audit trail that all access and activity to sensitive business material are accounted for. It is important to understand how critical logging and preparation are to meet Sections 404 and 409 for SOX. Many organizations invest a ton of resources dedicated to providing this type of data.

Here are a few terms you should be aware of in regard to understanding SOX compliance:

- The **Public Company Accounting Oversight Board (PCAOB)** develops auditing standards and trains auditors on best practices for assessing a company's internal controls. PCAOB publishes periodic recommendations and changes to the recommended audit process.

- The **Committee of Sponsoring Organizations (COSO)** is an auditing framework. COSO publishes periodic updates to its internal control framework and serves as the basis for the auditing standards developed by PCAOB.

- **COBIT** stands for **Control Objectives for Information and Related Technology** and is a framework published by ISACA. ISACA is responsible for guidelines for developing and accessing internal controls related to corporate information technology, which should make sense why it is used for SOX. Typically COBIT is used because it is seen as a more specific version of the COSO framework. COBIT outlines practices for 34 IT processes, which is far more detail than you will need for the Cyber Ops SECOPS exam.

- The **Information Technology Governance Institute (ITGI)** is another framework that publishes its own SOX compliance recommendations based on both COBIT and COSO guidelines. The key thing about ITGI is that this framework focuses only on security issues.

Now let's review some controls you should be familiar with in regard to a SOX audit.

SOX Auditing Internal Controls

IT administrators responsible for providing SOX compliance reporting to their C-level members should be focused on their **internal controls**. We can define internal controls as any computers, network equipment, and other electronic infrastructure that touches financial data. This means a SOX audit will review the following areas of technology and policy:

> **NOTE** We are not going to list all the controls for different frameworks because there are more than you need to know for the exam.

- **Access:** Access covers physical and electronic controls ensuring only authorized users can access sensitive information. Technology and concepts covered include secure physical locations of equipment, effective password policies, and network access control. Policies should follow the principle of least privilege, meaning only provide the minimal required access to perform a job.

- **IT security:** IT security covers various security technologies that prevent breaches and loss of sensitive data. Technology and concepts include firewalls, IPS/IDS, antivirus, honey pots, and content filters. The best way to meet this area is to spread the investment for layered protection and include both quality monitoring and reporting to prove the effectiveness of the IT security controls.

- **Change management:** Change management covers how an organization adds and removes users or workstations, software installation and maintenance, user database administration, and so on. When preparing for a SOX audit, you will need to show a record of changes, including who made the changes, when they were made, and how the integrity of such records is protected.

- **Backup:** This covers how sensitive data is protected while backed up in the event of a need for data recovery. SOX compliance includes data stored offsite or by a third-party data storage provider.

This should give you a general understanding of SOX requirements. Most likely the SECOPS exam will ask very basic questions about SOX; however, we included more details here for those looking to improve their understanding of SOX compliance.

The list that follows highlights the key SOX concepts:

- SOX applies to all publicly held American companies as well as any international organizations that have registered equity or debt securities within the U.S. Securities Exchange Commission.

- SOX also applies to any accounting firm or third-party service provider that is involved with financial services to all publicly held American companies and any international organizations responsible for SOX.

- SOX Section 302 requires the organization's C-level members to be responsible for enforcement.

- SOX Section 404 requires an annual audit of security controls by an outside auditor.

- SOX Section 409 requires disclosing changes on an urgent basis.

- Key security controls to be aware of in regard to a SOX audit are *access*, *IT security*, *change management*, and *backups*.

Summary

This chapter focused on a few top compliancy standards that have major impact on an organization's cybersecurity practice. There are many other compliance frameworks that were not covered; however, the Cyber Ops SECOPS exam has selected PCI DSS, HIPAA, and SOX based on their impact on a large number of organizations.

First we covered PCI DSS, which focused on the payment card industry. Next, we looked at HIPAA, targeting health care data. We concluded the chapter with a brief overview of SOX, which was designed to deal with financial fraud. Make sure you verify what version of PCI DSS, HIPAA, and SOX is referenced in the Cyber Ops SECOPS exam, even though it is very likely the questions you will see are very high level and don't require memorizing the specifics of each compliance standard.

In the next chapter, we will look at network and host profiles.

References

- http://www.hhs.gov/hipaa/for-professionals/security/laws-regulations/
- http://www.hhs.gov/hipaa
- http://www.dhcs.ca.gov/formsandpubs/laws/hipaa/Pages/1.00WhatisHIPAA.aspx
- https://www.pcisecuritystandards.org/pci_security/
- http://www.sarbanes-oxley-101.com/
- http://www.hipaajournal.com/no-insurance-cover-for-cottage-health-hipaa-breach-6778/
- http://www.thesecurityblogger.com/insurer-tells-hospitals-you-let-hackers-in-we-are-not-bailing-you-out/

Exam Preparation Tasks

As mentioned in the section "How to Use This Book" in the Introduction, you have a few choices for exam preparation: the exercises here, Chapter 11, "Final Preparation," and the exam simulation questions on the Pearson IT Certification Practice Test.

Review All Key Topics

Review the most important topics in this chapter, noted with the Key Topics icon in the outer margin of the page. Table 7-5 lists these key topics and the page numbers on which each is found.

Table 7-5   Key Topics for Chapter 7

Key Topic Element	Description	Page Number
List	Account data defined by PCI DSS 3.2	175
Table 7-4	A high-level overview of the PCI Data Security Standard	177
Paragraph	Testing for PCI DSS 3.2	178
List	PCI DSS key concepts	185
Paragraph	HIPAA security rule overview	186
Paragraph	HIPAA security rule safeguards	187
List	HIPAA key concepts	189
Paragraph	Section 302	190
Paragraph	Section 404	190
Paragraph	Section 409	190
Paragraph	SOX auditing internal controls	191
List	SOX key concepts	192

Complete Tables and Lists from Memory

Print a copy of Appendix B, "Memory Tables," (found on the book website), or at least the section for this chapter, and complete the tables and lists from memory. Appendix C, "Memory Tables Answer Key," also on the website, includes completed tables and lists to check your work.

Define Key Terms

Define the following key terms from this chapter and check your answers in the glossary:

Payment Card Industry Data Security Standard (PCI DSS), cardholder data environment (CDE), Health Insurance Portability and Accountability ACT (HIPAA), electronic protected health information (e-PHI), Sarbanes-Oxley Act of 2002 (SOX), Public Company Accounting Oversight Board (PCAOB), Committee of Sponsoring Organizations (COSO)

Review Questions

The answers to these questions appear in Appendix A. For more practice with exam format questions, use the exam engine on the website.

1. According to PCI DSS, cardholder data includes everything *but* which of following?

    a. Primary account number (PAN)

    b. Expiration date

    c. Image on the card

    d. Service code

2. Which of the following is *not* a HIPAA administrative safeguard?

    a. A company's CEO and CFO are required personally to certify that all financial reporting records are complete and accurate.

    b. There must be the appropriate supervision of anybody in contact with e-PHI.

    c. There must be a designated security officer responsible for developing and implementing security policies and procedures.

    d. Periodic assessments must be performed to evaluate HIPAA security rule requirements.

3. Cardholder data environment (CDE) can best be defined as which of the following?

    a. The people, processes, and technologies that store, process, or transmit cardholder data or authentication data

    b. The people, processes, and technologies that store, process, or transmit cardholder data

    c. The processes that store, process, or transmit cardholder data or authentication data

    d. The technologies that store, process, or transmit cardholder data or authentication data

4. Which of the following is *not* a requirement of the HIPAA security rule?

    a. Ensure the confidentiality, integrity, and availability of all e-PHI created, received, maintained, or transmitted.

    b. Protect against reasonably anticipated, impermissible uses or disclosures.

    c. Enforce automated access control using 802.1x-based technologies.

    d. Identify and protect against reasonably anticipated threats to the security or integrity of the information.

5. Which of the following is *not* part of the PCI Data Security Standard?

    a. Encrypt transmission of cardholder data across open, public networks.

    b. Restrict access to cardholder data by business need to know.

    c. Ensure that any deficiencies in the controls as well as information on fraud are disclosed.

    d. Track and monitor all access to network resources and cardholder data.

6. Which of the following is *not* part of SOX technology and policy monitoring?

    a. Access to physical and electronic controls, ensuring only authorized users have access to sensitive information

    b. Employing, hiring, and auditing for criminal history

    c. Change management for how an organization adds and removes users or workstations, software installation and maintenance, and user database administration

    d. How sensitive data is protected while backed up in the event of a need for data recovery

7. Which of the following is *not* a violation of PCI DSS?

    a. Sending e-PHI in an unencrypted method due to local law

    b. Installing the most secure software versus older PCI-approved software

    c. Hardening a PCI system due to being installed on a non-PCI approved network

    d. Running a PCI-approved application on a non-PCI-approved server

8. In regard to PCI DSS, sensitive authentication data does not include which of the following?

    a. PINs/PIN blocks

    b. Fingerprint scanning

    c. CAV2/CVC2/CVV2/CID

    d. Full track data, which can be magnetic strip or equivalent chip

9. Which of the following is *not* required for the PCI DSS requirement "Implement strong access control measures"?

    a. Restrict physical access to cardholder data.

    b. Identify and authenticate access to system components.

    c. Audit firewall configurations annually.

    d. Restrict access to cardholder data by business need to know.

10. The HIPAA security rule ensures the CIA of e-PHI. What does CIA stand for?

    a. Confidentiality, integrity, and access

    b. Confidentiality, integrity, and availability

    c. Confidentiality, indisputability, and access

    d. Control, integrity, and access

This chapter covers the following topics:

- Identifying elements used for network profiling
    - Understanding network throughput
    - How session duration is used for profiling
    - Monitoring port usage
    - Understanding and controlling critical asset address space
- Identifying elements used for server profiling
    - Learning about listening ports
    - Identifying logged-in users and used service accounts
    - Monitoring running processes, tasks, and applications on servers

Network and Host Profiling

Profiling is the process of collecting data about a target to better understand the type of system, who is using the system, and its intentions while on the network. The more profiling data collected typically means a better explanation can be made about the target being evaluated. For example, having basic information on a system found on your network might tell you that a computer is using an Ethernet connection. This limited data would make enforcing access control policies difficult. Having more data about a target system could reveal that the system is a corporate-issued Windows laptop being used by a trusted employee named Joey. Joey as an employee should be treated differently from an access control perspective when comparing Joey and his system to a Linux laptop run by an unknown guest (with the assumption that this sample organization's standard-issued laptop is Windows based). Also, knowing the types of devices on your network helps with making future business decisions, network and throughput sizing considerations, as well as what your security policy should look like.

The focus of this chapter is on understanding how network and host profiling are accomplished. The results may be used to determine the access rights that will be granted to the system, identify potentially malicious behavior, troubleshoot, audit for compliance, and so on. The focus on the SECOPS exam will be assessing devices based on the network traffic they produce, also known as their *network footprint*. However, we will also touch on profiling devices from the host level (meaning what is installed on the device) to round out the profiling concepts covered.

Let's start off by testing your understanding of profiling concepts.

"Do I Know This Already?" Quiz

The "Do I Know This Already?" quiz allows you to assess whether you should read this entire chapter thoroughly or jump to the "Exam Preparation Tasks" section. If you are in doubt about your answers to these questions or your own assessment of your knowledge of the topics, read the entire chapter. Table 8-1 lists the major headings in this chapter and their corresponding "Do I Know This Already?" quiz questions. You can find the answers in Appendix A, "Answers to the 'Do I Know This Already?' Quizzes and Q&A."

Table 8-1 "Do I Know This Already?" Foundation Topics Section-to-Question Mapping

Foundation Topics Section	Questions Covered in This Section
Network Profiling	1–5, 10
Host Profiling	6–9

1. Which of the following is true about NetFlow?

    a. NetFlow typically provides more details than sFlow.

    b. NetFlow typically contains more details than packet capturing.

    c. NetFlow is not available in virtual networking environments.

    d. NetFlow is only used as a network performance measurement.

2. Which of the following is *not* used to establish a network baseline?

    a. Determining the time to collect data

    b. Selecting the type of data to collect

    c. Developing a list of users on the network

    d. Identifying the devices that can provide data

3. Which of the following is an advantage of port security over automated NAC?

    a. Device profiling

    b. Ease of deployment

    c. Management requirements

    d. Technology cost

4. What is the best definition of session duration in terms of network profiling?

    a. The total time the user or device requests services from the network

    b. The total time the user connects to the network

    c. The total time a user or device connects to a network and later disconnects from it

    d. The total time the user logs in to a system and logs out of the system

5. Which of the following is *not* a tool or option for monitoring a host session on the network?

    a. Use firewall logs to monitor user connections to the network

    b. Use NetFlow to monitor user connections to the network

    c. Capture network packets and monitor user connections to the network

    d. Use SNMP tools to monitor user connections to the network

6. Which of the following is *not* true about listening ports?

    a. A listening port is a port held open by a running application in order to accept inbound connections.

    b. Seeing traffic from a known port will identify the associated service.

    c. Listening ports use values that can range between 1 and 65535.

    d. TCP port 80 is commonly known for Internet traffic.

7. A traffic substitution and insertion attack does which of the following?

    a. Substitutes the traffic with data in a different format but with the same meaning

    b. Substitutes the payload with data in the same format but with a different meaning

    c. Substitutes the payload with data in a different format but with the same meaning

    d. Substitutes the traffic with data in the same format but with a different meaning

8. Which of the following is *not* a method for identifying running processes?

    a. Reading network traffic from a SPAN port with the proper technology

    b. Reading port security logs

    c. Reading traffic from inline with the proper technology

    d. Using port scanner technology

9. Which of the following is *not* a tool that can identify applications on hosts?

    a. Web proxy

    b. Application layer firewall

    c. Using NBAR

    d. Using NetFlow

10. Which of the following statements is incorrect?

    a. Latency is a delay in throughput detected at the gateway of the network.

    b. Throughput is typically measured in bandwidth.

    c. A valley is when there is an unusually low amount of throughput compared to the normal baseline.

    d. A peak is when there is a spike in throughput compared to the normal baseline

8

Foundation Topics

Network Profiling

Profiling involves identifying something based on various characteristics specified in a detector. Typically, this is a weighted system, meaning that with more data and higher quality data, the target system can be more accurately profiled. An example might be using generic system data to identify that a system is possibly an Apple OS X product versus gaining enough information (such as detailed application or network protocol data) to distinguish an iPad from an iPhone. The results come down to the detector, data quality, and how the detectors are used.

The first section of this chapter focuses on network profiling concepts. These are methods used to capture network-based data that can reveal how systems are functioning on the network. The areas of focus for this section are determining throughput, ports used, session duration, and address space. Throughput directly impacts network performance. For most networks, it is mission critical to not over-utilize throughput; otherwise, the users will not be happy with the overall network performance. Network access comes from a LAN, VPN, or wireless connection; however, at some point that traffic will eventually connect to a network port. This means that by monitoring ports, you can tell what is accessing your network regardless of the connection type. Session duration refers to how long systems are on the network or how long users are accessing a system. This is important for monitoring potential security issues as well as for baselining user and server access trends. Lastly, address space is important to ensure critical systems are given priority over other systems when you're considering distributing network resources.

Let's start off by looking into profiling network throughput.

Throughput

Throughput is the amount of traffic that can cross a specific point in the network, and at what speed. If throughput fails, network performance suffers, and most likely people will complain. Administrators typically have alarms monitoring for situations where throughput utilization reaches a level of concern. Normal throughput levels are typically recorded as a *network baseline*, where a deviation from that baseline could indicate a throughput problem. Baselines are also useful for establishing real throughput compared to what is promised by your service provider. Having a network baseline may sound like a great idea; however, the challenge is establishing what your organization's real network baseline should be.

The first step in establishing a network baseline is identifying the devices on your network that can detect network traffic, such as routers and switches. Once you have an inventory, the next step is identifying what type of data can be pulled from those devices. The most common desired data is network utilization; however, that alone should not be your only source for building a network baseline. Network utilization has limitations, such as knowing what devices are actually doing on the network.

There are two common tactics for collecting network data for traffic analytic purposes. The first approach is *capturing packets* and then analyzing the data. The second approach is *capturing network flow*, also known as *NetFlow*, as explained in Chapter 4, "NetFlow for Cybersecurity." Both approaches have benefits and disadvantages. Packet capturing can provide more details than NetFlow; however, this approach requires storing packets as well as a method to properly analyze what is captured. Capturing packets can quickly increase storage requirements, making this option financially challenging for some organizations. Other times, the details provided by capturing packets are necessary for establishing baselines as well as security requirements and therefore is the best approach versus what limited data NetFlow can provide. For digital forensics requirements, capturing packets will most likely be the way to go due to the nature of the type of details needed to perform an investigation and to validate findings during the legal process.

NetFlow involves looking at network records versus actually storing data packets. This approach dramatically reduces storage needs and can be quicker to analyze. NetFlow can provide a lot of useful data; however, that data will not be as detailed as capturing the actual packets. An analogy of comparing capturing packets to NetFlow would be monitoring a person's phone. Capturing packets would be similar to recording all calls from a person's phone and spending time listening to each call to determine if there is a performance or security incident. This obviously would be time consuming and require storage for all the calls. Capturing NetFlow would be similar to monitoring the call records to and from the phone being analyzed, meaning less research and smaller storage requirements. Having the phone call (packet capture) would mean having details about the incident, whereas the call record (NetFlow) would show possible issues, such as multiple calls happening at 3 a.m. between the person and another party. In this case, you would have details such as the phone numbers, time of call, and length of call. If these call records are between a married person and somebody who is not that person's significant other, it could indicate a problem—or it could simply be planning for a surprise party. The point is, NetFlow provides a method to determine areas of concern quickly, whereas packet capturing determines concerns as well as includes details about the event since the actual data is being analyzed versus records of the data when using NetFlow. Also, it is important to note that some vendors offer hybrid solutions that use NetFlow but start capturing packets upon receiving an alarm. One example of a hybrid technology is Cisco's StealthWatch technology.

Once you have your source and data type selected, the final task for establishing a baseline is determining the proper length of time to capture data. This is not an exact science; however, many experts will suggest at least a week to allow for enough data to accommodate trends found within most networks. This requirement can change depending on many factors, such as how the business model of an organization could have different levels of traffic at different times of the year. A simple example of this concept would be how retailers typically see higher amounts of traffic during holiday seasons, meaning a baseline sample during peak and nonpeak business months would most likely be different. Network spikes must be accounted for if they are perceived to be part of the normal traffic, which is important if the results of the baseline are to be considered a true baseline of the environment. Time also impacts results in that any baseline taken today may be different in the future as the network changes, making it important to retest the baseline after a certain period of time.

Most network administrators' goal for understanding throughput is to establish a network baseline so throughput can later be monitored with alarms that trigger at the sign of a throughput valley or peak. *Peaks* are spikes of throughput that exceed the normal baseline, whereas *valleys* are periods of time that are below the normal baseline. Peaks can lead to problems, such as causing users to experience long delays when accessing resources, triggering redundant systems to switch to backups, breaking applications that require a certain data source, and so on. A large number of valleys could indicate that a part of the network is underutilized, representing a waste of resources or possible failure of a system that normally utilizes certain resources.

Many tools are available for viewing the total throughput on a network. These tools can typically help develop a network baseline as well as account for predicted peaks and valleys. One common metric used by throughput-measuring tools is bandwidth, meaning the data rate supported by a network connection or interface. *Bandwidth*, referred to as bits per second (bps), is impacted by the capacity of the link as well as latency factors, meaning things that slow down traffic performance.

Best practice for building a baseline is capturing bandwidth from various parts of the network to accommodate the many factors that impact bandwidth. The most common place to look at throughput is the gateway router, meaning the place that traffic enters and leaves the network. However, throughput issues can occur anywhere along the path of traffic, so only having a sample from the gateway could be useful for understanding total throughput for data leaving and entering the network, but this number would not be effective for troubleshooting any issues found within the network. For example, network congestion could occur between a host and network relay point prior to data hitting the network gateway, making the throughput at the gateway look slower than it actually would be if the administrator only tests for complications from the host network and doesn't validate the entire path between the host and gateway.

Measuring throughput across the network can lead to the following improvements:

- Understanding the impact of applications on the network
- Reducing peak traffic by utilizing network optimization tools to accommodate for latency-generating elements such as bandwidth hogs
- Troubleshooting and understanding network pain points, meaning areas that cause latency.
- Detecting unauthorized traffic
- Using security and anomaly detection
- Understanding network trends for segmentation and security planning
- Validating whether quality of service settings are being utilized properly

Let's look at some methods for measuring throughput.

Measuring Throughput

To capture packets and measure throughput, you will need a tap on the network before you can start monitoring. Most tools that collect throughput leverage a single point configured to provide raw data, such as pulling traffic from a switch or router. If the access point for the traffic is a switch, typically a network port is configured as a Switched Port Analyzer (SPAN) port, sometimes also called port mirroring or port monitoring. The probe capturing data from a SPAN port can be either a local probe or data from a SPAN port that is routed to a remote monitoring tool.

The following is an example of configuring a Cisco switch port as a SPAN port so that a collection tool can be set up to monitor throughput. The SPAN session for this example is ID 1 and is set to listen on the fastEthernet0/1 interface of the switch while exporting results to the fastEthernet0/10 interface of the switch. SPAN sessions can also be configured to capture more than one VLAN.

```
Switch(config)# no monitor session 1
Switch(config)# monitor session 1 source interface fastEthernet0/1
Switch(config)# monitor session 1 destination interface fastEthernet0/10
encapsulation dot1q
Switch(config)# end
```

Another method for capturing packets is to place a capturing device in the line of traffic. This is a common tactic for monitoring throughput from a routing point or security checkpoint, such as a firewall configured to have all traffic cross it for security purposes. Many current firewall solutions offer a range of throughput-monitoring capabilities that cover the entire network protocol stack. Figure 8-1 provides an example of Cisco Firepower application layer monitoring showing various widgets focused on throughput.

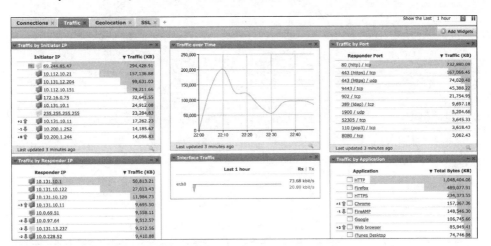

Figure 8-1 *Firepower Traffic Dashboard*

Routers can be leveraged to view current throughput levels. To see the current state of an interface on a standard Cisco IOS router, simply use the **show interface** command to display lots of data, including bps, packets sent, and so on. Some sample numbers from running this command might include the following information:

```
5 minute input rate 131000 bits/sec, 124 packets/sec
5 minute output rate 1660100 bit/sec, 214 packets/sec
```

This output provides details on throughput at that moment in time. Taking the average of samples across a span of time would be one method of calculating a possible network baseline.

Packet capture tools, sometimes referred to as *packet analyzers* or *packet sniffers*, are hardware or programs that intercept and log traffic as it passes over a digital network. This happens as a data stream crosses the network while the packet capture tool captures each packet and decodes the packet's raw data elements representing the various fields that can be interpreted to understand its content.

The requirements for capturing packets are having access to the data, the ability to capture and store the data, tools to interoperate the data, and capabilities to use the data. This means the tool must be able to access the data from a tap and have enough storage to collect the data, and it must be able to read the results and have a method to use those results for some goal. Failing at any of these will most likely result in an unsuccessful packet capture session. One of the most popular packet capture applications used by industry experts is Wireshark, as shown in Figure 8-2 and covered in Chapter 3, "Fundamentals of Intrusion Analysis." Wireshark can break down packets using various filters, thus aiding an analyst's investigation of a captured session.

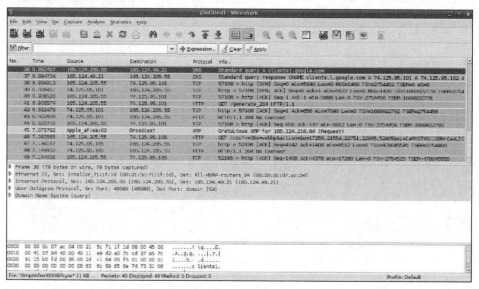

Figure 8-2 *Dashboard from Wireshark*

Capturing NetFlow is a different process than collecting network packets. NetFlow must be supported on the system to generate NetFlow data, and that data must be exported to a NetFlow collector that can translate NetFlow into usable data. Exceptions to this requirement are tools such as the Cisco StealthWatch Sensor. These tools offer the ability to convert raw data into NetFlow in a network-tap-like deployment. The typical sources of NetFlow are routers, switches, wireless access points, and virtual networking solutions that offer the ability to produce NetFlow upon proper configuration, meaning turning those devices into NetFlow producers rather than purchasing more equipment to create NetFlow. Note that some devices may require software upgrades or flat out do not support the ability to create NetFlow.

Enabling NetFlow typically requires two steps. The first step is to turn on NetFlow within the network device. An example of enabling NetFlow on a standard Cisco IOS router can be seen in the following example, which shows enabling NetFlow on the Ethernet 1/0 interface:

```
Router(config)# ip cef
Router(config)# interface Ethernet 1/0
Router(config-if)# ip flow ingress
```

The second step to enabling NetFlow is determining where the collected NetFlow should be sent. The next set of configurations is an example of exporting NetFlow from a Cisco IOS router to a NetFlow collector located at the IP address 10.1.1.40:

```
Router(config)# ip flow-export version 9
Router(config)# ip flow-export destination 10.1.1.40
```

One last important NetFlow concept is the fact that all versions of NetFlow do not provide the same level of data details. An example of this is comparing sFlow to NetFlow, where sFlow is a copy of flow, also called "sampled flow," and NetFlow is a direct capture. The details between sFlow and NetFlow are dramatically different. Let's look at location as an example: sFlow could inform you that a system is somewhere on the network, whereas NetFlow could provide the exact location of the system. The recommended best form of NetFlow at the time of this writing is using NetFlow version 9, as covered in Chapter 4.

The last throughput topic to consider is how to make improvements to your network baseline as well as accommodate for peaks and valleys. One tactic is implementing *quality of services (QoS)* tools designed to define different priory levels for applications, users, and data flows, with the goal of guaranteeing a certain level of performance to that data. For throughput, this could be guaranteeing a specific bit rate, latency, jitter, and packet loss to protect throughput levels from elements that could impact traffic types with a higher priority. An example would be providing high priority to video traffic since delays would be quickly noticed versus delays in delivering email. QoS is also important for defending against attacks directed at services such as denial-of-service and distributed denial-of-service attacks. Best practice is defining the data types on your network and configuring QoS properties for those deemed as high importance, which are commonly voice traffic, video traffic, and data from critical systems.

The list that follows highlights the key throughput concepts:

- A network baseline represents normal network patterns.
- Establishing a network baseline involves identifying devices that will collect throughput, pick the type of data available to be collected, and determine the time to collect data.
- The two common tactics for collecting data are capturing packets and harvesting NetFlow.
- Peaks and valleys are indications of a spike and a reduced amount of throughput from the network baseline, respectively. Both could represent a network problem.
- Network throughput is typically measured in bandwidth, and delays are identified as latency.

- Packet capture technologies are either inline to the network traffic being captured or positioned on a SPAN port.

- Enabling NetFlow on supported devices involves enabling NetFlow and pointing the collected NetFlow to a NetFlow analyzer tool.

- QoS can be used to prioritize traffic to guarantee performance of specific traffic types such as voice and video.

Used Ports

Controlling access to the network continues to be one of the most challenging yet important tasks for a network administrator. Networks will gradually increase in size, and the types of devices accessing the network will grow in diversity. Cyber attacks are also increasing in sophistication and speed, thus decreasing the time required to achieve a malicious goal such as stealing data or disrupting services. For these and many other reasons, access control must be a top priority for protecting your network. An example of a scary device you would not want to find on your network is the Pwnie Express attack arsenal disguised as a generic power plug (see Figure 8-3).

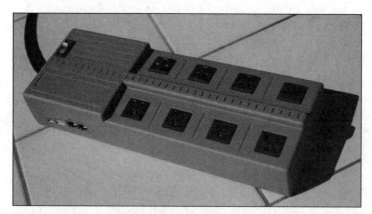

Figure 8-3 *Pwnie Express Power Plug*

Devices on the network tend to bypass many forms of traditional security solutions such as the network firewalls and intrusion prevention systems (IPSs) typically found at the gateway of the network. This gives physically connected devices some degree of trust, depending on the access control and resource-provisioning policies. Access control strategies should include not only identifying and controlling what can access the network but also some form of posture evaluation to properly provision access rights. Posture evaluation can include the topics in this chapter as well as applications running on the device, such as antivirus vendor and version. One example of why this is important would be preventing a host access to sensitive resources based on having unacceptable risks, such as lacking antivirus. Another example would be an unapproved device such as a mobile phone placed on the same network as the data center that hosts sensitive data. Posture concepts, meaning remediating devices out of policy, will not be covered in this chapter; however, profiling device types, which is typically part of a posture strategy, will be covered later.

Controlling network access starts with securing the network port. Similar concepts can apply to wireless and virtual private networks (VPNs); however, even those technologies eventually end up on a network port once the traffic is authenticated and permitted through a connection medium. The most basic form of controlling network access is the use of *port security*. Port security features provide a method to limit what devices will be permitted to access and send traffic on individual switch ports within a switched network.

Port security can be very useful yet also one of the most challenging practices to enforce due to misconfiguration and manual efforts to maintain. Many administrators responsible for large and dynamic networks manually managing port security strategies find they spend too much time addressing ports that have become disabled due to various reasons and must be manually reset by an authorized administrator. This makes the deployment methodology critical to the success of the access control practice. Enabling basic port security on a Cisco switch interface can be accomplished using the command **switchport port-security**. However, without other parameters being configured, this will only permit one MAC address that is dynamically learned. Any other MAC addresses found accessing that network port would cause an "err-disabled" state, meaning an administrator must reset the port before it can be used again. Other configuration and port security strategies can be enforced, such as providing a static list of devices that can access any port or dynamically learning about devices as they connect to the network using a sticky MAC configuration. However, maintaining a healthy state for multiple ports tends to be a challenge for most administrators using any of these strategies.

NOTE   An unauthorized device could spoof an authorized MAC address and bypass a port security configuration. Also, it is important to understand specific access levels granted when port security is used. These access levels are preconfigured or manually changed by the network administrator, meaning a device accessing VLAN10 must be manually predefined for a specific port by an administrator, making deploying a dynamic network policy across multiple ports using port security extremely difficult to maintain.

The challenges involved with port security led to a more advanced method to provide a similar goal by leveraging automation for enforcing port security. Per industry lingo, this is known as *network access control (NAC)*. NAC provides a method to have a network port automatically determine who and what is attempting to access a switch port and automatically provision specific network access based on a set of predefined policies. NAC can be enforced using various technologies, such as SNMP; however, 802.1x is one of the leading industry approaches at the time of this writing.

Regardless of the NAC technology being used, the goal for NAC is to determine the device type accessing the network using certain profiling approaches as well as to determine who is using the device. With 802.1x, users are identified using certificates validated by a backend authentication system. Policies can be defined for a user and device type, meaning a specific employee using a specific device could be granted specific access regardless of where he or she plugs in to the network. An example would be having employee Raylin Muniz granted access to VLAN10 if she is using her corporate-issued laptop regardless of the port she plugs in to. The process would work by having Raylin plug in to a port that is NAC enabled yet not granting any network access. The NAC solution would authenticate and authorize

Raylin to her specific access if she passes whatever checks are put in place to ensure she meets the NAC access policies. If Raylin unplugs her system and another system is plugged in to the same port, the NAC solution could evaluate that system and provision the proper network access. An example would be a guest plugging in a NAC-enabled port and being provisioned limited network privileges such as only Internet access.

The first step in deploying an access control strategy regardless of whether port security or automated NAC is used is capturing the current state of the network. This means identifying all devices that are currently connected to a network port. Capturing what is currently on the network is also important for meeting audits for compliance as well as network capacity validation. There are many approaches for capturing the current state of the network. The most basic method for collecting port information is identifying which ports are being used. For Cisco IOS devices, the **show interface status** command will display a summary of all ports' connection status, similar to the output shown in Example 8-1.

Example 8-1   *The show interfaces status Command*

```
Switch#show interfaces status


Port     Name              Status       Vlan      Duplex  Speed Type
Gi1/1                      notconnect   1          auto    auto No Gbic
Gi1/2                      notconnect   1          auto    auto No Gbic
Gi5/1                      notconnect   1          auto    auto 10/100/1000-TX
Gi5/2                      notconnect   1          auto    auto 10/100/1000-TX
Gi5/3                      notconnect   1          auto    auto 10/100/1000-TX
Gi5/4                      notconnect   1          auto    auto 10/100/1000-TX
Fa6/1                      connected    1         a-full  a-100 10/100BaseTX
Fa6/2                      connected    2         a-full  a-100 10/100BaseTX
```

Another option is to use the **show interface** command, which provides a ton of information, including whether the port is being used. To focus on whether the port is being used, you can use the pipe command following **show interface** to narrow down the output to the data of interest. An example would be using the command **show interface | i (FastEthernet|0 packets input)**. This command assumes the links of interest are using FastEthernet; **i** means "include" to match the following search expressions and items between the brackets to look for the conditions specified. The output of this command might look like that shown in Example 8-2, which is designed to specifically identify used ports.

Example 8-2   *Output of the show interface | i (FastEthernet|0 packets input) Command*

```
FastEthernet1/0/31 is up, line protocol is up (connected)       95445640 packets input,
18990165053 bytes, 0 no buffer FastEthernet1/0/32 is up, line protocol is up
(connected)
FastEthernet1/0/33 is up, line protocol is up (connected) FastEthernet1/0/34 is down,
line protocol is down (notconnect)       0 packets input, 0 bytes, 0 no buffer
FastEthernet1/0/35 is down, line protocol is down (notconnect)
FastEthernet1/0/36 is up, line protocol is up (connected) FastEthernet1/0/37 is down,


line protocol is down (notconnect)       0 packets input, 0 bytes, 0 no buffer
```

Another filter option you might include is when the port was last used by issuing the command **show interface | i proto|Last in**. The output might look like Example 8-3.

Example 8-3   *The show interface | i proto|Last in Command*

```
switch#show int | i proto|Last in
GigabitEthernet1/1 is down, line protocol is down (notconnect)    Last input 6w6d,
output 6w6d, output hang never
GigabitEthernet1/2 is down, line protocol is down (notconnect)    Last input 21w1d,
output 21w1d, output hang never
GigabitEthernet1/3 is up, line protocol is up (connected)    Last input 00:00:00,
output 00:00:24, output hang never
GigabitEthernet1/4 is up, line protocol is up (connected)    Last input 00:00:58,
output 00:00:24, output hang never
GigabitEthernet1/5 is down, line protocol is down (notconnect)    Last input never,
output never, output hang never
```

These network-based **show** commands are useful for identifying used ports; however, they do not explain what type of device is attached or who is using the device. Other protocols such as *Cisco Discovery Protocol (CDP), Link Layer Discovery Protocol (LLDP),* and *Dynamic Host Configuration Protocol (DHCP)* can be used to learn more about what is connected. CDP is used to share information about other directly connected Cisco equipment, such as the operating system, hardware platform, IP address, device type, and so on. The command **show cdp neighbors** is used in Figure 8-4.

```
Router#show cdp neighbors

Capability Codes: R - Router, T - Trans Bridge, B - Source Route Bridge
                  S - Switch, H - Host, I - IGMP, r - Repeater

Device ID          Local Intrfce    Holdtme    Capability    Platform    Port ID
device1.cisco.com    Eth 0/1        122           T S         WS-C2900    2/11
device2.cisco.com    Eth 0/1        179           R           4500        Eth 0
device3.cisco.com    Eth 0/1        155           R           2500        Eth 0
device4.cisco.com    Eth 0/1        155           R           2509        Eth 0
```

Figure 8-4   *show cdp neighbors*

LLDP is a neighbor discovery protocol that has an advantage over CDP by being a vendor-neutral protocol. LLDP can be used to capture identity, capabilities, and neighbors through LLDP advertisements with their network neighboring devices and to store that data in their internal database. SNMP can be used to access this information to build an inventory of devices connected to the network as well as applications.

Other protocols such as DHCP and domain browsing are also used to identify routers, subnets, potential clients, and other connected devices. Typically, discovery tools harvest this type of information based on what is available to determine details of the device connected.

Cisco Identity Services Engine is an example of a technology that uses various protocol probes to discover device types, as shown in Figure 8-5.

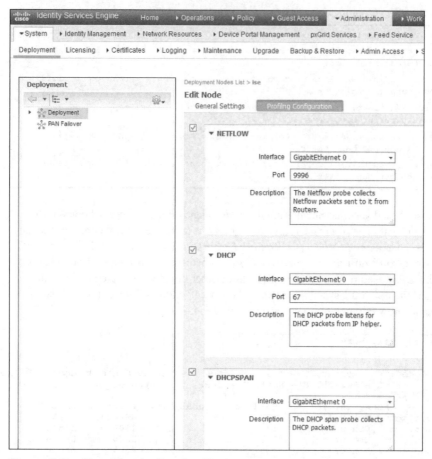

Figure 8-5 *Cisco Identity Services Engine*

Many other discovery solutions are available on the market that can leverage various protocols to determine the device types plugged in to a port such as Ipswitch's WhatsUp Gold, SolarWinds, OpManager, and so on. Also, port-scanning applications such as Nmap can be used to identify the devices connected to a network, which will be covered later in this chapter.

Once you have an idea of what devices are on the network, the next step is enforcing a basic policy. Typically, a basic policy's goal is to connect corporate devices and/or employees with full network access while limiting guest users as well as denying other unauthorized devices. A basic policy does not include complicated configurations (such as multiple user policy types) or consider posture. The purpose is to introduce NAC concepts to the network slowly to avoid disrupting business process as well as to let administration become familiar with using NAC technology. It is very rare and not recommended to start enforcing multiple policies during an initial NAC deployment due to the risk of impacting business and causing a negative outlook on the overall security mission.

After a basic policy is successfully deployed for a specific time, the remaining step to provision NAC is tuning the policy to be more granular in identifying device types, user groups, and what is provisioned. For example, a NAC policy could be developed for a specific device type such as employee mobile devices, which may have less access rights than employees using a corporate-issued device. Another example would be segmenting critical devices or devices requiring unique services such as Voice over IP phones. This step is typically slowly deployed and tested as the environment adopts the NAC technology.

The SECOPS exam will not test you on configuring or deploying access control technology; however, it is important that you understand these concepts before considering deploying this technology into your network.

The list that follows highlights the key used port concepts:

- Port security is a basic form of controlling what devices can plug in to a network port.

- Basic port security uses MAC addresses, which is labor intensive to manage and can be bypassed using MAC spoofing.

- NAC technology automates port security to simplify port security management as well as adds additional security elements such as profiling and host posture checks.

- Best practices for enabling a NAC solution is to discover what is on the network, establish a basic NAC policy, and then later tune that policy with more granular checks and policies.

Session Duration

Another important network topic is monitoring how long devices are connected to the network. The value in knowing this can be learning how long users utilize network resources during different periods of the workday, identifying when a critical system goes offline, and identifying how to enforce usage policies, such as limiting access to the network to approved times. An example of limiting access could be controlling guest access to only work hours. We will focus in this section on viewing the session duration of devices connecting to a network rather than on the time users are logged in to a host system.

Session duration in network access terms is the total time a user or device connects to a network and later disconnects from that network. The session average is the total duration of all sessions at a time divided by the number of sessions. Taking the average of a host's session duration for a period of time can provide a baseline of how that system utilizes network resources. This can be a very valuable tool for monitoring for anomalies that could represent a technical issue or security breach. An example is identifying that for the first time in eight months, one system starts connecting to other systems it has never connected to in the past. Malicious software is typically designed to spread through the network. Also, attackers tend to seek other systems when compromising a network. Seeing authorized yet "weird" behavior or behavior outside of normal sessions can indicate an insider threat. The same approach can be used to identify whether any critical systems are identified as leaving the network, indicating a problem such as internal network complications or power loss.

Identifying sessions starts with knowing what devices are connected to the network. The "Used Ports" section of this chapter showed various methods for identifying used ports.

Session duration is a little different in that you need to use SNMP or a port-monitoring solution to gather exact utilization data. Cisco IOS offers the ability to show how long an IP address is mapped to a MAC address using the command **show ip arp**, as shown in Figure 8-6. This command indicates how long the device has been seen on the network. As you can see in this example, two IP addresses have been seen for less than 20 minutes.

```
funktribe#show ip arp
Protocol   Address          Age  (min)   Hardware  Addr    Type    Interface
Internet   10.0.2.1             -         0022.be20.f140   ARPA    Vlan1
Internet   10.0.2.61           15         a820.660c.dfff   ARPA    Vlan1
Internet   10.0.2.63            0         000c.2975.a143   ARPA    Vlan1
Internet   10.0.2.254          12         0021.a009.96b7   ARPA    Vlan1
Internet   10.0.3.1             -         0022.be20.f142   ARPA    Vlan10
Internet   10.0.4.1             -         0022.be20.f143   ARPA    Vlan20
Internet   10.0.5.1             -         0022.be20.f144   ARPA    Vlan30
funktribe#
```

Figure 8-6   *A show ip arp Example*

Identifying the session duration for the entire network using the command line is a challenging task. The industry typically uses tools that pull SNMP and port logs to calculate the duration of a connected device. An example of a network-monitoring application with this capability is Cisco Prime LAN Manager. Other protocols can also be used to monitor ports such as NetFlow and packet-capturing technology, as long as the monitoring starts before the host connects to the network. The SECOPS exam won't ask you about the available tools on the market for monitoring sessions because this is out of scope, and there are way too many to mention.

The list that follows highlights the key session duration concepts:

■ Session duration in network access terms is the total time a user or device connects to a network and later disconnects from that network.

■ Identifying sessions starts with knowing what devices are connected to the network.

■ Many tools are available on the market that leverage SNMP, NetFlow, packet captures, and so on, to monitor the entire session a host is seen on the network.

Critical Asset Address Space

The last topic for the network section of this chapter involves looking at controlling the asset address space. This is important to ensure that critical assets are provisioned network resources, limit devices from interfering with devices deemed a higher importance, and possibly control the use of address spaces for security or cost purposes.

Address space can be either Internet Protocol version 4 (IPv4) or 6 (IPv6). IPv4 uses 32-bit addresses broken down into 4 bytes, which equals 8 bits per byte. An IPv4 address is written in a dotted-decimal notation, as shown in Figure 8-7. The address is divided into two parts, where the highest order octet of the address identifies the class of network, and the rest of the address represents the host. There are five classes of networks: Classes A, B, C, D, and

E. Classes A, B, and C have different bit lengths for the new network identification, meaning the rest of the network space will be different regarding the capacity for address hosts. Certain ranges of IP addresses defined by the Internet Engineering Task Force (IETF) and the Internet Assigned Numbers Authority (IANA) are restricted from general use and reserved for special purposes. *Network address translation (NAT)* was developed as a method to remap one IP address space into another by modifying network address information; however, this still doesn't deal with the increasing demand for new IP addresses. Details about creating IPv4 networks is out of scope for this section of the book and for the SECOPS exam.

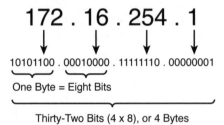

An IPv4 Address (Dotted-Decimal Notation)

172 . 16 . 254 . 1

10101100 . 00010000 . 11111110 . 00000001

One Byte = Eight Bits

Thirty-Two Bits (4 x 8), or 4 Bytes

Figure 8-7   *IPv4 Network Address*

To tackle the issue of available IPv4 address depletion, IPv6 was created as a replacement. It offers a much larger address space that ideally won't be exhausted for many years. This also removes the need for NAT, which has its own inherent problems. IPv6 is made up of a 128-bit address format logically divided into a network prefix and host identifier. The number of bits in a network prefix is represented by a prefix length, while the remaining bits are used for the host identifier. Figure 8-8 shows an example of an IPv6 address using the default 64-bit network prefix length. Adoption of IPv6 has been slow, and many administrators leverage IPv4-to-IPv6 transition techniques, such as running both protocols simultaneously, which is known as **dual stacking** or translating between IPv4 and IPv6 approaches. The details for developing IPv6 address ranges are out of scope for this chapter and for the SECOPS exam.

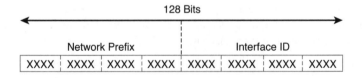

128 Bits

Network Prefix | Interface ID

| XXXX | XXXX | XXXX | XXXX | XXXX | XXXX | XXXX | XXXX |

XXXX = 0000 Through FFFF

3.4×10^{38} = ~340,282,366,920,938,463,374,607,432,768,211,456 IPv6 Addresses

Figure 8-8   *Example of IPv6 Addressing*

Key Topic

Regardless of the version of IP addressing being used, IP address management (IPAM) will be a topic to tackle. Factors that impact address management include the version of IP addresses deployed, DNS security measures, and DHCP support. IPAM can be broken down into three major areas of focus.

- **IP address inventory:** Obtaining and defining the public and private IPv4 and IPv6 address space as well as allocating that address space to locations, subnets, devices, address pools, and users on the network.

- **Dynamic IP address services management:** The parameters associated with each address pool defined within the IP address space management function as well as how DHCP servers supply relevant IP addresses and parameters to requesting systems. This function also includes managing capacity of address pools to ensure dynamic IP addresses are available.

- **IP name services management:** Managing domain name system (DNS) assignment so devices can access URL resources by name. This also includes other relevant DNS management tasks.

Each of these areas is critical to the proper operation of an IP-based network. Any device accessing the network regardless of connection type will need an IP address and the ability to access internal and/or external resources to be productive. Typically, this starts with an organization obtaining a public IPv4 or IPv6 address space from an Internet service provider (ISP). Administrators must spend time planning to accommodate current and future IP address capacity requirements in user accessible and mission-critical subnets on the network. Once those numbers are calculated, proper address allocation needs to be enforced. This means considering the routing infrastructure and avoiding issues such as duplicated IP addresses being assigned, networks rendered unreachable due to route summarization conflicts, and IP space rendered unusable due to errors in providing IP addresses in a hierarchical manager while still preserving address space for use on other parts of the network.

Address planning can be challenging and best accomplished by using a centralized IP inventory database, DHCP, and DNS policy. This provides one single, holistic view of the entire address space that is deployed across the network, regardless of the number of locations and required address pools, DHCP servers, and DNS servers. *Dynamic Host Configuration Protocol (DHCP)* automatically provisions hosts with an IP address and other related configurations, such as a subnet mask and default gateway. Centralizing DHCP can improve configuration accuracy and consistency of address pool allocation as well as IP reallocation, as needed for ongoing address pool capacity management.

The same centralized deployment practice should be enforced for *domain name servers (DNS)* responsible for resolving IP addresses to domain names, and vice versa. Leveraging a single DNS database simplifies deploying configuration parameters to the appropriate master or slave configuration as well as aggregating dynamic updates to keep all servers up to date. These and other strategies should make up your *IP inventory assurance* practice for enforcing the accuracy of IP inventory through periodic discovery, exception reporting, and selective database updates. IP assurance must be a continuous process to confirm the integrity of the IP inventory for effective IP planning.

Critical devices need additional measures to ensure other devices don't impact their availability and functionality. Typically, two approaches are used to ensure critical devices don't lose their IP address. One is to manually configure the IP information on those devices, and the other approach is reserving those IP addresses in DHCP. Manually setting the IP address, sometimes called *statically setting* or *hard coding* the IP address, ensures that the critical system does not rely on an external system to provide it IP information. Reserving IP addresses to the MAC address of a critical system in DHCP can accomplish the same thing; however, there is the low risk that the critical asset is relying on DHCP to issue the correct IP address, which could go down or be compromised. The risk of using static IP assignment is based on the concept that any system manually configured is not aware of how the IP address it is using impacts the rest of the network. If another device has the same IP address, there will be an IP address conflict and thus network issues. Static assignments also are manually enforced, which means this approach has a risk of address planning errors.

Once IP address sizing and deployment is complete, IP space management will become the next and ongoing challenge. This is due to various reasons that can occur and potentially impact the IP address space. New locations may open or existing locations may close. New IT services may be requested, such as Voice over IP (VoIP) requiring a new dedicated IP range. New security requirements such as network segmentation demands may be pushed down from leadership. One change that many administrators are or will eventually face is converting IPv4 networks to IPv6, as all networks are slowly adapting to the future of the Internet. The success of maintaining an effective IP address space is staying on top of these and other requests.

Here is a summary of IP address inventory management best practices:

- Use a centralized database for IP address inventory.
- Use a centralized DHCP server configuration and include failover measures.
- Document all IP subnet and address space assignments.
- Use basic security practices to provide selective address assignment.
- Track address space allocations in accordance with the routing topology.
- Deploy consistent subnet addressing policies.
- Develop network diagrams that include a naming convention for all devices using IP space.
- Continuously monitor address and pool utilization as well as adapt to capacity issues.
- Plan for IPv6 if using IPv4.

Host Profiling

Profiling hosts on the network is similar to profiling network behavior. The focus for the remaining topics in this chapter will be on viewing devices connected to the network versus the actual network itself. This can be valuable in identifying vulnerable systems, internal threats, what applications are installed on hosts, and so on. We will touch upon how to view details directly from the host; however, the main focus will be on profiling hosts as an outside entity by looking at a host's network footprint.

Let's start off by discussing how to view data from a network host and the applications it is using.

Listening Ports

The first aspect people look at when attempting to learn about a host system over a network—regardless of whether it is a system administrator, penetration tester, or malicious attacker—is determining which ports are "listening." A *listening port* is a port held open by a running application in order to accept inbound connections. From a security perspective, this may mean a vulnerable system that could be exploited. A worst-case scenario would be an unauthorized active listening port to an exploited system permitting external access to a malicious party. Because most attackers will
be outside your network, unauthorized listening ports are typically evidence of an intrusion.

Let's look at the fundamentals behind ports: Messages associated with application protocols use TCP or UDP. Both of these employ port numbers to identify a specific process to which an Internet or other network message is to be forwarded when it arrives at a server. A port number is a 16-bit integer that is put in the header appended to a specific message unit. Port numbers are passed logically between the client and server transport layers and physically between the transport layer and the IP layer before they are forwarded on. This client/server model is typically seen as web client software. An example is a browser communicating with a web server listening on a port such as port 80. Port values can range between 1 and 65535, with server applications generally assigned a valued below 1024.

The following is a list of well-known ports used by applications:

- **TCP 20 and 21**: File Transfer Protocol (FTP)
- **TCP 22**: Secure Shell (SSH)
- **TCP 23**: Telnet
- **TCP 25**: Simple Mail Transfer Protocol (SMTP)
- **TCP and UDP 53**: Domain Name System (DNS)
- **UDP 69**: Trivial File Transfer Protocol (TFTP)
- **TCP 79**: Finger
- **TCP 80**: Hypertext Transfer Protocol (HTTP)
- **TCP 110**: Post Office Protocol v3 (POP3)
- **TCP 119**: Network News Protocol (NNTP)
- **UDP 161 and 162**: Simple Network Management Protocol (SNMP)
- **UDP 443**: Secure Sockets Layer over HTTP (HTTPS)

NOTE: These are just industry guidelines, meaning administrators do not have to run the following services over these ports. Typically administrators will follow these guidelines; however, these services can run over other ports. The services do not have to run on the known port to service list.

There are two basic approaches for identifying listening ports on the network. The first approach is accessing a host and searching for which ports are set to a listening state. This requires a minimal level of access to the host and being authorized on the host to run commands. This could also be done with authorized applications that are capable of showing all possible applications available on the host. The most common host-based tool for checking systems for listening ports on Windows and UNIX systems is the **netstat** command. An example of looking for listening ports using the **netstat** command is **netstat –an,** as shown in Figure 8-9. As you can see, two applications are in the "LISTEN" state. Another host command to view similar data is the **lsof –i** command.

```
[JOMUNIZ-M-91SU:~ jomuniz$ netstat -an
Active Internet connections (including servers)
Proto Recv-Q Send-Q  Local Address         Foreign Address        (state)
tcp6      0      0  2001:420:c0c4:10.64706 2620:106:e003:f0.80    ESTABLISHED
tcp6      0      0  2001:420:c0c4:10.64705 2607:f8b0:4004:8.443   ESTABLISHED
tcp4      0      0  10.82.175.174.64704    17.154.66.69.443       ESTABLISHED
tcp4      0      0  127.0.0.1.631          *.*                    LISTEN
tcp6      0      0  ::1.631                *.*                    LISTEN
tcp6      0      0  2001:420:c0c4:10.64700 2607:f8b0:4004:8.443   ESTABLISHED
tcp4      0      0  10.82.175.174.64699    173.37.102.6.443       ESTABLISHED
tcp4      0      0  10.82.175.174.64698    173.37.102.6.443       ESTABLISHED
```

Figure 8-9 *A netstat –an Command Example*

A second and more reliable approach to determining what ports are listening from a host is to scan the host as an outside evaluator with a **port scanner** application. A port scanner probes a host system running TCP/IP to determine which TCP and UDP ports are open and listening. One extremely popular tool that can do this is the **nmap** tool, which is a port scanner that can determine whether ports are listening, plus provide many other details. The **nmap** command **nmap-services** will look for more than 2,200 well-known services to fingerprint any applications running on the port.

It is important to be aware that port scanners are providing a best guess, and the results should be validated. For example, a security solution could reply with the wrong information or an administrator could spoof information such as the version number of a vulnerable server to make it appear to a port scanner that the server is patched. Newer breach detection technologies such as advanced honey pots will attempt to attract attackers that have successfully breached the network by leaving vulnerable ports open on systems in the network. They will then monitor those systems for any connections. The concept is that attackers will most likely scan and connect to systems that are found to be vulnerable, thus being tricked into believing the fake honey pot is really a vulnerable system. Figure 8-10 shows an example of using the **nmap –sT –O localhost** command to identify ports that are open or listening for TCP connections.

8

```
root@kali:~# nmap -sT -O 10.0.0.14

Starting Nmap 7.12 ( https://nmap.org ) at 2016-08-09 20:54 EDT
Nmap scan report for 10.0.0.14
Host is up (0.0099s latency).
Not shown: 990 closed ports
PORT      STATE SERVICE
135/tcp   open  msrpc
139/tcp   open  netbios-ssn
445/tcp   open  microsoft-ds
8099/tcp  open  unknown
49152/tcp open  unknown
49153/tcp open  unknown
49154/tcp open  unknown
49157/tcp open  unknown
49158/tcp open  unknown
49159/tcp open  unknown
MAC Address: 00:24:D7:9F:EC:78 (Intel Corporate)
Device type: general purpose
Running: Microsoft Windows 7|2008|8.1
OS CPE: cpe:/o:microsoft:windows_7:: cpe:/o:microsoft:windows_7::sp1 cpe:/o:microsoft:windows_serve
r_2008::sp1 cpe:/o:microsoft:windows_8 cpe:/o:microsoft:windows_8.1
OS details: Microsoft Windows 7 SP0 - SP1, Windows Server 2008 SP1, Windows 8, or Windows 8.1 Update
 1
Network Distance: 1 hop

OS detection performed. Please report any incorrect results at https://nmap.org/submit/ .
Nmap done: 1 IP address (1 host up) scanned in 1.73 seconds
```

Figure 8-10 *The nmap –sT –O localhost Command*

If attackers are able to identify a server with an available port, they can attempt to connect to that service, determine what software is running on the server, and check to see if there are known vulnerabilities within the identified software that potentially could be exploited, as previously explained. This tactic can be effective when servers are identified as unadvertised because many website administrators fail to adequately protect systems that may be considered "non-production" systems yet are still on the network. An example would be using a port scanner to identify servers running older software, such as an older version of Internet Information Service (IIS) that has known exploitable vulnerabilities. Many penetration arsenals such as Metasploit carry a library of vulnerabilities matching the results from a port scanner application. Based on the port scan in Figure 8-10, an attacker would be particularly interested in the open TCP ports listed with unknown services. This is how many cyber attacks are delivered, meaning the attacker identifies applications on open ports, matches them to a known vulnerability, and exploits the vulnerability with the goal of delivering something such as malware, a remote access tool, or ransomware.

Another option for viewing "listening" ports on a host system is to use a network device such as a Cisco IOS router. A command similar to **netstat** on Cisco IOS devices is **show control-plan host open-ports**. A router's control plane is responsible for handling traffic destined for the router itself, versus the data plane being responsible for passing transient traffic. This means the output from the Cisco IOS command is similar to a Windows **netstat** command, as shown in Figure 8-11, which lists a few ports in the LISTEN state.

```
Router# show control-plane host open-ports
Active internet connections (servers and established)
Prot      Local Address     Foreign Address          Service    State
 tcp         *:23              *:0                    Telnet     LISTEN
 tcp         *:80              *:0                 HTTP CORE     LISTEN
 udp         *:67              *:0            DHCPD Receive     LISTEN
 udp         *:2887            *:0                      DDP     LISTEN
```

Figure 8-11 *A show control-plan host open-ports Example*

Best practice for securing any listening and open ports is to perform periodic network assessments on any host using network resources for open ports and services that might be running and are either unintended or unnecessary. The goal is to reduce the risk of exposing vulnerable services and to identify exploited systems or malicious applications. Port scanners are very common and widely available for the Windows and UNIX platforms. Many of these programs are open source projects, such as **nmap**, and have well-established support communities. A risk evaluation should be applied to identified listening ports because some services may be exploitable but wouldn't matter for some situations. An example would be a server inside a closed network without external access that's identified to have a listening port that an attacker would never be able to access.

The following list shows some of the known "bad" ports that should be secured:

- 1243/tcp: SubSeven server (default for V1.0-2.0)
- 6346/tcp: Gnutella
- 6667/tcp: Trinity intruder-to-master and master-to-daemon
- 6667/tcp: SubSeven server (default for V2.1 Icqfix and beyond)
- 12345/tcp: NetBus 1.x
- 12346/tcp: NetBus 1.x
- 16660/tcp: Stacheldraht intruder-to-master
- 18753/udp: Shaft master-to-daemon
- 20034/tcp: NetBus Pro
- 20432/tcp: Shaft intruder-to-master
- 20433/udp: Shaft daemon-to-master
- 27374/tcp: SubSeven server (default for V2.1-Defcon)
- 27444/udp: Trinoo master-to-daemon
- 27665/tcp: Trinoo intruder-to-master
- 31335/udp: Trinoo daemon-to-master
- 31337/tcp: Back Orifice
- 33270/tcp: Trinity master-to-daemon
- 33567/tcp: Backdoor rootshell via inetd (from Lion worm)
- 33568/tcp: Trojaned version of SSH (from Lion worm)
- 40421/tcp: Masters Paradise Trojan horse
- 60008/tcp: Backdoor rootshell via inetd (from Lion worm)
- 65000/tcp: Stacheldraht master-to-daemon

One final best practice we'll cover for protecting listening and open ports is implementing security solutions such as firewalls. The purpose of a firewall is to control traffic as it enters and leaves a network based on a set of rules. Part of the responsibility is protecting listening ports from unauthorized systems—for example, preventing external attackers from having the ability to scan internal systems or connect to listening ports. Firewall technology has come a long way, providing capabilities across the entire network protocol stack and the ability to evaluate the types of communication permitted. For example, older firewalls can permit or deny web traffic via port 80 and 443, but current application layer firewalls can also permit or deny specific applications within that traffic, such as denying YouTube videos within a Facebook page, which is seen as an option in most application layer firewalls. Firewalls are just one of the many tools available to protect listening ports. Best practice is to layer security defense strategies to avoid being compromised if one method of protection is breached.

The list that follows highlights the key listening port concepts:

- A listening port is a port held open by a running application in order to accept inbound connections.

- Ports use values that range between 1 and 65535.

- Using **netstat** and **nmap** are popular methods for identifying listening ports.

- **Netstat** can be run locally on a device, whereas **nmap** can be used to scan a range of IP addresses for listening ports.

- Best practice for securing listening ports is to scan and evaluate any identified listening port as well as to implement layered security, such as combining a firewall with other defensive capabilities.

Logged-in Users/Service Accounts

Identifying who is logged in to a system is important for knowing how the system will be used. Administrators typically have more access to various services than other users because their job requires those privileges. Human Resources may need more access rights than other employees to validate whether an employee is violating a policy. Guest users typically require very little access rights because they are considered a security risk to most organizations. In summary, best practice for provisioning access rights is to enforce the concept of **least privilege**, meaning to provision the absolute least amount of access rights required to perform a job.

People can be logged in to a system in two ways. The first method is to be physically at a keyboard logged in to the system. The other method is to remotely access the system using something like a Remote Desktop Connection (RDP) protocol. Sometimes the remote system is authorized and controlled, such as using a Citrix remote desktop solution to provide remote users access to the desktop, whereas other times it's a malicious user who has planted a remote access tool (RAT) to gain unauthorized access to the host system. Identifying post-breach situations is just one of the many reasons why monitoring remote connections should be a priority for protecting your organization from cyber breaches.

Identifying who is logged in to a system can be accomplished by using a few approaches. For Windows machines, the first method involves using the *Remote Desktop Services Manager* suite. This approach requires the software to be installed. Once the software is running, an administrator can remotely access the host to verify who is logged in. Figure 8-12 shows an example of using the Remote Desktop Services Manager to remotely view that two users are logged in to a host system.

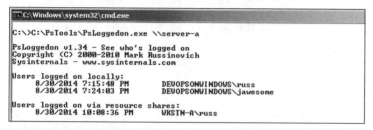

Figure 8-12   *Remote Desktop Services Manager Example*

Another tool you can use to validate who is logged in to a Windows system is the **PsLoggedOn** application. For this application to work, it has to be downloaded and placed somewhere on your local computer that will be remotely checking hosts. Once it's installed, simply open a command prompt and execute the command **C:\PsTools\psloggedon.exe \\ HOST_TO_CONNECT**. Figure 8-13 shows an example of using PsTools to connect to "server-a" and finding that two users are logged in to the host system.

```
C:\Windows\system32\cmd.exe

C:\>C:\PsTools\PsLoggedon.exe \\server-a

PsLoggedon v1.34 - See who's logged on
Copyright (C) 2000-2010 Mark Russinovich
Sysinternals - www.sysinternals.com

Users logged on locally:
     8/30/2014 7:15:48 PM        DEVOPSONWINDOWS\russ
     8/30/2014 7:24:03 PM        DEVOPSONWINDOWS\jawesome

Users logged on via resource shares:
     8/30/2014 10:08:36 PM       WKSTN-A\russ
```

Figure 8-13   *PsTools Example*

One last method to remotely validate who is logged in to a Windows system is using the Windows **Query** application, which is executed using the command **query user / server:server-a**. Figure 8-14 shows an example of using this command to see who is logged into server-a.

```
C:\Windows\system32\cmd.exe

C:\>query user /server:server-a
 USERNAME              SESSIONNAME        ID  STATE    IDLE TIME  LOGON TIME
 russ                  console            1   Active      none    9/1/2014 7:20 PM
 jawesome              rdp-tcp#0          2   Active        11    9/1/2014 7:25 PM
```

Figure 8-14   *Query Example*

For Linux machines, various commands can show who is logged in to a system, such as the **w** command, **who** command, **users** command, **whoami** command, and the **last "user name"** command, as shown in Figure 8-15. Each option shows a slightly different set of information about who is currently logged in to a system. One command that displays the same information on a Windows system is the **whoami** command.

```
Last login: Fri Aug 19 11:42:32 on ttys000
JOMUNIZ-M-91SU:~ jomuniz$ w
11:42  up 2 days, 12:16, 2 users, load averages: 1.93 2.04 2.15
USER      TTY      FROM             LOGIN@  IDLE WHAT
jomuniz  console   -                Tue23   2days -
jomuniz  s001      -                11:42      - w
JOMUNIZ-M-91SU:~ jomuniz$ who
jomuniz  console  Aug 16 23:26
jomuniz  ttys001  Aug 19 11:42
JOMUNIZ-M-91SU:~ jomuniz$ users
jomuniz
JOMUNIZ-M-91SU:~ jomuniz$ whoami
jomuniz
JOMUNIZ-M-91SU:~ jomuniz$ last jomuniz
jomuniz   ttys001               Fri Aug 19 11:42   still logged in
jomuniz   ttys000               Fri Aug 19 11:42 - 11:42  (00:00)
jomuniz   ttys000               Wed Aug 17 22:56 - 22:56  (00:00)
jomuniz   ttys000               Wed Aug 17 21:24 - 21:24  (00:00)
jomuniz   console               Tue Aug 16 23:26   still logged in

wtmp begins Tue Aug 16 23:26
JOMUNIZ-M-91SU:~ jomuniz$ 
```

Figure 8-15 *Various Linux Commands to See Logged-in Users*

Many administrative tools can be used to remotely access hosts, so the preceding commands can be issued to validate who is logged in to the system. One such tool is a *virtual network computing (VNC)* server. This method requires three pieces. The first part is having a VNC server that will be used to access clients. The second part is having a VNC viewer client installed on the host to be accessed by the server. The final part is an SSH connection that is established between the server and client once things are set up successfully. SSH can also be used directly from one system to access another system using the **ssh "remote_host"** or **ssh "remote_username@remote_host"** command if SSH is set up properly. There are many other applications, both open source and commercial, that can provide remote desktop access service to host systems.

It is important to be aware that validating who is logged in to a host can identify when a host is compromised. According to the kill chain concept, attackers that breach a network will look to establish a foothold through breaching one or more systems. Once they have access to a system, they will seek out other systems by pivoting from system to system. In many cases, attackers want to identify a system with more access rights so they can increase their privilege level, meaning gain access to an administration account, which typically can access critical systems. Security tools that include the ability to monitor users logged in to systems can flag whether a system associated with an employee accesses a system that's typically only accessed by administrator-level users, thus indicating a concern for an internal attack through a compromised host. The industry calls this type of security breach detection, meaning technology looking for post compromise attacks.

The list that follows highlights the key concepts covered in this section:

■ Employing least privilege means to provision the absolute minimum amount of access rights required to perform a job.

- The two methods to log in to a host are locally and remotely.

- Common methods for remotely accessing a host are using SSH and using a remote access server application such as VNC.

Running Processes

Now that we have covered identifying listening ports and how to check users that are logged in to a host system, the next topic to address is how to identify which processes are running on a host system. A *running process* is an instance of a computer program being executed. There's lots of value in understanding what is running on hosts, such as identifying what is consuming resources, developing more granular security policies, and tuning how resources are distributed based on QoS adjustments linked to identified applications. We will briefly look at identifying processes with access to the host system; however, the focus of this section will be on viewing applications as a remote system on the same network.

In Windows, one simple method for viewing the running processes when you have access to the host system is to open the **Task Manager** using the **Ctrl+Shift+Esc**, as shown in Figure 8-16.

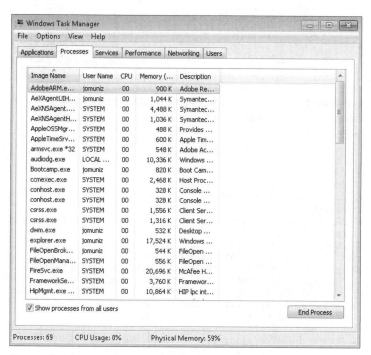

Figure 8-16 *Windows Task Manager*

A similar result can be achieved using the Windows command line by opening the command terminal with the **cmd** command and issuing the **tasklist** command, as shown in Figure 8-17.

```
C:\Users\jomuniz>tasklist

Image Name                     PID Session Name     Session#    Mem Usage
========================= ======== ================ =========== ============
System Idle Process              0 Services                  0         24 K
System                           4 Services                  0        552 K
smss.exe                       304 Services                  0        212 K
csrss.exe                      520 Services                  0      2,624 K
wininit.exe                    568 Services                  0        496 K
csrss.exe                      576 Console                   1      3,428 K
services.exe                   624 Services                  0      7,128 K
lsass.exe                      632 Services                  0      9,084 K
lsm.exe                        648 Services                  0      2,728 K
winlogon.exe                   668 Console                   1        892 K
svchost.exe                    784 Services                  0      5,220 K
svchost.exe                    860 Services                  0      6,400 K
svchost.exe                    952 Services                  0     14,388 K
svchost.exe                    272 Services                  0      8,324 K
svchost.exe                    340 Services                  0     12,392 K
svchost.exe                    500 Services                  0     54,032 K
svchost.exe                   1228 Services                  0     22,500 K
spoolsv.exe                   1340 Services                  0      3,272 K
svchost.exe                   1368 Services                  0      8,116 K
armsvc.exe                    1480 Services                  0      1,172 K
AeXNSAgent.exe                1516 Services                  0     10,872 K
AppleOSSMgr.exe               1548 Services                  0      1,064 K
AppleTimeSrv.exe              1576 Services                  0      1,644 K
FireSvc.exe                   1616 Services                  0     26,488 K
FileOpenManager64.exe         1672 Services                  0      1,104 K
HipMgmt.exe                   1716 Services                  0     14,216 K
```

Figure 8-17 *Running the tasklist Command on the Windows Command Line*

For UNIX systems, the command **ps -e** can be used to display a similar result as the Windows commands previously covered. Figure 8-18 shows executing the **ps -e** command to display running processes on an OS X system.

```
[JOMUNIZ-M-91SU:~ jomuniz$ ps -e
  PID TTY           TIME CMD
    1 ??        36:52.58 /sbin/launchd
   41 ??         1:29.32 /usr/libexec/UserEventAgent (System)
   42 ??         8:35.81 /usr/sbin/syslogd
   44 ??       351:47.29 /Applications/CrashPlan.app/Contents/MacOS/CrashPlanSe
   45 ??         0:38.11 /usr/libexec/kextd
   46 ??         5:23.07 /System/Library/Frameworks/CoreServices.framework/Vers
   48 ??         0:04.52 /usr/local/McAfee/AntiMalware/VShieldUpdate
   49 ??        12:49.16 /usr/local/jamf/bin/jamf launchDaemon -monitorNetworkS
   50 ??       168:45.27 /opt/cisco/anyconnect/bin/vpnagentd -execv_instance
   51 ??         0:00.65 /opt/cisco/hostscan/bin/ciscod -d
   54 ??         0:04.23 /System/Library/CoreServices/appleeventsd --server
   55 ??         2:23.07 /usr/libexec/configd
   56 ??         0:29.05 /System/Library/CoreServices/powerd.bundle/powerd
   57 ??         0:10.18 /Library/McAfee/agent/bin/macmnsvc self_start
   58 ??         0:31.76 /Library/McAfee/agent/bin/masvc self_start
   65 ??         1:34.29 /usr/libexec/airportd
   66 ??        55:10.95 /Library/McAfee/agent/bin/macompatsvc self_start
   68 ??         0:02.87 /usr/libexec/warmd
   69 ??        29:19.91 /System/Library/Frameworks/CoreServices.framework/Fram
   74 ??         0:00.13 /System/Library/CoreServices/iconservicesagent
   75 ??         0:00.30 /System/Library/CoreServices/iconservicesd
   76 ??         0:07.15 /usr/libexec/diskarbitrationd
   79 ??         1:11.95 /usr/libexec/coreduetd
```

Figure 8-18 *Using the ps -e Command on an OS X System*

These approaches are very useful when you can log in to the host and have the privilege level to issue such commands. The focus for the SECOPS exam is identifying these processes from an administrator system on the same network versus administrating the host directly. This requires evaluation of the hosts based on traffic and available ports. There are known services associated with ports, meaning that simply seeing a specific port being used indicates it has a known associated process running. For example, if port 25 is showing SMTP traffic, it is expected that the host has a mail process running.

Identifying traffic from a host and the ports being used by the host can be handled using methods we previously covered, such as using a port scanner, having a detection tool inline, or reading traffic from a SPAN port. An example is using **nmap** commands that include application data, such as the **nmap –sV** command shown in Figure 8-19. This **nmap** command searchers the port against more than 2,200 well-known services. It is important to note that a general **nmap** scan will just provide a best guess for the service based on being linked to a known port, whereas the **nmap –sV** command will interrogate the open ports using probes that the specific service understands to validate what is really running. This also holds true for identifying the applications, which we will cover in the next section.

```
root@kali:~# nmap -sV 64.90.49.201

Starting Nmap 7.12 ( https://nmap.org ) at 2017-03-03 17:29 EST
Nmap scan report for apache2-emu.myrtlepoint.dreamhost.com (64.90.49.201)
Host is up (0.096s latency).
Not shown: 993 filtered ports
PORT     STATE SERVICE   VERSION
21/tcp   open  ftp       ProFTPD
22/tcp   open  ssh       OpenSSH 5.9p1 Debian 5ubuntu1.10 (Ubuntu Linux; protocol
 2.0)
80/tcp   open  http      Apache httpd
443/tcp  open  ssl/http  Apache httpd
587/tcp  open  smtp      Postfix smtpd
5222/tcp open  jabber    ejabberd (Protocol 1.0)
5269/tcp open  jabber    ejabberd
Service Info: Host: myrtlepoint.dreamhost.com; OS: Linux; CPE: cpe:/o:linux:linu
x_kernel

Service detection performed. Please report any incorrect results at https://nmap
.org/submit/ .
Nmap done: 1 IP address (1 host up) scanned in 43.45 seconds
```

Figure 8-19   *Using the nmap –sV Command*

The list that follows highlights the key concepts covered in this section:

- A running process is an instance of a computer program being executed.

- Identifying traffic and ports from a host can be accomplished by using a port scanner, having a detection tool inline, or reading traffic from a SPAN port.

- Identifying running processes uses similar tools as discovering listening ports.

Applications

The final topic for this chapter is detecting and monitoring host applications. An application is software that performs a specific task. Applications can be found on desktops, laptops, mobile devices, and so on. They run inside the operating system and can be simple tasks or complicated programs. Identifying applications can be done using the methods previously covered, such as identifying which protocols are seen by a scanner, the type of clients (such as the web browser or email client), and the sources they are communicating with (such as what web applications are being used).

> **NOTE**   Applications operate at the top of the OSI and TCP/IP layer models, whereas traffic is sent by the transport and lower layers, as shown in Figure 8-20.

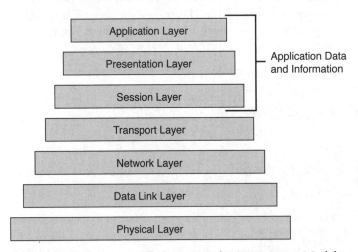

Figure 8-20   *Representing the OSI and TCP/IP Layer Models*

To view applications on a Windows system with access to the host, you can use the same methods we covered for viewing processes. The *Task Manager* is one option, as shown in Figure 8-21. Notice in this example I'm running two applications: a command terminal and the Google Chrome Internet Browser.

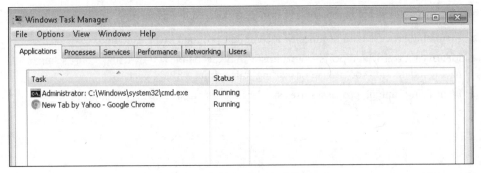

Figure 8-21   *Windows Task Manager Showing Applications*

For OS X systems, you can use *Force Quit Applications* (accessed with **Command+Option+Escape**), as shown in Figure 8-22, or the Activity Monitor tool.

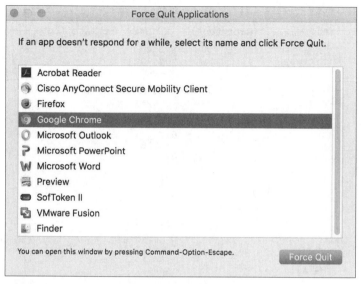

Figure 8-22   *Force Quit Applications OS X*

Once again, these options for viewing applications are great if you have access to the host as well as the proper privilege rights to run those commands or applications; however, let's look at identifying the applications as an outsider profiling a system on the same network.

The first tool to consider is a port scanner that can also interrogate for more information than port data. *Nmap version scanning* can further interrogate open ports to probe for specific services. This tells **nmap** what is really running versus just the ports that are open. For example, running **nmap –v** could display lots of details, including the following information showing which port is open and the identified service:

```
PORT        STATE      SERVICE
80/tcp      open       http
631/tcp     open       ipp
3306/tcp    open       mysql
```

A classification engine available in Cisco IOS software that can be used to identify applications is *Network-Based Application Recognition (NBAR)*. This works by enabling an IOS router interface to map traffic ports to protocols as well as recognize traffic that doesn't have a standard port, such as various peer-to-peer protocols. NBAR is typically used as a means to identify traffic for QoS policies; however, you can use the **show ip nbar protocol-discovery** command, as shown in Figure 8-23, to identify what protocols and associated applications are identified by NBAR.

```
                      Input                      Output
                      -----                      ------
Protocol              Packet Count               Packet Count
                      Byte Count                 Byte Count
                      5min Bit Rate (bps)        5min Bit Rate (bps)
                      5min Max Bit Rate (bps)    5min Max Bit Rate (bps)
----------------------------------------------------------------------------
http                  31694                      31895
                      32263992                   29905994
                      314000                     298000
                      314000                     304000
smtp                  1857                       2779
                      604514                     3485245
                      0                          35000
                      12000                      86000
secure-http           430                        617
                      45760                      830228
                      0                          0
                      2000                       8000
ldap                  267                        281
                      72466                      69587
                      0                          0
                      5000                       5000
socks                 113                        99
                      46356                      55212
                      0                          0
                      3000                       5000
telnet                424                        213
                      18934                      54442
                      0                          0
                      2000                       6000
unknown               25934                      43559
                      3055485                    56297141
                      29000                      525000
                      33000                      531000
Total                 63115                      81627
                      36403523                   91018830
                      343000                     859000
                      386000                     960000
```

Figure 8-23   *Using the show ip nbar protocol-discovery Command*

Many other tools with built-in application-detection capabilities are available. Most content filters and network proxies can provide application layer details, such as Cisco's *Web Security Appliance (WSA)*.

Even NetFlow can have application data added when using a Cisco StealthWatch Flow Sensor. The Flow Sensor adds detection of 900 applications while it converts raw data into NetFlow. Application layer firewalls also provide detailed application data, such as Cisco Firepower, which is shown in Figure 8-24.

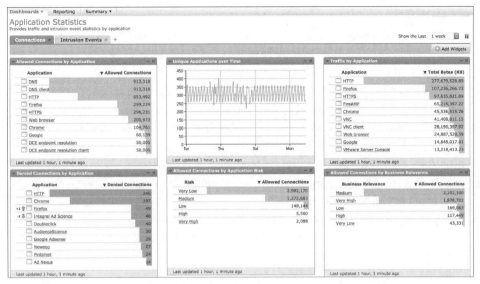

Figure 8-24 *Cisco Firepower Application-Focused Dashboard*

In summary, networks tools that can detect application layer data must have access to network traffic both to and from a host, such as being inline or off a SPAN port. Examples of tools that can detect application layer data are content filters, application layer firewalls, and tools that have custom application-detection capabilities built in. Also, network scanning can be used to evaluate the ports on host and link traffic to known associated applications.

The list that follows highlights the key concepts covered in this section:

■ An application is software that performs a specific task.

■ Applications operate at the top of the OSI and TCP/IP layer models, whereas traffic is sent by the transport layer.

■ NBAR in Cisco IOS devices can be used to identify applications.

■ Network tools that can detect application layer data must have access to network traffic both to and from a host, such as being inline or off a SPAN port.

Summary

The focus of this chapter was to review the various methods to profile devices found on networks. We started off by looking at throughput to determine what should be considered for creating a network baseline. After establishing a baseline, we covered how to view what devices are connected to the network by analyzing used ports. Next, we reviewed the session time a device uses while on the network, and then closed the first part of this chapter with provisioning and securing available address space.

The second part of this chapter looked at how to profile hosts found on the network. We started off with looking at how to evaluate listening ports found on hosts through various detection methods. Next, we covered tactics for identifying users logged in to a system. The final two sections identified running processes and applications found on hosts.

Now that we've covered profiling, the next chapter will look at data analysis.

References

- https://msdn.microsoft.com/en-us/library/windows/desktop/ms681917(v=vs.85).aspx
- http://www.cisco.com/c/en/us/td/docs/interfaces_modules/services_modules/ace/vA5_1_0/configuration/rtg_brdg/guide/rtbrgdgd/ipv6.html
- http://www.cisco.com/c/en/us/products/collateral/cloud-systems-management/prime-network-registrar/white_paper_c11-728639.html
- https://access.redhat.com/documentation/en-US/Red_Hat_Enterprise_Linux/3/html/Security_Guide/s1-server-ports.html
- http://packetlife.net/blog/2008/dec/3/listing-open-sockets-ios/
- http://www.cisco.com/c/en/us/td/docs/ios-xml/ios/qos_nbar/configuration/15-mt/qos-nbar-15-mt-book/clsfy-traffic-nbar.html
- https://www.lancope.com/products/StealthWatch-flowsensor

Exam Preparation Tasks

Review All Key Topics

Review the most important topics in the chapter, noted with the Key Topic icon in the outer margin of the page. Table 8-2 lists these key topics and the page numbers on which each is found.

Table 8-2   Key Topics

Key Topic Element	Description	Page
List	Throughput concepts	200
List	Used ports concepts	206
List	Session duration concepts	211
Bullet Points	IPAM focus areas	213
List	IP address inventory management best practices	215
List	Listening port concepts	216
List	Well-known ports by the IT industry	216
List	Running process concepts	223
List	Applications concepts	226

Define Key Terms

8

Define the following key terms from this chapter and check your answers in the glossary:

network baseline, bandwidth, latency, quality of service (QoS), switch port security, session duration, network address translation (NAT), Dynamic Host Configuration Protocol (DHCP), domain, domain name server (DNS), listening port, port scanner, least privilege

Q&A

The answers to these questions appear in Appendix A, "Answers to the 'Do I Know This Already' Quizzes and Q&A." For more practice with exam format questions, use the exam engine on the website.

1. Which statement is true?

   a. NetFlow provides more details than capturing network packets.

   b. Capturing network packets provides more details than NetFlow.

   c. Capturing packets provides the same data as NetFlow.

   d. Technology cannot offer both packet capture and NetFlow capabilities.

2. Which of the following is *not* used to collect data for measuring throughput?

   a. Pulling data from a SPAN port

   b. Capturing data from a device that is in the line of traffic

   c. Gathering the number of routers, switches, and hosts on the network

   d. Capturing traffic from a gateway firewall

3. Which of the following protocols would provide the least value in explaining the type of device connected to a port?

   a. CDP

   b. LLDP

   c. DHCP

   d. DNS

4. What is the least valuable benefit for using session duration?

   a. Triggering when a critical system goes down

   b. Baselining network performance

   c. Detecting network breaches

   d. Identifying unusual network behavior

5. Which is *not* a reason for controlling asset address space?

   a. Segmenting hosts

   b. Network resource management

   c. Protecting critical assets

   d. Reducing costs

6. Which of the following is *not* an IPAM factor to consider?

   a. IP address inventory

   b. Endpoint posture

   c. Dynamic IP address services management

   d. IP name services management

7. Which of the following is *not* a value from profiling hosts on the network?

   a. Identifying devices that are potentially compromised

   b. Alerting to internal threats

   c. Understanding bandwidth utilization

   d. Identifying installed applications

8. Which of the following is *not* a method for identifying and securing listening ports?

   a. Implementing firewall technology

   b. Implementing strong access control policies

   c. Periodically scanning the network for listening ports

   d. Evaluating listening ports for risk

9. Which of the following is *not* a tool used for profiling host applications?

    a. Nmap version scanning

    b. Using content filters

    c. Using NetFlow

    d. Using NBAR

10. Which is *not* a tool for seeing running processes on a host?

    a. who

    b. tasklist

    c. ps -e

    d. Task Manager

8

This chapter covers the following topics:

■ Normalizing data

■ Using the 5-tuple correlation to respond to security incidents

■ Retrospective analysis and identifying malicious files

■ Mapping threat intelligence with DNS and other artifacts

■ Deterministic versus probabilistic analysis

CHAPTER 9

The Art of Data and Event Analysis

This chapter starts with details about how you can normalize security events and other data generated by different sources such as intrusion prevention systems (IPSs), firewalls, routers, and other infrastructure devices across your organization. In this chapter, you will also learn how to use the 5-tuple correlation to respond to security incidents. You will learn what retrospective analysis is and how to use it to reconstruct what happened after an attack has taken place. This chapter also teaches you how to use security tools to identify malicious files as well as how to map DNS, HTTP, and threat intelligence to identify and respond to attacks. Finally, this chapter ends with an explanation of the differences between deterministic and probabilistic analysis.

"Do I Know This Already?" Quiz

The "Do I Know This Already?" quiz helps you identify your strengths and deficiencies in this chapter's topics. The seven-question quiz, derived from the major sections in the "Foundation Topics" portion of the chapter, helps you determine how to spend your limited study time. Table 9-1 outlines the major topics discussed in this chapter and the "Do I Know This Already?" quiz questions that correspond to those topics.

Table 9-1 "Do I Know This Already?" Foundation Topics Section-to-Question Mapping

Foundation Topics Section	Questions Covered in This Section
Normalizing Data	1, 2
Using the 5-Tuple Correlation to Respond to Security Incidents	3
Retrospective Analysis and Identifying Malicious Files	4, 5
Mapping Threat Intelligence with DNS and Other Artifacts	6
Deterministic Versus Probabilistic Analysis	7

1. Which of the following is the process of capturing, storing, and analyzing data so that it exists in only one form?

    a. Data normalization

    b. Data correlation

    c. Big data analytics

    d. Retrospective analysis

2. Which of the following is not a data normalization method used in the industry?

    a. First normal form (1NF)

    b. First data ingest (FDI)

    c. Second normal form (2NF)

    d. Third normal form (3NF)

3. Which of the following is not an element in the 5-tuple?

    a. Source IP address

    b. Source port

    c. Protocol

    d. IP option

4. Which of the following describes the security event log shown here?

Timestamp	Signature ID	Src IP	Dst IP	Event
2018-10-30 T 10:45 UTC	1:41636	10.1.1.20	10.2.1.22	FILE-OTHER Adobe AcrobatDC EMF buffer underflow attempt (file-other.rules)

    a. NetFlow record

    b. Traditional firewall syslog

    c. WSA log

    d. Intrusion prevention system (IPS) or intrusion detection system (IDS) log

5. Which of the following statements is true about retrospective analysis?

    a. Cisco Talos uses threat intelligence from Cisco to perform retrospective analysis and protection. Cisco AMP also provides device and file trajectory capabilities to allow the security administrator to analyze the full spectrum of an attack.

    b. Cisco AMP for Endpoints uses threat intelligence from Cisco to perform retrospective analysis and protection. However, Cisco AMP for Networks does not support device and file trajectory capabilities to allow the security administrator to analyze the full spectrum of an attack.

    c. Cisco AMP uses threat intelligence from Cisco Talos to perform retrospective analysis and protection. Cisco AMP also provides device and file trajectory capabilities to allow the security administrator to analyze the full spectrum of an attack.

    d. Cisco AMP uses threat intelligence from Cisco WSA to perform retrospective analysis and protection. Cisco WSA also provides device and file trajectory capabilities to allow the security administrator to analyze the full spectrum of an attack.

6. Which of the following can be combined with security event logs to identify compromised systems and communications to command and control (CnC) servers?

   a. PII

   b. PHI

   c. AH/ESP

   d. DNS

7. In which type of analysis do you know and obtain "facts" about the incident, breach, and affected applications?

   a. Probabilistic

   b. Compound

   c. Deterministic

   d. Dynamic

Foundation Topics

Normalizing Data

Data normalization is the process of capturing, storing, and analyzing data (security-related events, in this case) so that it exists in only one form. One of the main goals of data normalization is to purge redundant data while maintaining data integrity. The normalized data is protected by making sure that any manifestation of the same data elsewhere is only making a reference to the data that is being stored.

Another goal of security data normalization is to eliminate the risk of evasions and ambiguities. There are different types of normalization, depending on levels of increasing complexity. The following are three different types of data normalization categories used in the industry:

- First normal form (1NF)
- Second normal form (2NF)
- Third normal form (3NF)

These categories can continue to increase in form and complexity, depending on your requirements and environmental needs.

Intrusion prevention systems (IPSs) focus on throughput for the most rapid and optimal inline performance. While doing so, in most cases, it is impossible for full normalization to take place. Traditional IPS devices often rely on shortcuts that only implement partial normalization and partial inspection. However, this increases the risk of evasions. Fragmentation handling is an example of such an evasion.

Next-generation IPS devices perform data normalization in a very effective way. They analyze data as a normalized stream instead of as single or combined packets. This ensures there is a unique way to interpret network traffic passing through the security appliance.

Interpreting Common Data Values into a Universal Format

It is important that you have a way to interpret common data values into a universal format and have a good data model. Okay, so what's a data model? It is a hierarchically structured mapping of semantic knowledge about one or more datasets. Having a good data model for all your security event data allows you to build an assortment of specialized (and fast) queries of those datasets.

In order for you to be able to create an effective data model, you must first understand the sources of security event data in your infrastructure. Figure 9-1 illustrates a security information and event management (SIEM) system receiving data from different sources, including IPS devices, firewalls, NetFlow generating devices, servers, endpoints, and syslogs from infrastructure devices.

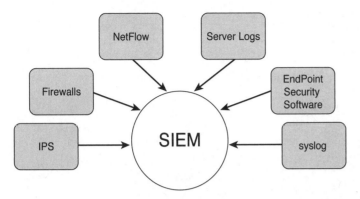

Figure 9-1   *SIEM Receiving Security Event Data from Different Sources*

Your data model architecture can be affected by how the security event data is structured from each of these sources and by your data semantics (how the different fields in your data are extracted, related, and organized).

Tools such as Splunk already accept data from well-known security devices and other sources. Such tools allow you to arrange the data to have it get additional fields at search time through regex-based field extractions, lookups, and evaluation expressions, once you have a data model created.

There's also a problem within the industry concerning the different ways security tools and humans refer to security events, incidents, and related information. This is why specifications such as the Vocabulary for Event Recording and Incident Sharing (VERIS) have been created. Per the website http://veriscommunity.net/veris-overview.html, "VERIS is a set of metrics designed to provide a common language for describing security incidents in a structured and repeatable manner. The overall goal is to lay a foundation on which we can constructively and cooperatively learn from our experiences to better manage risk."

> **NOTE**   Chapter 5, "Introduction to Incident Response and the Incident Handling Process," covers the VERIS model in greater detail.

Using the 5-Tuple Correlation to Respond to Security Incidents

While studying for the CCNA Cyber Ops SECFND exam, you learned about the concept of the 5-tuple. As a refresher, the 5-tuple refers to the following five elements:

- Source IP address
- Source port
- Destination IP address
- Destination port
- Protocol

This is also illustrated in Figure 9-2.

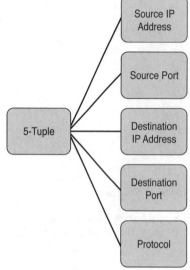

Figure 9-2 *The 5-Tuple*

Traditional firewalls typically provide security event logs that are mostly based on the 5-tuple. For instance, in traditional Cisco ASA logs, you might see logs similar to the following:

```
%ASA-3-106010: Deny inbound protocol
src [interface_name:source_address/source_port]([ idfw_user | FQDN_string ],
sg_info)] dst [ interface_name : dest_address / dest_port }
[(([ idfw_user | FQDN_string ], sg_info)]
```

The following is another example:

```
%ASA-6-106015: Deny TCP (no connection) from IP_address /port to IP_address /port
flags tcp_flags on interface interface_name
```

In the second example, the Cisco ASA dropped a TCP packet that didn't have any associated connection in its connection table. In short, the Cisco ASA looks for a SYN flag in the first packet of a TCP connection. The Cisco ASA will drop the packet if the SYN flag is not set and there is no existing connection.

TIP You also see the 5-tuple in IPS events, NetFlow records, and other event data. In fact, on the exam you may need to differentiate between a firewall log versus a traditional IPS or IDS event. One of the things to remember is that traditional IDS and IPS use signatures, so an easy way to differentiate is by looking for a signature ID (SigID). If you see a signature ID, then most definitely the event is a traditional IPS or IDS event.

Retrospective Analysis and Identifying Malicious Files

Cisco Advanced Malware Protection (AMP) for Networks and AMP for Endpoints provide mitigation capabilities that go beyond point-in-time detection. They use threat intelligence from Cisco TALOS to perform retrospective analysis and protection. Cisco AMP also provides device and file trajectory capabilities to allow the security administrator to analyze the full spectrum of an attack.

You can track the transmission of any file with an AMP cloud-assigned disposition. The system can use information related to detecting and blocking malware from both AMP for Networks (utilizing FirePOWER) and AMP for Endpoints to build the trajectory. The Network File Trajectory List page displays the malware most recently detected on your network, as well as the files whose trajectory maps you have most recently viewed. From these lists, you can view when each file was most recently seen on the network as well as the file's SHA-256 hash value, name, type, current file disposition, contents (for archive files), and the number of events associated with the file. The page also contains a search box that lets you locate a file based on SHA-256 hash value or filename or by the IP address of the host that transferred or received the file. After you locate a file, you can click the file SHA-256 value to view the detailed trajectory map.

Identifying a Malicious File

Figure 9-3 shows the Network File Trajectory screen of the Cisco Firepower Management Center (FMC) for some malware (in this case, a Trojan) called Win.Trojan.Wootbot-199.

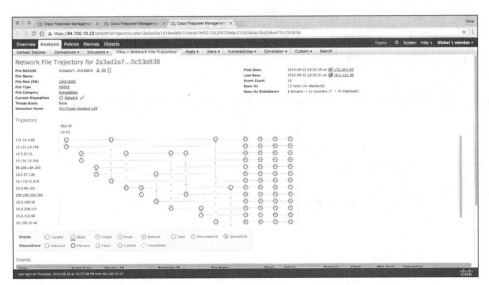

Figure 9-3 *Cisco FMC Network File Trajectory and Retrospective Analysis*

In Figure 9-3, you can see that the file was first seen on September 3 at 23:02 on two hosts (172.16.0.83 and 10.131.15.146). It then subsequently spread to several other hosts in the network, and you can see their IP addresses in the screen.

Mapping Threat Intelligence with DNS and Other Artifacts

Security threat intelligence is extremely useful when correlating events and to gain an insight into what known threats are in your network. DNS intelligence and URL reputation are used in many security solutions such as the Cisco Firepower appliances, Cisco Firepower Threat Defense (FTD), the Cisco Web and Email security appliances, and Cisco Umbrella. For instance, you can correlate security events based on threat intelligence to identify communications to known malicious command and control (CnC) servers based on DNS information. Figure 9-4 shows different security threat intelligence events in the Cisco FMC.

Figure 9-4 *Cisco FMC Security Intelligence Events*

In Figure 9-4, you can see that a host (10.112.70.34) is communicating to a known CnC server based on DNS threat intelligence data.

Deterministic Versus Probabilistic Analysis

Two methods for security analysis have been described and implemented in the industry: deterministic and probabilistic.

In deterministic analysis, all data used for the analysis is known beforehand. Probabilistic analysis, on the other hand, is done assuming the likelihood that something will or has happened, but you don't know exactly when or how.

Probabilistic methods institute powerful tools for use in many kinds of decision-making problems—in this case, cybersecurity event analysis. In this type of analysis, the analysis components suggest a "probabilistic answer" to the results of the investigation, which is not a definitive result.

In deterministic analysis, you know and obtain "facts" about the incident, breach, affected applications, and so on. For instance, by analyzing applications using port-based analysis and similar methods, you can assume that the process is deterministic—especially when applications conform to the specifications of the standards. Unfortunately, some applications do not follow the standards. A good example is peer-to-peer (P2P) applications, which try to evade firewalls by using ephemeral ports. This is why, in many cases, probabilistic analysis is done.

9

Exam Preparation Tasks

Review All Key Topics

Review the most important topics in the chapter, noted with the Key Topic icon in the outer margin of the page. Table 9-2 lists these key topics and the page numbers on which each is found.

Table 9-2 Key Topics

Key Topic Element	Description	Page
Summary	Describe what data normalization is.	238
Summary	Understand how to interpret common data values into a universal format.	238
Summary	Describe how to use the 5-tuple correlation to respond to security incidents.	239
Figure 9-2	The five elements that make up the 5-tuple.	240
Summary	Define what retrospective analysis is and how to identify malicious files.	241
Summary	How to map threat intelligence with DNS and other artifacts.	242
Summary	Contrast probabilistic versus deterministic analysis.	242

Complete Tables and Lists from Memory

Print a copy of Appendix B, "Memory Tables," (found on the book website), or at least the section for this chapter, and complete the tables and lists from memory. Appendix C, "Memory Tables Answer Key," also on the website, includes completed tables and lists to check your work.

Define Key Terms

Define the following key terms from this chapter and check your answers in the glossary:

Data normalization, 5-tuple

Q&A

The answers to these questions appear in Appendix A, "Answers to the 'Do I Know This Already' Quizzes and Q&A." For more practice with exam format questions, use the exam engine on the website.

1. What is the type of security or event log or record described in the following table?

Source IP Address	Destination IP Address	Source Port	Destination Port	IP Protocol	Next Hop	TCP Flags
10.10.1.8	10.8.7.2	48392	443	6	10.10.1.1	0x1A

   a. NetFlow record

   b. IPS event

   c. IDS event

   d. Traditional firewall log

2. What type of security event log is the following?

   ```
   %ASA-6-106015: Deny TCP (no connection) from 192.168.1.22/7263 to 10.1.2.3/80
   flags 0xA1 on interface dmz.
   ```

   a. A firewall syslog

   b. IDS event

   c. IPS event

   d. NetFlow

3. Which of the following can be identified by correlating DNS intelligence and other security events? (Choose two.)

   a. Communication to CnC servers

   b. Configuration issues

   c. Malicious domains based on reputation

   d. Routing problems

4. Cisco Advanced Malware Protection (AMP) for Networks and AMP for Endpoints provide mitigation capabilities that go beyond point-in-time detection. Which of the following is an example of this capability?

   a. Hashing

   b. DLP

   c. Using threat intelligence to perform retrospective analysis and protection

   d. Encryption

5. Which of the following is one of the main goals of data normalization?

   a. To save duplicate logs for redundancy

   b. To purge redundant data while maintaining data integrity

   c. To correlate IPS and IDS logs with DNS

   d. To correlate IPS/IDS logs with firewall logs

9

This chapter covers the following exam topics:

- Classify intrusion events based on the Diamond Model of Intrusion

- Define the Cyber Kill Chain Model

  - Understand reconnaissance as the first stage of an attack

  - Touch on developing attacks known as weaponization

  - Identify when an attack is delivered as it's related to the kill chain

  - What exploitation means in regard to the Kill Chain Model

  - Installation as a step following exploitation

  - What it means to have command and control access to a network

- Understand defense best practices against the threats represented by the Cyber Kill Chain Model

CHAPTER 10

Intrusion Event Categories

Now that we have covered analyzing data and events, let's look at how to handle categorizing an incident that is identified during the monitoring process. A *security incident* is any event that threatens the security, confidentiality, integrity, or availability of something of value, such as assets, technical systems, networks, and so on. Things that can be identified as threats and would trigger an incident are violations of security policies, user policies, or general security practices. Examples would be unauthorized access to a system, denying services, exploiting vulnerabilities, and removing sensitive data.

Today's IT market offers dozens of options for tools and many documented methods that can be used to develop how your organization categorizes an incident, which is the core of an incident management practice. The SECOPS exam was designed to follow industry best practices and therefore identified the *Diamond Model of Intrusion* as a trusted approach to categorizing security incidents. The reason behind creating the Diamond Model was to develop a repeatable way to characterize and organize threats, consistently track identified threats, and eventually develop measures to counter them. Basically, the Diamond Model of Intrusion provides a structured method for the IT security analyst to use.

The end result of the Diamond Model is to increase the cost on the adversary while reducing the cost of the defender. When it comes to IT security, the concept of reducing the risk of being compromised by a cyber attack means nothing is 100%, so the best-case scenario for the defender is to make the cost of attacking his or her assets higher than the value of an adversary achieving a successful attack. This is accomplished by blending information assurance strategies (reducing risk) with cyber threat intelligence (adapting to the adversary). Having this data gives the incident response team the ability to identify elements of the attack structure as well as highlight intelligence gaps, making it easier to proactively plan the best defense actions. Let's take a closer look at how the Diamond Model works.

"Do I Know This Already?" Quiz

The "Do I Know This Already?" quiz allows you to assess whether you should read this entire chapter thoroughly or jump to the "Exam Preparation Tasks" section. If you are in doubt about your answers to these questions or your own assessment of your knowledge of the topics, read the entire chapter. Table 10-1 lists the major headings in this chapter and their corresponding "Do I Know This Already?" quiz questions. You can find the answers in Appendix A, "Answers to the 'Do I Know This Already?' Quizzes and Q&A."

Table 10-1 "Do I Know This Already?" Section-to-Question Mapping

Foundation Topics Section	Questions
Diamond Model of Intrusion	1–3
Cyber Kill Chain Model	4–10

1. Which of the following is *not* true about the Diamond Model of Intrusion?

   a. Adversaries use an infrastructure or capability to access a victim.

   b. Meta-features are not a required component of the Diamond Model.

   c. Technology and social metadata features establish connections between relations.

   d. A diamond represents a single event.

2. Which of the following is a false statement about activity threads in the Diamond Model?

   a. Activity threads are the relationship between diamonds.

   b. Activity threads can spread across to other attacks.

   c. Activity threads can involve more than one victim.

   d. Activity threads are possible attacks the attacker could use against the victim.

3. An activity-attack graph is useful for determining which of the following?

   a. Logging attacks seen by an adversary

   b. Highlighting the attacker's preferences for attacking the victim as well as alternative paths that could be used

   c. Developing reactive but not proactive security planning

   d. An alternative to threat intelligence

4. Which of the following is *not* a step in the kill chain?

   a. Weaponization

   b. C2

   c. Installation

   d. Data exfiltration

5. What is the difference between delivery and exploitation according to the kill chain?

   a. Delivery is how the attacker communicates with the victim whereas exploitation is the attack used against the victim.

   b. Exploitation is an example of a delivery step in the kill chain.

   c. Exploitation and delivery are different names for the same step.

   d. Delivery is how the attack is delivered whereas exploitation is the type of attack.

6. Which of the following is *not* an example of reconnaissance?

   a. Searching the robots.txt file

   b. Redirecting users to a source and scanning traffic to learn about the target

   c. Scanning without completing the three-way handshake

   d. Communicating over social media

7. Which of the following is the best explanation of the command and control phase of the kill chain?

   a. When the compromised system opens ports for communication

   b. When the attacker accesses the breached network using a keyboard

   c. When the malware reaches back to a remote server for instructions

   d. When the attacker breaches a network

8. Which of the following is an example of an action step from the kill chain?

   a. Attacking another target

   b. Taking data off the network

   c. Listening to traffic inside the network

   d. All of the above

9. Which of the following is the best explanation of early detection of threats in the kill chain?

   a. Starting analysis at the reconnaissance phase to begin detection weaponization

   b. Starting analysis at the delivery phase to begin detection at the exploitation phase

   c. Starting analysis at the reconnaissance phase to begin detection at the delivery phase

   d. Starting analysis at the exploitation phase to begin detection at the installation phase

10. Which of the following is a true statement?

   a. Firewalls are best for detecting insider threats.

   b. Behavior-based technologies are best for detecting insider threats.

   c. Antivirus is effective for detecting known threats.

   d. Insider threats are best detected with signature-based security.

10

Foundation Topics

Diamond Model of Intrusion

The Diamond Model is designed to represent an incident, also called an event, and is made up of four parts. Active intrusions start with an adversary who is targeting a victim. The adversary will use various capabilities along some form of infrastructure to launch an attack against the victim. Capabilities can be various forms of tools, techniques, and procedures, while the infrastructure is what connects the adversary and victim. The lines connecting each part of the model depict a mapping of how one point reached another. For example, the analyst could see how a capability such as a phishing attack is being used over an infrastructure such as email and then relate the capabilities back to the adversary. Moving between each part of an attack is called *analytic pivoting* and is key for modeling the event.

The Diamond Model also includes additional meta-features of an event, such as a timestamp, kill chain phase, result of the attack, direction of the attack, attack method, and resources used. An example of a meta-feature list might show a timestamp of 1:05 p.m. The kill chain phase could be exploitation, the result could be successful, the direction could be adversary to victim, the attack method could be spear-phishing, and the resources could be a specific vulnerability on the victim's host system. Meta-features provide useful context but are not core to the model, so they can be disregarded and augmented as necessary. Figure 10-1 shows a graphical view of the Diamond Model with metadata features.

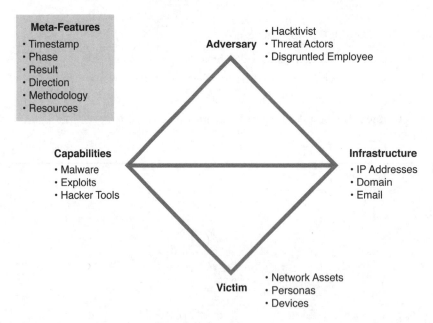

Figure 10-1   *The Diamond Model of Intrusion*

The Diamond Model can be expanded further by adding two additional meta-features that establish connections between relations. The *technology* meta-feature connects capabilities and infrastructure by describing the technology used between these two parts of the model. An example of a technology meta-feature could be the domain name system (DNS) if it is used by malware to determine its command-and-control point. The *social-political* meta-feature represents the relationship between the adversary and victim. This is critical to determine the intent behind the attack so the analyst can understand the reason the victim was selected and the value the adversary sees in the victim, as well as sometimes identify a *shared threat space*, meaning a situation where multiple victims link back to the same adversaries. A shared threat space equates to threat intelligence—that is, understanding threat actors in a specific space to potentially forecast and react to future malicious activity. An example might be threat actors identified for launching an attack campaign against hospitals. Figure 10-2 represents the extended version of the Diamond Model.

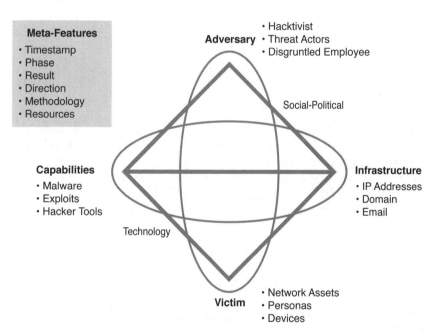

Figure 10-2   *The Extended Diamond Model of Intrusion*

Each event is considered a diamond using this model. An incident management practice should use the Diamond Model as the basis for grouping and organizing incidents. The goal would be to review multiple diamonds and identify a common adversary. For example, let's consider an attack where the adversary is delivering ransomware to a victim. The first part of the attack could involve the adversary using a malicious email to trick the victim into accessing a website. The goal is to have the website scan the victim for vulnerabilities and deliver ransomware by exploiting one of those weaknesses. The first stage of the attack could be represented as one diamond, as shown in Figure 10-3.

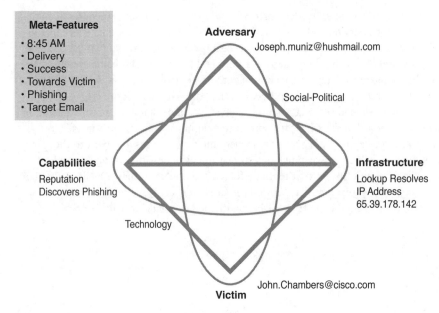

Figure 10-3   *Stage 1 of Ransomware Attack*

Stage 2 of the attack follows the phishing email that redirected the victim's system to the malicious website. Now that the victim's system has accessed the website, the malicious website will push down the ransomware by exploiting a vulnerability. The adversary is still the same attacker; however, the capabilities and infrastructure involved with the second part of the security incident have changed, which is common when identifying all stages of an attack according to the kill chain concept. Figure 10-4 showcases a diamond for stage 2 of this attack.

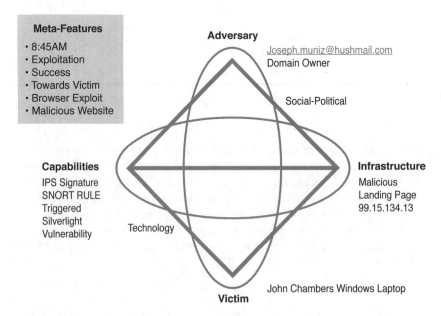

Figure 10-4   *Stage 2 of the Ransomware Attack*

Instances of the same event occurring over the course of a few weeks could be linked together through multiple diamonds and then linked back to the same adversary. Linking the spear-phishing attack to the delivery of ransomware can give an analyst a method to diagram the attack and all associated adversaries. The incident response team should create an activity group based on the various connected diamonds and attempt to define what combinations of elements are criteria for grouping diamonds together. As new diamonds appear, activity groups can grow as diamonds are grouped together based on newly available data. The relationships between diamonds are known as *activity threads*, which can spread across the same attack as well as connect other attacks, depending on intelligence gathered that meets activity group requirements. Figure 10-5 provides an example of building an activity thread based on the previous sample attack data.

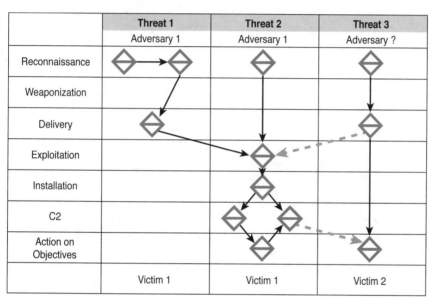

Figure 10-5 *Developing an Activity Thread*

Figure 10-5 shows an adversary is linked to two different attacks against the same victim as well as possibly another victim, represented with the dashed line. There is also another possible adversary attacking a similar victim as the previously identified adversary. This visibility into the attack data gives analysts the ability to integrate any hypotheses that can be tested as additional evidence is gathered. The activity thread process displays the current research status, which can help an analyst identify knowledge gaps and adversary campaigns through documentation and testing proposed attack hypotheses.

Once the incident management team builds a decent sized activity group mapping out multiple incidents, the team can better analyze the data to fill in missing knowledge gaps and start to potentially predict future attack paths. This threat intelligence data can be built into a graph, known as an *attack graph*, representing the paths an adversary could take against the victim. Within the attack graph are *activity threats*, which are paths the adversary has already taken. Combining the attack and activity data gives the team an *activity-attack graph*, which is useful for highlighting the attacker's preferences for attacking the victim

10

as well as alternative paths that could be used. This gives the incident response team a way to focus efforts on defending against the adversary, by knowing where to likely expect the attack as well as being aware of other possible risks to the victim. Figure 10-6 is an example of an activity-attack group for our ransomware example.

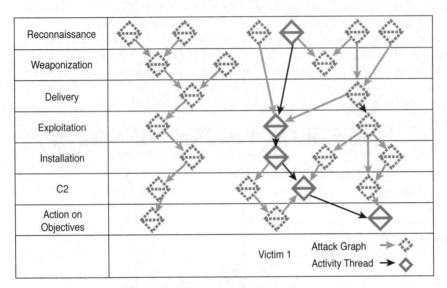

Figure 10-6 *Activity-Attack Group Example*

If the analyst was concerned that this was a persistent attack, using the activity-attack group could show not only where defenses should be considered for the identified active attack but also additional areas that could be used by the adversary and therefore should be secured proactively. By grouping common malicious events, adversary processes, and threads, the analyst can create activity groups. Figure 10-6 would help the analyst determine which combination of events make up an activity group based on similar characteristics. Activity groups can then be grouped into activity group families used to model the organizations behind the various incidents, such as identifying a particular organization crime syndicate. The end result could be the identification of a particular group out of Ukraine attempting to plant ransomware at a specific U.S.-based hospital through the analyst grouping together various events against multiple hosts linked to the hospital.

Cyber Kill Chain Model

Looking back at Figure 10-5 and Figure 10-6, you will notice along the left edge of the graph a list of steps representing the progress of the adversary's attack. This chain of events, known as the *Cyber Kill Chain Model*, represents steps taken by an adversary to accomplish an intrusion. The Cyber Kill Chain Model was first introduced by Lockheed Martin and is continuously referenced as a method to explain cyber intrusions activity. The model can be summarized as follows: In order for an adversary to accomplish an intrusion, the aggressor must develop some form of a payload that will be used to breach the victim's trusted boundary, establish a foothold inside the trusted environment, and take some form of malicious action. Here are the steps of the Kill Chain Model:

- Reconnaissance
- Weaponization
- Delivery
- Exploitation
- Installation
- Command and control (C2)
- Actions on objectives

The goal for any incident management practice is to catch an attack as early in the kill chain as possible. This includes improvising existing incident response capabilities so that repeating threats are caught earlier in the kill chain as the management practice matures in capabilities and technology. Figure 10-7 demonstrates detecting an incident early and late in the kill chain, where the lighter line is early detection and darker line is late. Look back at our attack example: Early detection could be identifying the website attempting to exploit the host, whereas late detection could be the network IPS identifying an internally breached host system with ransomware installed that's communicating out to a remote server that will initiate the encryption handshake process. Possible actions for identifying this attack earlier in the kill chain could be patching the vulnerability that was exploited and blocking where the attack was delivered using reputation-based security.

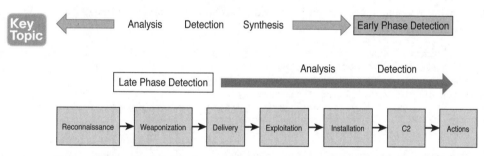

Figure 10-7 *Early and Late Detection in the Kill Chain Example*

Now that you have an understanding of the Diamond Model, let's look closer at each step of the Kill Chain Model. The following is a list of some key points to remember before moving forward:

- The Diamond Model was developed as a repeatable way to characterize and organize threats, consistently track identified threats, and develop measures to counter them.
- The Diamond Model represents an event and is made up of an adversary, victim, capability, and infrastructure. Lines between these items represent how the adversary reaches the victim.
- Meta-features provide useful context but are not core to the model.
- The Extended Diamond Model includes two additional meta-features—technology and social-political—thus further establishing a connection between relations.

- Diamonds can be grouped together into activity threads to identify related attacks.

- Activity-attack graphs can be used to highlight the attacker's preferences for attacking the victim as well as alternative paths that could be used for predicting future attacks.

Reconnaissance

The first and by far the most critical step to an attack is the quality of reconnaissance. Reconnaissance is research on a target and typically is the most time-consuming yet most rewarding step of the kill chain. Goals for this phase are to identify targets, associations to the targets, and as much data as possible about each target. The more data that's found provides more options for planning a more effective attack. For example, an adversary's goal may be to breach a network; however, there are many ways this could be accomplished. Knowing as much as possible about the target would help determine the best approach— meaning the easiest, least costly, and lowest risk to being identified. An example would be identifying multiple web-facing servers and uncovering a vulnerable version of software installed on one of the servers, making it the ideal target to exploit.

Some examples of valuable data adversaries target to capture during the reconnaissance phase are identified targets, applications, systems, available ports, running services, information about people, and documents. There are many methods adversaries could use to gather this information. The first common place that is researched is the target's website. This can divulge tons of information, including data that was not intended to be publicly available. An example of this is pulling up the robots.txt file of a website, which tells search engines what should and what should not be visible. Figure 10-8 is an example of the robots.txt file from Facebook, showing a bunch of areas of interest that the Facebook IT team has designated as "Disallow," meaning "hide from spiders."

```
← → C  🔒 https://www.facebook.com/robots.txt

# Notice: if you would like to crawl Facebook you can
# contact us here: http://www.facebook.com/apps/site_scraping_tos.php
# to apply for white listing. Our general terms are available
# at http://www.facebook.com/apps/site_scraping_tos_terms.php

User-agent: baiduspider
Disallow: /ac.php
Disallow: /ae.php
Disallow: /ajax/
Disallow: /album.php
Disallow: /ap.php
Disallow: /autologin.php
Disallow: /checkpoint/
Disallow: /feeds/
Disallow: /l.php
Disallow: /o.php
Disallow: /p.php
Disallow: /photo.php
Disallow: /photo_comments.php
Disallow: /photo_search.php
Disallow: /photos.php
Disallow: /share.php
Disallow: /sharer/
```

Figure 10-8 *Facebook Robots.txt*

Another method for finding data that isn't intended to be publicly available is looking at an older version of a website using the WayBack Machine found at http://archive.org. Older versions of a website could reveal employees who left the company, information about IT services from previous recruiting efforts, associations with other organizations, and so on. Another place to find sensitive documents and information is the EDGAR database, which contains registration statements, periodic reports, and other forms of information on American-based companies since 1994.

One popular source for reconnaissance is social media sources. Most humans are trusting by default and tend to share too much information about where they work and what they are interested in. This data tends to bleed into how they access and secure their data, such as disclosing what experience they have on LinkedIn profiles or hobbies on Facebook, which could also be terms used for passwords. The same goes for companies, meaning recruiting efforts tend to present too much data about what systems are being protected. For example, a job posting stating a need for a Cisco FirePOWER engineer would probably mean that this is one of the security solutions an adversary would have to be prepared to bypass.

Other techniques can be used to gather the vast amount of data left behind on the Internet. Specific searches on Google, known as Google hacking, can pull up unsecure systems connected to the public Internet. An example could be using the search "inurl:main.cgi Linksys" to pull up publicly available Linksys cameras. Figure 10-9 shows an accessed, unsecured Linksys camera displaying a highway from a condo's balcony. I was also able to move the camera to get a view of the entire landscape. This may seem like a low threat; however, we have found much more interesting cameras using this tactic, such as the cameras monitoring the information security group of a customer we were performing a penetration test against! Check out the Google Hacking Database found at www.hackersforcharity.org for more information on Google hacking.

Metadata tools such as Foca and Shodan can be useful for finding unintended data about target systems. The Shodan search engine can identify a specific device, such as a server or network router using metadata from system banners. An example might be pulling up the model and software version of a target's router, such as a Cisco 3850 running IOS version 15.0(1)EX. This level of data is great for mapping vulnerabilities to systems running older software.

10

Other network-based reconnaissance activities could include DNS, ICMP, and port research using tools such as Nmap and Maltego, or just basic requests such as issuing **dig**, which queries DNS servers associated with a target. Figure 10-10 shows a **dig** request against www. thesecurityblogger.com.

Figure 10-9 *Unsecure Linksys Camera*

```
root@kali:~/Desktop# dig www.thesecurityblogger.com

; <<>> DiG 9.9.5-12.1-Debian <<>> www.thesecurityblogger.com
;; global options: +cmd
;; Got answer:
;; ->>HEADER<<- opcode: QUERY, status: NOERROR, id: 40358
;; flags: qr rd ra; QUERY: 1, ANSWER: 1, AUTHORITY: 0, ADDITIONAL: 1

;; OPT PSEUDOSECTION:
; EDNS: version: 0, flags:; udp: 512
;; QUESTION SECTION:
;www.thesecurityblogger.com.      IN      A

;; ANSWER SECTION:
www.thesecurityblogger.com. 14400 IN     A        64.90.49.201

;; Query time: 39 msec
;; SERVER: 75.75.75.75#53(75.75.75.75)
;; WHEN: Mon Sep 12 21:50:57 EDT 2016
;; MSG SIZE  rcvd: 71

root@kali:~/Desktop# 
```

Figure 10-10 *Dig Reconnaissance Example*

The end result of good reconnaissance should be a list of possible targets, with details regarding what software they are running, open ports, available services, associated administrators, and so on. At this point, the adversary can select the best method for the attack, thus moving things to the weaponization phase of the kill chain.

Weaponization

Once an adversary has identified the easiest and best target and approach to launch an attack, the next step is to develop and test how the attack will be executed. Typically, reconnaissance will provide guidance for how the attack is developed based on identified vulnerabilities that could be exploited. An example might be researching a vulnerability on the server found during the reconnaissance stage and matching a known exploit to use against it. A lab could be built where the adversary installs a similar version of software on a test system as what was found on the target's network. He or she could then attempt to exploit it and confirm a successful exploitation of the vulnerability is possible.

One popular tool used by adversaries to develop exploits against vulnerabilities is the Metasploit framework. Metasploit has many functions, including a large list of exploits for known vulnerabilities. An adversary could use the search command to identify a specific vulnerability, or he or she could leverage Nessus, which will uncover vulnerabilities during a scan of the system and automatically map possible exploits. Metasploit also provides options to perform upon executing the exploit, such as delivering a remote access tool (RAT), gaining root-level access on the target, and so on. Figure 10-11 shows an example of searching Metasploit for the term "usermap_script" and identifying one exploit ranked as "excellent," meaning it's very likely to be successful against the target. You can learn more about Metasploit by visiting https://www.offensive-security.com/metasploit-unleashed.

```
msf > search usermap_script

Matching Modules
================

    Name                                Disclosure Date   Rank        Description
    ----                                ---------------   ----        -----------
    exploit/multi/samba/usermap_script  2007-05-14        excellent   Samba "username map script" Command Execution

msf >
```

Figure 10-11 *Example of Searching Metasploit*

It is important to realize that this is how real-world breaches occur. TV shows such as *24* feature scenes where cast members ask so called "elite hackers" to breach an unknown target within seconds. Yes, attacks can happen within seconds; however, the attacks that are executed in the real world are typically planned and tested before being launched against a target. It is rare in the real world that an adversary can blindly pick a target and successfully exploit the victim. Rare does not mean impossible, though. There are examples of getting a victim to click something (an email, web link, and so on) that will instantaneously own them. Metasploit can also be used to generate payloads using the msfpayload options. Figure 10-12 shows an example of a malicious executable we created called important.exe that will provide us a backdoor to any system it is executed on. You might think antivirus will catch such an attack. However, Metasploit also includes encoders that add additional data to the payload to make it look unique and thus not like anything antivirus would be capable of detecting.

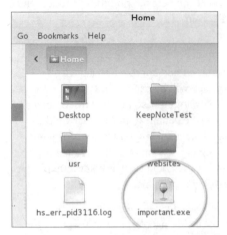

Figure 10-12   *Malicious Executable Created in Metasploit*

The key to the success of an adversary's attack is how it is executed. The example showing important.exe may be effective; however, it must somehow get onto the target's system. The delivery of the attack represents the next phase of the kill chain process.

Delivery

Having a great exploit won't do you any good if you can't properly deliver it against your intended target. For example, the adversary's goal could be to place the backdoor titled important.exe on a host; however, the malicious software must somehow get to the target and be installed through some form of exploitation. Delivering an attack can follow many steps and leverage a combination of physical, digital, and social methods. Some common delivery methods are communicating over a network to a target, redirecting a target to a malicious source, and placing the payload onto a mobile storage medium such as a USB stick. Sometimes the adversary can just ask the target to install the malicious software using social engineering tactics.

Many adversaries use a combination of delivery methods to sneak the payload over. For example, an adversary could exploit a victim's server directory from the adversary's computer; however, that would possibly expose the attacker's location, providing a possible method to be tracked. As an alternative, to avoid detection from the target's incident management team, the adversary could first attempt to breach a trusted host on the victim's network and launch the attack from that system post-compromise. To breach the host without directly attacking it, the adversary could set up a malicious website and send an email to the target claiming the host has missed a USPS package delivery, however they can "click the link" to check the status of the package. Clicking the link would direct the victim's system to a malicious web page designed to breach the host based on identified vulnerabilities in installed versions of Java or Flash. This social engineering tactic is very effective for moving an attack to a remote server that can be hidden behind deep web resources, thus concealing the origin of the adversary. Figure 10-13 is an example of a phishing email designed to get the target to click a link that takes him or her to a malicious server.

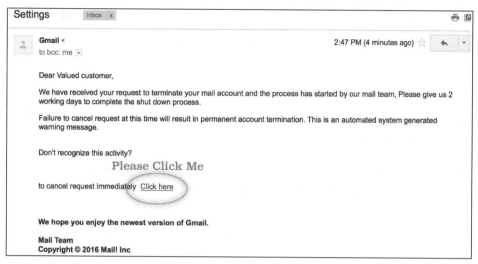

Figure 10-13   *Phishing Email Example*

Once the adversary delivers the attack, the next phase of the kill chain maps how the attack exploits the target.

Exploitation

Avoiding exploitation tends to be the focus of many security administrators, yet it is the most challenging step of the kill chain to defend against because there are just too many things that can be vulnerable to exploitation. A security administrator could perform a thorough assessment of the network, but a new vulnerability could become available to an adversary as soon as the assessment is complete. New vulnerabilities could originate from a new user coming on the network, the misconfiguration of a device, an industry vulnerability announcement requiring a patch to fix, and so on. This is why infrastructure maintenance practices such as patch management are so critical to the quality of security for an organization.

Many attacks seen in the wild leverage known vulnerabilities, meaning there usually is a patch to fix them as well as a signature to enable on security devices to prevent these vulnerabilities from being exploited. An example is the recent outbreak of the ransomware known as SamSam, which targets a 2007/2010 vulnerability found in JBoss systems. RedHat has released patches for this vulnerability and security vendors such as Cisco have released signatures (Snort signatures 18794, 24642, 21516, 24342, and 24343), yet you can search Google using the term "/status&full=true" and find thousands of systems that have been or will be compromised by the SamSam ransomware due to this JBoss vulnerability. Figure 10-14 shows an example of a JBoss server that was found using the previously mentioned Google search with a possible SamSam backdoor installed.

10

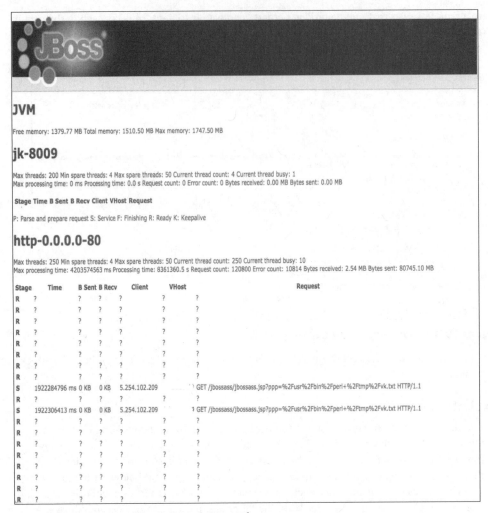

Figure 10-14 *JBoss Server Search Example*

Most quality intrusion detection and prevention systems have more signatures available to use for defense than the solution can enforce, meaning a security administrator can only tune the system to match what is considered the most important vulnerabilities to defend against. Turning on all the signature checks on quality security tools would render the security solution useless based on the sheer number of checks available. This highlights the need for proper tuning of security devices to avoid a gap between what it is configured to defend against versus what vulnerabilities actually exist on the network. The same concepts apply to other signature-based technologies such as antivirus. An example would be having industry signatures such as heartbleed and shellshock automatically enabled by the vendor; however, a specific vulnerability in a web server might not be part of the vendor's auto-enablement list, meaning proper tuning would be required to ensure these and other additional vulnerabilities are protected against.

The exploitation step, in summary, is when an attack is delivered to a target and launched against a vulnerability. This often involves abusing a weakness in an operating system or application, but could be something the victim decides to execute, such as the important.exe malicious application example covered previously.

Once the exploitation completes, something needs to be done following the successful exploitation. Adversaries don't exploit systems just to see if it can be done. Typically something is delivered through the exploitation process, which leads us to the next step in the kill chain process.

Installation

The installation step of the kill chain tends to be an area that is overlooked by security operations teams because administrators tend to by hyper-focused on avoiding exploitation using tools such as antivirus and IPS, not thinking about what happens if something gets past those security products. This is why companies will appear in the news claiming they have been compromised for years yet have invested in security solutions to protect their network. The issue is they probably didn't balance out their security defense investments and were, for example, lacking breach detection capabilities. The industry average for most organizations to identify a security breach takes anywhere from 100 to 200 days, giving an adversary plenty of time to accomplish the remaining steps of the kill chain. The goal for an incident management team for this stage of the attack is to include products and practices that reduce the time to identify and remediate a breach to a reasonable amount of time. A reasonable amount of time could be less than 24 hours, which would make it very difficult for an adversary to accomplish the remaining steps of the kill chain. Think of breach detection as a method to reduce the exposure time to a breach versus preventing an attack.

NOTE It is important to be aware that all steps after the exploitation phase of the kill chain involve a breach, meaning that any security features designed to prevent an exploit will most likely not help at this stage of the attack.

The installation step of the kill chain can simply be seen as an adversary successfully installing the previously developed weapon and being capable of maintaining persistence inside the target system or environment. Sometimes this step is referred to as "establishing a foothold," meaning the adversary can now access the network through the newly established communication channel. Examples of backdoors are remote access tools (RATs), unauthorized VPN sessions (such as an SSH tunnel from a server), and simply having login rights (possibly from stealing the target system's authentication credentials). It is common for an adversary to pivot to other systems and establish similar communication channels to further improve the foothold on the network since any breached system could eventually be patched or leave the network.

Once the adversary has installed the malicious software and has persistent access to the system, he or she must take control of the system to start attempting to accomplish the end goal of attacking the victim. This leads us to the next phase of the kill chain.

10

Command and Control

This phase of the kill chain is when the attacker accesses the breached system. Sometimes this is accomplished by listening for a beacon coming from the target, informing the adversary that a command and control (C2) channel is available to access. Sometimes the adversary must manually attempt to connect to the target system using a specific port to test whether the installation of the malicious software was successful. The end result of this phase is providing the adversary "hands-on-keyboard" access inside the target environment.

It is important to point out that there are various levels of user and network rights that may or may not be available to an adversary at this stage of the attack. This is why identity management and access control are extremely important for ensuring that only the necessary services are provisioned to hosts and systems. If an adversary gets keyboard access to a host that is limited to a specific part of the network, that adversary must attempt some form of network pivoting if the attack is to move beyond the limited area of the currently owned network. Sometimes the level of access on the breached server is only for a guest account, meaning the adversary will have limited keyboard commands available unless he or she can perform a privilege escalation attack to gain more access rights on the target system. This example stresses the need for not giving all users within the organization administrative rights to their systems.

Insider threats are on the rise today as most all devices are now enabled with IP capabilities. Each new device requires the same level of defenses; otherwise, it will become your weakest link, thus potentially leading to a breach. This is challenging for administrators based on the possible lack of security tools available for certain device types, not to mention laziness for securing the products or associated applications. Examples of uncommon devices I have in my home with IP capabilities are my Ring doorbell and Nest thermostat (see Figure 10-15). These devices not only could lead to access to my internal network, but they also contain sensitive data, such as when I leave my home. The Ring doorbell triggers when there is movement in front of my house, and the Nest thermostat switches to Away mode when my phone is out of home range.

Once the adversary has keyboard access, he or she is ready to start working toward the goal for attacking the victim, which is the final stage of the kill chain.

Figure 10-15 *Ring Doorbell and Nest Thermostat iPhone Applications*

Action and Objectives

This is the point of the kill chain that keeps executives up at night. The last stage of the kill chain represents when an adversary is inside the network and starting to achieve his or her objective for launching the attack. An adversary could use this opportunity to steal data. The process for doing this typically takes many more steps, as the adversary needs to locate the data, gain access to it, and remove it without being interrupted. Sometimes the adversary just wants to listen on the network and collect sensitive information versus pivoting around the network. An example of this was when a group of Ukraine hackers breached servers owned by the Newswire Association LLC, MarketWired, and Business Wire to pilfer corporate press announcements. The hackers traded on the inside information, raking in close to $30 million over a five-year period.

Sometimes the goal of a particular event is a smaller step in a larger attack. This means that the objective of one attack could be just to establish an internal point to launch the next layer of a bigger attack that will start at the beginning of the kill chain, but now within the target's environment. This is why the Diamond Model of Intrusion leverages the Kill Chain Model and offers the ability to develop activity-attack groups to identify the true intentions of the identified adversaries as well as to potentially get ahead of future attacks.

Defending against a breach should include a handful of best practices. The first is a need for identity management and network segmentation. This limits what systems and resources are available to anything that is compromised. An example of a Cisco solution that provides this capability is Cisco Identity Services Engine (ISE). Some benefits of a solution such as this include knowing who or what is accessing the network, controlling what they can access, and assessing those devices for risks.

The next best practice is having behavior- and anomaly-based monitoring within the network, looking for unusual and possibly malicious behavior. Malicious behavior should be understood as actions that are seen as threatening, including many of the steps in the kill chain. For example, identifying internal network scanning or attempts to exploit a vulnerable internal server would most likely indicate malicious behavior. Anomaly behavior, however, is slightly different. An example would be a user doing something that is potentially authorized but weird and atypical of that user—for instance, a user attempting to log in to various servers as an administrator when that user has never expressed needing those privileges. Another example could be based on the timing of the action, such as establishing a VPN to a remote server at 3:00 on a Saturday morning.

Cisco offers a handful of technologies that have breach-detection capabilities. Cisco Advanced Malware Protection (AMP) analyzes any file seen on the network or endpoint looking for malicious behavior. This goes beyond what typical antivirus and other signature-based technologies use to identify threats. A key capability AMP offers is not only identifying threats but also providing retrospective security. This is accomplished by developing a hash of any file seen, so if a threat is identified, a hash record can be traced to identify any system, including the first system infected with the file. This is critical to not only removing the threat but also learning how the first system was exploited to remediate and avoid future compromises. Figure 10-16 shows an example of Cisco AMP detecting multiple systems infected with a malicious file. The pop-up shown in the figure represents the first system with the infection, revealing the details of how that system was compromised.

Another solution from Cisco involves using NetFlow, as covered earlier in this book. Cisco StealthWatch uses NetFlow to baseline the network with the goal of identifying unusual behavior, which could represent an insider threat. An example would be data-loss detection from an unusual behavior viewpoint. This could be triggered if a user is seen exporting large amounts of data using an unusual protocol, at an unusual time, for the first time in over a year of profiling the system. Maybe this action is okay, but it would be something an administrator should be concerned about and is worth investigating. Figure 10-17 represents the StealthWatch dashboard showing some examples of malicious and unusual activities that would represent a potential breach within the network.

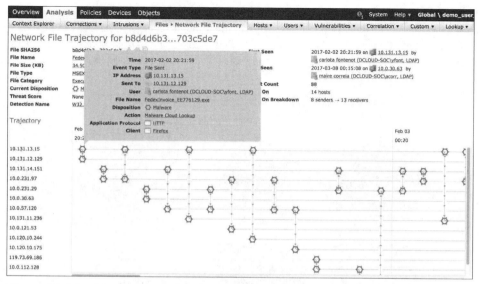

Figure 10-16 *Cisco Advanced Malware Protection File Trajectory*

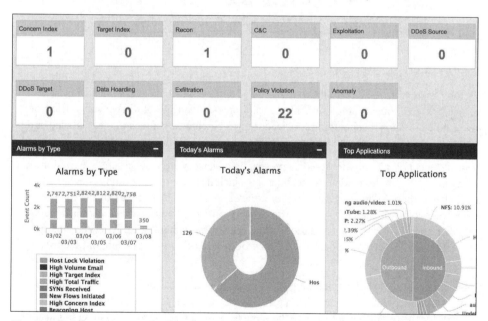

Figure 10-17 *Cisco StealthWatch Events Dashboard*

Many other industry tools are available to combat breaches. For example, **honey pots** are systems planted on the network that are highly vulnerable to attack. The hope is that an attacker would identify one of these systems during internal reconnaissance and attempt to breach it, which will trigger alarms and alert administration of an internal breach.

It is recommended that an organization invest in security capabilities that can defend against all steps of the kill chain. Cisco defines properly investing in security as having capabilities that defend before, during, and after the attack. This is called the BDA strategy. Figure 10-18 represents Cisco's BDA strategy with aligned industry security technologies.

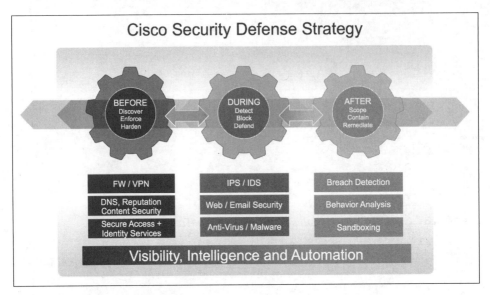

Figure 10-18   *Cisco BDA Strategy*

"Before" represents the capability to deny the adversary the chance to launch an attack against a target. Some examples of this concept include using VPN to encrypt traffic from being stolen in transit, using reputation security to block web sources that are labeled as a high risk, and using access control to deny access to unauthorized systems.

"During" technologies are designed to prevent an adversary from successfully exploiting a vulnerability. Examples of defense technologies include antivirus, IPS, and other signature- and behavior-based defenses that look for attack behaviors. The last part of the BDA is "after" technology, which aims to identify activity post-exploitation, meaning insider and unknown threats that have passed the "during" detection technologies. After technology examples include NetFlow monitoring, honey pots, and other types of internal security sensors.

There are many options for obtaining BDA capabilities, and it is recommended that an organization consider having a BDA design for all areas of security. For example, having layered security for the perimeter but lacking the same level of defense for wireless communication would base the grade of this security posture on the weakest area, meaning a likely future breach would occur through the wireless network. Adversaries following the kill chain would identify this weakness during the reconnaissance phase and select wireless as the easiest and best route for success to attack the target network.

Here are some key points to remember about the Kill Chain Model:

- The kill chain represents the steps taken by an adversary to accomplish an intrusion.
- The steps in the kill chain are reconnaissance, weaponization, delivery, exploitation, installation, command and control (C2), and actions on objectives.
- Reconnaissance is an information-gathering stage focused on researching the target.
- Weaponization is when an attack is developed based on data found during the reconnaissance phase.
- The delivery phase determines how the attack developed during the weaponization phase is delivered.
- The exploitation phase is when the attack is launched against a vulnerability in the targeted victim.
- Installation in regard to the kill chain refers to installing the previously developed weapon and being capable of maintaining persistence inside the target system or environment.
- The command and control phase is when the adversary connects to the compromised system and has "hands-on-keyboard" access inside the environment.
- The final stage of the kill chain is action and objectives, which represents the adversary moving on to accomplishing the goal for launching the attack.
- The goal for an incident response team is to identify an event as early as possible in the kill chain.

Summary

The focus of this chapter included how an incident response team should categorize an identified incident. We started off by introducing the Diamond Model of Intrusion, which is an industry standard for modeling the lifecycle of an attack. We covered how to build diamonds and group them into activity-attack groups so a security analyst can highlight the attacker's preferences as well as alternative paths that could be used for predicting future attacks.

Next, we looked at the steps of the Kill Chain Model to better understand how an adversary compromises a target system. We reviewed each step—both from the attacker's viewpoint and from the analyst's viewpoint—and provided a general overview of how real-world cyber attacks are carried out along with how to identify each step of the kill chain. We closed with an introduction to Cisco's recommended security strategy for defending against modern cyber threats, giving the defender multiple chances to prevent an adversary from completing the kill chain.

Next up, we will look at how to consider your final preparation for the exam.

References

- https://access.redhat.com/solutions/2205341
- http://www.bloomberg.com/news/articles/2015-08-11/u-s-identifies-insider-trading-ring-including-ukraine-hackers
- www.hackersforcharity.org

10

- https://www.paterva.com/web7/
- https://www.shodan.io/
- https://www.offensive-security.com/metasploit-unleashed
- http://www.slideshare.net/cybersquared/diamond-model-methodology
- http://www.activeresponse.org/wp-content/uploads/2013/07/diamond_summary.pdf
- https://www.threatconnect.com/wp-content/uploads/ThreatConnect-The-Diamond-Model-of-Intrusion-Analysis.pdf
- http://www.cisco.com/c/en/us/solutions/collateral/enterprise-networks/rapid-threat-containment/solution-overview-c22-736229.html
- http://www.lockheedmartin.com/us/what-we-do/aerospace-defense/cyber/cyber-kill-chain.html

Exam Preparation Tasks

As mentioned in the section "How to Use This Book" in the Introduction, you have a few choices for exam preparation: the exercises here, Chapter 11, "Final Preparation," and the exam simulation questions on the Pearson IT Certification Practice Test.

Review All Key Topics

Review the most important topics in this chapter, noted with the Key Topics icon in the outer margin of the page. Table 10-2 lists these key topics and the page numbers on which each is found.

Table 10-2   Key Topics for Chapter 10

Key Topic Element	Description	Page Number
Figure 10-2	Extended Diamond Model diagram	251
Figure 10-5	Developing an activity thread	253
Figure 10-7	Kill Chain Model	255
List	Diamond Model summary	255
List	Kill chain key points	269

Define Key Terms

Define the following key terms from this chapter and check your answers in the glossary:

Diamond Model of Intrusion, security incident, adversary, metadata, Cyber Kill Chain Model, reconnaissance, weaponization, delivery, exploitation, installation, command and control (C2), incident response

Q&A

The answers to these questions appear in Appendix A, "Answers to the 'Do I Know This Already' Quizzes and Q&A." For more practice with exam format questions, use the exam engine on the website.

1. Which of the following is *not* an example of weaponization?

   a. Connecting to a command and control server

   b. Wrapping software with a RAT

   c. Creating a backdoor in an application

   d. Developing an automated script to inject commands on a USB device

10

2. Which of the following steps in the kill chain would come before the others?

    a. C2

    b. Delivery

    c. Installation

    d. Exploitation

3. Which is true regarding the difference between Installation and Command and Control?

    a. Installation does not provide keyboard access to the attacker

    b. Installation is a form of exploitation

    c. Command and Control comes prior to Installation

    d. Command and Control is the final step of the kill chain

4. Which of the following is *not* an example of a capability in the Diamond Model?

    a. Hacker tools

    b. Exploit kits

    c. Malware

    d. Email

5. Which of the following statements would represent the delivery stage of a ransomware attack?

    a. The ransomware encrypts the hard drive.

    b. Ransomware is pushed onto a system through an exploit.

    c. The user connects to a malicious website that attacks the system.

    d. The exploit page identifies a vulnerability and launches an attack.

6. Which statement is true about the C2 stage of an attack?

    a. The malware post-compromise phoning back to the attacker is the C2 stage.

    b. The attacker accesses the internal network through a breached system.

    c. The attacker pivots inside the network.

    d. The attacker connects to another internal system inside the breached network.

7. Which is a false statement about the Diamond Model?

    a. Lines in the Diamond Model represent how the attacker reaches the victim.

    b. Diamonds represent an adversary, victim, capability, and infrastructure.

    c. Diamonds can be grouped together, known as activity threads.

    d. Meta-features provide useful context and are core to the model.

8. What is the main value of activity-attack graphs?

    a. Used to make security product purchasing decisions

    b. To predict future attacks

    c. An alternative to threat intelligence

    d. To map out an attacker's attack history

9. Which technology would not be considered part of the "during" phase of the Cisco BDA model?

   a. Antivirus

   b. Intrusion prevention

   c. Application layer firewall threat detection

   d. Port security

10. Which of the following is *not* a metadata feature of the Diamond Model?

   a. Direction

   b. Result

   c. Devices

   d. Resources

10

CHAPTER 11

Final Preparation

The first 10 chapters of this book covered the technologies, protocols, design concepts, and considerations required to be prepared to pass the CCNA Cyber Ops 210-255 SECOPS exam. Although these chapters supplied the detailed information, most people need more preparation than just reading the first 10 chapters of this book. This chapter details a set of tools and a study plan to help you complete your preparation for the exam.

This short chapter has two main sections. The first section lists the exam preparation tools useful at this point in the study process. The second section lists a suggested study plan now that you have completed all the earlier chapters in this book.

> **NOTE** Note that Appendix B, "Memory Tables and Lists," and Appendix C, "Memory Tables and Lists Answers," exist as soft-copy appendixes on the website for this book, which you can access by going to www.pearsonITcertification.com/register, registering your book, and entering this book's ISBN: 9781587147036.

Tools for Final Preparation

This section lists some information about the available tools and how to access them.

Pearson Cert Practice Test Engine and Questions on the Website

Register this book to get access to the Pearson IT Certification test engine (software that displays and grades a set of exam-realistic, multiple-choice questions). Using the Pearson Cert Practice Test Engine, you can either study by going through the questions in Study mode or take a simulated (timed) SECOPS exam.

The Pearson Test Prep practice test software comes with two full practice exams. These practice tests are available to you either online or as an offline Windows application. To access the practice exams that were developed with this book, please see the instructions in the card inserted in the sleeve in the back of the book. This card includes a unique access code that enables you to activate your exams in the Pearson Test Prep software.

Accessing the Pearson Test Prep Software Online

The online version of this software can be used on any device with a browser and connectivity to the Internet, including desktop machines, tablets, and smartphones. To start using your practice exams online, simply follow these steps:

Step 1. Go to: http://www.PearsonTestPrep.com.

Step 2. Select **Pearson IT Certification** as your product group.

Step 3.   Enter your email/password for your account. If you don't have an account on PearsonITCertification.com or CiscoPress.com, you will need to establish one by going to PearsonITCertification.com/join.

Step 4.   In the **My Products** tab, click the **Activate New Product** button.

Step 5.   Enter the access code printed on the insert card in the back of your book to activate your product.

Step 6.   The product will now be listed in your My Products page. Click the **Exams** button to launch the exam settings screen and start your exam.

Accessing the Pearson Test Prep Software Offline

If you wish to study offline, you can download and install the Windows version of the Pearson Test Prep software. There is a download link for this software on the book's companion website, or you can just enter this link in your browser:

http://www.pearsonitcertification.com/content/downloads/pcpt/engine.zip

To access the book's companion website and the software, simply follow these steps:

Step 1.   Register your book by going to PearsonITCertification.com/register and entering the ISBN: 9781587147036.

Step 2.   Respond to the challenge questions.

Step 3.   Go to your account page and select the **Registered Products** tab.

Step 4.   Click the **Access Bonus Content** link under the product listing.

Step 5.   Click the **Install Pearson Test Prep Desktop Version** link under the Practice Exams section of the page to download the software.

Step 6.   Once the software finishes downloading, unzip all the files on your computer.

Step 7.   Double-click the application file to start the installation; then follow the onscreen instructions to complete the registration.

Step 8.   Once the installation is complete, launch the application and select **Activate Exam** button on the My Products tab.

Step 9.   Click the **Activate a Product** button in the Activate Product Wizard.

Step 10. Enter the unique access code found on the card in the sleeve in the back of your book and click the **Activate** button.

Step 11. Click **Next** and then the **Finish** button to download the exam data to your application.

Step 12. You can now start using the practice exams by selecting the product and clicking the **Open Exam** button to open the exam settings screen.

Note that the offline and online versions will synch together, so saved exams and grade results recorded on one version will be available to you on the other as well.

Customizing Your Exams

Once you are in the exam settings screen, you can choose to take exams in one of three modes:

- Study mode
- Practice Exam mode
- Flash Card mode

Study mode allows you to fully customize your exams and review answers as you are taking the exam. This is typically the mode you would use first to assess your knowledge and identify information gaps. Practice Exam mode locks certain customization options, as it is presenting a realistic exam experience. Use this mode when you are preparing to test your exam readiness. Flash Card mode strips out the answers and presents you with only the question stem. This mode is great for late-stage preparation when you really want to challenge yourself to provide answers without the benefit of seeing multiple-choice options. This mode will not provide the detailed score reports that the other two modes will, so it should not be used if you are trying to identify knowledge gaps.

In addition to these three modes, you will be able to select the source of your questions. You can choose to take exams that cover all of the chapters or you can narrow your selection to just a single chapter or the chapters that make up a specific part in the book. All chapters are selected by default. If you want to narrow your focus to individual chapters, simply deselect all the chapters and then select only those on which you wish to focus in the Objectives area.

You can also select the exam banks on which to focus. Each exam bank comes complete with a full exam of questions that cover topics in every chapter. The two exams printed in the book are available to you as well as two additional exams of unique questions. You can have the test engine serve up exams from all four banks or just from one individual bank by selecting the desired banks in the exam bank area.

There are several other customizations you can make to your exam from the exam settings screen, such as the time of the exam, the number of questions served up, whether to randomize questions and answers, whether to show the number of correct answers for multiple-answer questions, and whether to serve up only specific types of questions. You can also create custom test banks by selecting only questions that you have marked or questions for which you have added notes.

Updating Your Exams

If you are using the online version of the Pearson Test Prep software, you should always have access to the latest version of the software as well as the exam data. If you are using the Windows desktop version, every time you launch the software, it will check to see if there are any updates to your exam data and automatically download any changes that were made

11

since the last time you used the software. This requires you to be connected to the Internet at the time you launch the software.

Sometimes, due to many factors, the exam data might not fully download when you activate your exam. If you find that figures or exhibits are missing, you may need to manually update your exams.

To update a particular exam you have already activated and downloaded, simply select the **Tools** tab and select the **Update Products** button. Again, this is only an issue with the desktop Windows application.

If you wish to check for updates to the Pearson Test Prep exam engine software, Windows desktop version, simply select the **Tools** tab and select the **Update Application** button. This will ensure you are running the latest version of the software engine.

Premium Edition

In addition to the free practice exam provided on the website, you can purchase additional exams with expanded functionality directly from Pearson IT Certification. The Premium Edition of this title contains an additional two full practice exams and an eBook (in both PDF and ePub format). In addition, the Premium Edition title also has remediation for each question to the specific part of the eBook that relates to that question.

Because you have purchased the print version of this title, you can purchase the Premium Edition at a deep discount. There is a coupon code in the book sleeve that contains a one-time-use code and instructions for where you can purchase the Premium Edition.

To view the premium edition product page, go to www.informit.com/title/9781587147036.

The Cisco Learning Network

Cisco provides a wide variety of CCNA Cyber Ops preparation tools at a Cisco Systems website called the Cisco Learning Network. This site includes a large variety of exam preparation tools, including sample questions, forums on each Cisco exam, educational video games, and information about each exam.

To reach the Cisco Learning Network, go to www.cisco.com/go/learnnetspace, or just search for "Cisco Learning Network." You must use the logon you created at Cisco.com. If you do not have such a logon, you can register for free. To register, simply go to Cisco.com, click **Register** at the top of the page, and supply the required information.

Memory Tables and Lists

Like most *Official Cert Guides* from Cisco Press, this book purposely organizes information into tables and lists for easier study and review. Rereading these tables and lists can be very useful before the exam. However, it is easy to skim over them without paying attention to every detail, especially when you remember having seen the table's or list's contents when reading the chapter.

Instead of just reading the tables and lists in the various chapters, this book's Appendixes B and C give you another review tool. Appendix B, "Memory Tables and Lists," lists partially completed versions of many of the tables from the book. You can open Appendix B (a PDF available on the book website after registering) and print the appendix. For review, you can attempt to complete the tables. This exercise can help you focus on the review. It also exercises the memory connectors in your brain; plus it makes you think about the topic without as much information, which forces a little more contemplation about the facts.

Appendix C, "Memory Tables and Lists Answers," also a PDF located on the book website, lists the completed tables to check yourself. You can also just refer to the tables as printed in the book.

Chapter-Ending Review Tools

Chapters 1 through 10 each have several features in the "Exam Preparation Tasks" and "Q&A" sections at the end of the chapter. You might have already worked through these in each chapter. It can also be useful to use these tools again as you make your final preparations for the exam.

Suggested Plan for Final Review/Study

This section lists a suggested study plan from the point at which you finish reading through Chapter 10 until you take the 210-255 SECOPS exam. Certainly, you can ignore this plan, use it as is, or just take suggestions from it.

The plan uses four steps:

Step 1.   **Review key topics and DIKTA questions:** You can use the table that lists the key topics in each chapter, or just flip through the pages looking for key topics. Also, reviewing the "Do I Know This Already" (DIKTA) questions from the beginning of the chapter can be helpful for review.

Step 2.   **Complete memory tables:** Open Appendix B from the book's website and print the entire thing, or print the tables by major part. Then complete the tables.

Step 3.   **Review the "Q&A" sections:** Go through the Q&A questions at the end of each chapter to identify areas where you need more study.

Step 4.   **Use the Pearson Cert Practice Test engine to practice:** The Pearson Cert Practice Test engine on the book's companion website can be used to study using a bank of unique exam-realistic questions available only with this book.

Summary

The tools and suggestions listed in this chapter have been designed with one goal in mind: to help you develop the skills required to pass the CCNA Cyber Ops 210-255 SECOPS exam. This book has been developed from the beginning to not just tell you the facts but to also help you learn how to apply the facts. Regardless of your experience level leading up to when you take the exam, it is our hope that the broad range of preparation tools, and even the structure of the book, helps you pass the exam with ease. We hope you do well on the exam.

Answers to the "Do I Know This Already?" Quizzes and Q&A

Do I Know This Already? Answers

Chapter 1

1. C. Encryption is often used to maintain confidentiality. An example is the use of encryption in virtual private networks (VPNs).

2. B. Integrity protection encompasses more than just data; it not only protects data, but also operating systems, applications, and hardware from being altered by unauthorized individuals.

3. A and C. STRIDE, DREAD, and attack trees are examples of threat modeling techniques.

4. C. Damage potential, reproducibility, exploitability, affected users, and discoverability are the components of DREAD.

5. A. Spoofing, tampering, repudiation, information disclosure, denial of service, and elevation of privilege are the components of STRIDE.

6. A, B, C. All three are examples of attack vectors.

7. C. CVAL does not exist. The rest are examples of tools that can help analyze the attack surface of a system.

8. B. The attack complexity is categorized as low when specialized access conditions or mitigating circumstances do not exist.

9. B. The risk is considered low (not high) if the attacker is already authorized or is required to have privileges on the system.

10. B. A VM escape vulnerability is an example of a vulnerability that could lead to an attack scope change.

Chapter 2

1. A. The three broad categories of cybersecurity investigations are public, private, and individual.

2. D. Evidence found on a system or network may be presented in a court of law to support accusations of crime or civil action, including all the options presented.

3. B. A suspect-led approach is pejorative and often biased to the disadvantage of those being investigated.

4. D. The reliability of the digital evidence is vital to supporting or refuting any hypothesis put forward, including the attribution of threat actors.

5. C. Each process starts with a single thread, known as the primary thread, but can also create additional threads from any of its threads.

6. D. A job is a group of processes.

7. D. NTFS is more secure, scalable, and advanced in comparison to FAT32. FAT64 and uFAT do not exist.

8. C. Ext4 supports journaling and features for better performance. LILO and GRUB are not file systems; they are boot loaders.

9. A and C. GRUB and LILO are examples of commonly used Linux boot loaders.

10. C. The journal is the most used part of the disk, making the blocks that form part of it more prone to hardware failure.

Chapter 3

1. A and D. Source and destination IP addresses, along with source and destination ports, are part of NetFlow records. Usernames and signature IDs are not part of NetFlow or IPFIX data.

2. A and D. Signature IDs as well as source and destination IP addresses are typically shown in IDS and IPS events. Passwords and PII should not be shown in IDS and IPS events.

3. A. The regular expression [bcr]at will pick up any words with "at," starting with a *b*, *c*, or *r*.

4. B. The "*" will pick up any characters after the 10.1.2. string.

5. C. Protocol header analysis has better detection of both known and unknown attacks. This is done by alerting and blocking traffic on anomalies within the protocol transactions, instead of just simply matching traffic on signatures of security vulnerability exploits.

6. A. Wireshark is one of the most popular packet capture programs used in the industry.

7. A and C. The output shows a TCP connection (HTTP) from a host with the FQDN omar.cisco.com to a destination server called www1.cisco.com.

Chapter 4

1. A, B, and C. NetFlow can be used to see what is actually happening across the entire network, to identify DoS attacks, and to quickly identify compromised endpoints and network infrastructure devices. It is not a scanning technology or solution.

2. A, B, C, and D. Flexible NetFlow can track a wide range of Layer 2, IPv4, and IPv6 flow information, including the following:

    - Source and destination MAC addresses
    - Source and destination IPv4 or IPv6 addresses
    - Source and destination ports
    - ToS
    - DSCP
    - Packet and byte counts

- Flow timestamps
- Input and output interface numbers
- TCP flags and encapsulated protocol (TCP/UDP)
- Sections of packet for deep packet inspection
- All fields in an IPv4 header
- All fields in an IPv6 header
- Routing information

3. A, C, D. Normal, immediate, and permanent are the three types of NetFlow cache.

4. D. IPFIX is an IETF standard based on NetFlow v9, with several extensions.

5. B. Templates provide a vendor-neutral support for companies that create applications that provide collector or analysis capabilities for NetFlow so that they are not required to reinvent their product each time a new NetFlow feature is added. Additionally, templates allow for new features to be added to NetFlow more quickly, without breaking current implementations and with backward compatibility.

6. C. IPFIX uses the Stream Control Transmission Protocol (SCTP), which provides a packet transport service designed to support several features beyond TCP or UDP capabilities.

7. C. NetFlow, along with other telemetry features, can be enabled within your infrastructure to provide the necessary data used for identifying and classifying threats and anomalies. Before implementing these anomaly-detection capabilities, you should perform traffic analysis to gain an understanding of general traffic rates and patterns. This is often referred to as a traffic baseline.

8. A and B. Both DHCP logs and VPN logs are examples of other telemetry sources that can be correlated with NetFlow.

9. A, B, D. SiLK, ELK, and Graylog are open source tools that can be used for NetFlow analysis.

10. A and B. StealthWatch Management Console, FlowCollector, FlowSensor, FlowReplicator, and StealthWatch IDentity are components of the Cisco Lancope StealthWatch solution.

Chapter 5

1. A. NIST's Special Publication 800-61 was created to provide guidelines for incident response and all related processes and procedures.

2. D. Definition of QoS policies in network infrastructure devices is not part of NIST's Special Publication 800-61.

3. B. An SOP is a delineation of the specific technical processes, techniques, checklists, and forms used by the incident response team.

4. D. Although network monitoring is part of the preparation phase, it is not a phase as a whole of the incident response process, as defined by NIST.

5. D. Incident prioritization is part of the detection and analysis phase.

6. B. Identifying the attacking hosts is not part of the post-incident phase.

A

7.   D. The FS-ISAC is a good example of an information-sharing community.

8.   A, B, C, and D. All of these are examples of external parties you may need to communicate with during the resolution of a security incident.

9.   D. Product Security Incident Response Teams (PSIRTs), National CSIRTs and Computer Emergency Response Teams (CERTs), and the incident response teams of security vendors and managed security service providers (MSSPs) are all examples of incident response teams.

10.   A. Centralized incident response teams, distributed incident response teams, and coordinating teams are all examples of the most common incident response team structures.

Chapter 6

1.   B, C, D, and E. Incident classification and handling, information classification and protection, information dissemination, and record retentions and destruction are the responsibilities of a CSIRT or policies it helps create. Typically, corporate CSIRTs do not scan the network of vendors or their customers.

2.   C. One of the main goals of a CSIRT is to minimize risk, contain cyber damage, and save money by preventing incidents from happening—and if they do occur, to mitigate them efficiently.

3.   B, C, and D. The base, temporal, and environmental scores are the three main components of the CVSS.

4.   D. PSIRTs are typically responsible for disclosing vulnerabilities in products and services sold by the organization to its customers.

5.   B. National CSIRTs and CERTs aim to protect their citizens by providing security vulnerability information, security awareness training, best practices, and other information.

6.   C. The CERT division of the Software Engineering Institute (SEI) is an example of a coordination center. Both Cisco PSIRT and Microsoft MSRC are PSIRTs, and FIRST is a forum for incident response teams.

7.   B. The Cisco ATA service offers customers 24-hour continuous monitoring and advanced-analytics capabilities, combined with threat intelligence and security analysts and investigators to detect security threats in the customer networks. More information about Cisco ATA can be obtained at https://www.cisco.com/c/en/us/products/security/managed-services.html.

Chapter 7

1.   B. PCI DSS is designed to protect financial transactions, meaning the primary account number (PAN), account data on the magmatic strip, and data on the embedded chip.

2.   D. In this case, D is the best answer. B is incorrect because someone's personal home network doesn't impact the networks they work on during their day job, unless those networks are connected and are the responsibility of the employer (IE working from home).

3. C. PCI is related to financial data and includes the full account number. A health condition would be something related to HIPAA.

4. A. Answer A is a good practice; however, it is not specifically called out as a high-level PCI DSS 3.2 requirement. Encryption would fall under protecting cardholder data; however, PCI DSS states that encryption does not remove PCI compliance requirements.

5. D. Answer D is the best answer. Answers A and B do not consider the installed software. Answer C includes a false aspect (that is, contractors).

6. C. HIPAA is designed to guard protected health information (PHI) and electronic PHI (e-PHI).

7. D. PHI is protected health information.

8. C. Any health condition is protected by HIPAA.

9. B. SOX is a U.S.-based compliance requirement. Answer B could mean organizations outside the U.S. The other answers are associated with U.S.-based financial services and therefore must be SOX compliant.

10. B. The Open Web Application Security Project (OWASP) creates web application security content and is not related to SOX compliance.

Chapter 8

1. A. sFlow (also called sampled flow) provides fewer details than NetFlow.

2. C. Developing a list of users on the network is not necessary for developing a network baseline.

3. D. Port security is a feature that is available with most modern switches, meaning it does not have an additional cost. Automated NAC typically is purchased, meaning it has a higher cost to acquire the technology.

4. C. Session is the total time a user or device connects to a network and later disconnects from a network.

5. A. Answer A would not help with monitoring connections to the network because firewalls tend not to see switch layer data, depending on how they are deployed.

6. B. Although the statement in answer B is usually true, this is not always the case. Administrators can choose to use other ports. Although it is common to use industry ports, this is not required.

7. C. Answer C is the best answer. Answers A and D do not include a payload, meaning there isn't an associated attack. Answer B is incorrect because if the same payload is used, it will be detected by most security solutions.

8. B. Answer B has nothing to do with running processes due to port security being only MAC address based.

9. D. NetFlow does not have application layer data.

10. A. Answer A is not always true, meaning latency can be introduced anywhere in the network.

A

Chapter 9

1. A. Data normalization is the process of capturing, storing, and analyzing data (security-related events, in this case) so that it exists in only one form.

2. B. First normal form (1NF), second normal form (2NF), and third normal form (3NF) are data normalization categories used in the industry.

3. D. IP option is not part of the 5-tuple.

4. D. The event shown is an IPS/IDS log. One key field in recognizing this is the presence of a signature ID.

5. C. Cisco AMP uses threat intelligence from Cisco to perform retrospective analysis and protection. Cisco AMP also provides device and file trajectory capabilities to allow the security administrator to analyze the full spectrum of an attack.

6. D. DNS intelligence and URL reputation are used in many security solutions like the Cisco Firepower appliances, Cisco Firepower Threat Defense (FTD), the Cisco Web and Email security appliances, and others. For instance, you can correlate security events based on threat intelligence to identify communications to known malicious command and control (CnC) servers based on DNS information.

7. C. In deterministic analysis, you know and obtain "facts" about the incident, breach, affected applications, and other information.

Chapter 10

1. A. Adversaries must use both some form of infrastructure and the capability to access the victim.

2. D. Activity threads represent attacks that the attacker has already used.

3. B. Answer B defines what an activity-attack graph is best for. Answers A and C lack the proactive planning value offered by activity-attack graphs. Answer D is simply incorrect.

4. D. The final step is "action." One example of an action could be to remove data. Action is not a required step of an attack and not part of the kill chain. For example, an attacker's goal could be to take down the network from within.

5. A. Although answer D is close, answer A provides the best definition. Delivery is how the attacker communicates while exploitation is the attacker taking advantage of a vulnerability.

6. B. This is a man-in-the-middle attack and is something done as an attack, not as research.

7. B. The command and control (C2) stage is best defined as when the attacker completes the delivery of the attack and now can access the breached network.

8. D. Attacking internal targets or stealing data could be goals. Sometimes listening to traffic is the goal. For example, hackers might breach a company and use inside information to affect stock trading decisions. This was done by a group, which is believed to have made millions doing this.

9. C. It's best to start doing analysis early so you can detect when an adversary attempts to communicate with you and then attack. Waiting for the attack is okay, but proactive measures, such as making it hard for attackers to communicate with you, is the best and earliest detection approach.

10. B. An insider threat could be an attacker who has breached the network and is now moving around like other users. The best approach to detect this is to look for unusual behavior, such as systems connecting to new systems for the first time, internal recon, data exfiltration, and so on.

Q&A Answers

Chapter 1

1. A. A DoS attack against a web server affects availability; the attack by itself does not affect integrity, repudiation, or confidentiality.

2. C. Integrity covers any changes to a system or its data.

3. B. Confidentiality is the promise that data is not unveiled to unauthorized users, applications, or processes. Depending on the type of information, a higher level of confidentiality might be required, depending on how sensitive it is.

4. A. An attack against a VM escape vulnerability is an example of an attack whose scope has potentially been changed. This scope is defined in CVSSv3 and later.

5. A and B. STRIDE and DREAD are examples of thread modeling techniques.

6. C. Malicious web page content, malicious email attachments and malicious email links, and social engineering are all attack vectors. DDoS is a type of attack.

Chapter 2

1. A. **VirtualAlloc** is a specialized allocation of the Windows virtual memory system, meaning it allocates straight into virtual memory via reserved blocks of memory.

2. D. **HeapAlloc** allocates any size of memory that is requested dynamically in Windows, and is a concept of Microsoft Windows.

3. A and C. When you're performing forensics, the storage device you are investigating should immediately be write-protected before it is imaged and should be labeled to include the investigator's name and the date when the image was created.

4. A. In cyber forensics, the original device can be returned to the owner or stored for trial, normally without having to be examined repeatedly.

5. A. Evidence that can be presented in court in the original form is referred to as "best evidence."

6. C. Swap is extra memory on the hard disk drive or SSD that is an expansion of the system's physical memory.

7. C. A file system that supports journaling maintains a record of changes not yet committed to the file system's main part.

8. A. Indirect or circumstantial evidence is a type of evidence that relies on an extrapolation to a conclusion of fact.

A

9. D. Ext4 is one of the most used Linux file systems. It has several improvements over its predecessors and supports journaling. NTFS is typically used in Windows. Ext5 does not exist as of the time of writing, and exFAT does not support journaling.

10. D. Heaps are set up by **VirtualAlloc** and are used to initially reserve allocation space from the operating system.

Chapter 3

1. C. The packet capture shown includes a Telnet connection attempt from omar.cisco.com that eventually times out due to no answer from the server (93.184.216.34).

2. A. A true positive is a successful identification of a security attack or a malicious event.

3. B. A true negative is when the intrusion detection device identifies an activity as acceptable behavior and the activity is actually acceptable.

4. C. A false positive is when a security device triggers an alarm but there is no malicious activity or an actual attack taking place.

5. D. Fragmentation has traditionally been used by attackers to evade IDS and IPS devices.

6. C. A Flow record is an element in NetFlow, not an example of an element in an IDS alert or event.

7. B and C. The 5-tuple refers to source and destination IP addresses, source and destination ports, and protocols.

Chapter 4

1. A and B. Using NetFlow along with identity management systems, an administrator can detect the person who initiated the data transfer and the host involved.

2. A, B, and D. Each forensics team needs to have awareness of assets, risks, impact, and the likelihood of events. In addition, the team needs to know incident response policies and procedures in mock events and collect NetFlow on a regular basis to analyze what is happening in the network. Other items the team should be aware of are how to handle evidence and what chain of custody is.

3. A, B, and C. DHCP server logs, VPN server logs, and 802.1x authentication logs are good telemetry sources for attribution for who is the potential threat actor in a security incident or attack.

4. A and B. The following are the steps required to configure Flexible NetFlow in Cisco IOS or Cisco IOS-XE:

    1. Configure a flow record.

    2. Configure a flow monitor.

    3. Configure a flow exporter for the flow monitor.

    4. Apply the flow monitor to an interface.

5. D. Network Time Protocol, or NTP, is used to make sure that time is synchronized effectively in network infrastructure devices, servers, and any other computing devices.

6. C. Flow records, monitors, and samplers are examples of Flexible NetFlow components.

7. C. Source and destination IP addresses and ports as well as the protocol are part of the 5-tuple.

8. A. The default cache in NetFlow is the "normal cache."

9. D. Encryption security association serial numbers are not part of NetFlow or Flexible NetFlow.

10. D. Flexible NetFlow is based on NetFlow Version 9 and it uses the concept of templates.

Chapter 5

1. D. According to NIST, a computer security incident is a violation or imminent threat of violation of computer security policies, acceptable use policies, or standard security practices.

2. B. An SOP is a delineation of the specific technical processes, techniques, checklists, and forms used by the incident response team.

3. A. A security event is any observable occurrence in a system or network.

4. D. PSIRT is not an example of the most common incident response team staffing models. Staffing models are employees, partially outsourced team, and fully outsourced team.

5. C and D. The containment, eradication, and recovery phase includes choosing a containment strategy and evidence gathering and handling.

6. A. The post-incident activity phase in the incident response process includes lessons learned, how to use collected incident data, and evidence retention.

7. A. The preparation phase is the phase in the incident response process that includes creating processes for incident handler communications and the facilities that will host the security operation center (SOC) and incident response team.

8. A and D. Centralized and distributed are examples of the most common incident response team structures.

9. D. The main five sections of the VERIS schema are:
   - Incident Tracking
   - Victim Demographics
   - Incident Description
   - Discovery & Response
   - Impact Assessment

10. C. The Incident Description section of the VERIS schema includes the following elements:
   - Actors
   - Actions
   - Assets
   - Attributes

A

Chapter 6

1. A. National CERTs aim to protect their citizens by providing security vulnerability information, security awareness training, best practices, and other information. PSIRTs are vendor Product Security Incident Response Teams. ATA is a Cisco-managed security service, and global CERTs do not exist.

2. D. Product Security Incident Response Teams (PSIRTs) are the ones that handle the investigation, resolution, and disclosure of security vulnerabilities in vendor products and services.

3. C. CERT/CC is an example of a coordination center.

4. B. The Common Vulnerability Scoring System (CVSS) is the most widely adopted standard to calculate the severity of a given security vulnerability.

5. C, D, E. Confidentiality, integrity, and availability (CIA) are part of the CVSS base score metrics.

Chapter 7

1. C. Images presented on cards are not part of what PCI DSS is responsible to protect.

2. A. Answer A is a SOX requirement.

3. A. Answer A is the best definition of CDE.

4. C. Answer C is a great practice; however, it is not a requirement listed for the HIPAA security rule.

5. C. Answer C relates to SOX compliance.

6. B. Answer B is a good practice to enforce but not part of SOX compliance. Remember compliance can offer good practices but should be considered the minimal best practices. There are usually other areas that can be improved beyond what is required for compliance.

7. A. PCI does not supersede legal requirements.

8. B. Currently, biometrics isn't listed as part of a PCI DSS 3.2 security requirement.

9. C. Answer C is a good best practice; however, it is not part of the PCI DSS 3.2 Implementing strong access control measure requirements.

10. B. Answer B is the correct CIA breakdown.

Chapter 8

1. B. Capturing network packets offers more details than NetFlow.

2. C. Knowing the number of devices can help; however, devices can have different impacts on throughput. An example would be comparing a user browsing the Internet versus another user streaming video. The video user would have a larger impact on the network; hence, it's more important to see the type of traffic versus types of devices when establishing throughput requirements.

3. D. DNS provides name resolution when searching the web; however, it doesn't have the same value as the others in regard to identifying the types of devices connected to the network.

4. B. Baselining typically is about how users impact network performance versus how long they use a system. This can help with baselining, but the other answers are more valuable uses of session duration data.

5. A. Segmenting hosts has to do with controlling traffic between address spaces versus provisioning addresses to hosts.

6. B. Endpoint posture is a good thing to consider for an access control policy; however, it is not required for IP address management (IPAM).

7. C. Understanding bandwidth utilization could possibly help a little; however, bandwidth utilization is typically something developed from a network baseline versus the types of devices on the network.

8. B. Implementing strong access control policies is helpful for controlling access to the network, but this does not help with securing systems already authorized that have listening ports.

9. C. Native NetFlow does not have application layer data.

10. A. Answer A shows who is logged in, not what is running.

Chapter 9

1. A. The table includes a NetFlow record. You can see information such as the 5-tuple and next-hop router information, as well as TCP flags, which are supported by NetFlow.

2. A. The ASA syslog shown is an example of a firewall log.

3. A and C. You can identify communications to CnC servers and malicious domains based on reputation by correlating DNS intelligence and other security events.

4. C. AMP for Networks and AMP for Endpoints use threat intelligence to allow you to perform retrospective analysis and protection.

5. B. Purging redundant data while maintaining data integrity is one of the main goals of data normalization.

Chapter 10

1. A. Connecting to a command and control server would be C2, not weaponization.

2. B. Delivery is the earliest option out of the choices listed.

3. A. Installation is when the malware is installed while Command and Control is when that software provides keyboard access to the attacker.

4. D. Email would be an infrastructure.

5. C. The user connecting to a malicious website would represent how the attack is delivered. You might think answer B is correct; however, that is how the ransomware is installed—hence, the installation stage post-exploitation.

6. B. The attacker accessing the internal network through a breached system is an example of C2. Answers C and D are actions that happen *after* the attacker gets network access. Answer A doesn't give the attacker keyboard access yet.

A

7. D. Meta-features are not required.

8. A. Activity-attack graphs are good for both current and future attack data. That data, however, is always changing and wouldn't typically represent a single product that is needed for purchase. Deciding what to purchase would require more than this type of information.

9. D. Port security would be more of a "before" technology. It involves preventing attackers from having the chance to attack the network by physically plugging in an unauthorized device.

10. C. Devices are the victim, or what is attacked. Direction is additional data about delivery. Result is extra data about the attack. Resources provide more details about what is being used to attack the victim.

Numbers

5-tuple   The 5-tuple refers to the following five elements:

- Source IP address
- Source port
- Destination IP address
- Destination port
- Protocol

A

Adversary   An attacker, hacktivist, disgruntled employee, and so on.

Attack vector   According to NIST, an attack vector is "a segment of the entire pathway that an attack uses to access a vulnerability. Each attack vector can be thought of as comprising a source of malicious content, a potentially vulnerable processor of that malicious content, and the nature of the malicious content itself."

Availability   Availability means that systems, applications, and data must be available to users without impacting productivity.

B

Bandwidth   The data rate supported by a network connection or interface.

C

Cardholder data environment (CDE)   The people, processes, and technologies that store, process, or transmit cardholder data or authentication data.

Command and control (C2)   In terms of the kill chain, C2 occurs when the attacker accesses the breached system. It represents the attacker having keyboard access to inside the breached system or network.

Committee of Sponsoring Organizations (COSO)   An auditing framework. COSO publishes periodic updates to its internal control framework and serves as the basis for the auditing standards developed by PCAOB.

Confidentiality   Confidentiality is the promise that data is not unveiled to unauthorized users, applications, or processes. Depending on the type of information, a higher level of confidentiality might be required, depending on how sensitive it is. You must have adequate control mechanisms in order to enforce and ensure that data is only accessed by the individuals who should be allowed to access it, and nobody else.

CSIRT   CSIRT is typically the team that is in charge of working hand-in-hand with the information security teams (often called InfoSec). In smaller organizations, InfoSec and CSIRT may be the same team. In large organizations, the CSIRT is specialized in the investigation of computer security incidents, and the InfoSec team is tasked with the implementation of security configurations, monitoring, and policies within the organization.

CVSS   The Common Vulnerability Scoring System (CVSS) is one of the most widely adopted standards to calculate the severity of a given security vulnerability.

Cyber Kill Chain Model   A model representing the steps taken by an adversary to accomplish an intrusion.

D

Data normalization   Data normalization is the process of capturing, storing, and analyzing data so that it exists in only one form. One of the main goals of data normalization is to purge redundant data while maintaining data integrity.

Delivery   In terms of the kill chain, delivery is the method of contact used to transmit an attack. Examples are email, across a network, and physically plugging in a device.

Diamond Model of Intrusion   A trusted approach to categorizing security incidents.

Domain name server (DNS)   Responsible for resolving IP addresses to domain names.

Dynamic Host Configuration Protocol (DHCP)   Automatically provisions IP hosts with an IP address and other related configurations such as a subnet mask and default gateway.

E

Electronic protected health information (e-PHI)   The first process during the boot sequence.

Exploitation   Involves attacking a weakness or vulnerability within a system, application, network, and so on.

Ext4   Ext4 is one of the most used Linux file systems. It has several improvements over its predecessors Ext3 and Ext2. Ext4 not only supports journaling but also modifies important data structures of the file system, such as the ones destined to store the file data. This is done for better performance, reliability, and additional features.

F

False negative   *False negative* is the term used to describe a network intrusion device's inability to detect true security events under certain circumstances—in other words, a malicious activity that is not detected by the security device.

False positive   The term *false positive* is a broad term that describes a situation in which a security device triggers an alarm but there is no malicious activity or an actual attack taking place. In other words, false positives are "false alarms." They are also called "benign triggers." False positives are problematic because by triggering unjustified alerts, they diminish the value and urgency of real alerts. If you have too many false positives to investigate, it becomes an operational nightmare and you most definitely will overlook real security events.

FAT   FAT was the default file system of the Microsoft DOS operating system back in the 1980s. Then other versions were introduced, including FAT12, FAT16, FAT32, and exFAT. Each version overcame some of the limitations of the file system until the introduction of the New Technology File System (NTFS). One of the FAT file system limitations is that no modern properties can be added to the file, such as compression, permissions, and encryption. The number after each version of FAT, such as FAT12, FAT16, or FAT32, represents the number of bits that are assigned to address clusters in the FAT table.

Flow collector   A device that collects, processes, and stores NetFlow records from infra-structure devices.

H

Health Insurance Portability and Accountability Act (HIPAA)   Protects health-care-related data being transferred in digital form. This is the focus of the HIPAA security rules.

I

Incident response   The process and tools defenders use to respond to a cybersecurity incident.

Installation   In terms of the kill chain, installation is what is delivered by a successful exploi-tation. Examples might be ransomware and remote access tools.

Integrity   Integrity is the second component of the CIA triad. It is very important that sys-tems and the data they maintain be accurate, complete, and protected from unauthorized modification. Integrity protection encompasses more than just data; it not only protects data, but also operating systems, applications, and hardware from being altered by unauthorized individuals.

IPFIX   An industry flow-based standard that's based on NetFlow v9.

J

Journaling   A journaling file system maintains a record of changes not yet committed to the file system's main part. This data structure is referred to as a "journal," which is a circular log. One of the main features of a file system that supports journaling is that if the system crashes or experiences a power failure, it can be restored back online a lot quicker while also avoiding system corruption.

L

Latency   Factors that slow down traffic performance.

Least privilege   To provision the absolute least amount of access rights required to perform a job.

Listening port   A port held open by a running application in order to accept inbound connections.

M

Master boot record   The master boot record (MBR) is the first sector (512 bytes) of the hard drive. It contains the boot code and information about the hard drive itself. The MBR contains the partition table, which includes information about the partition structure in the hard disk drive. The MBR can tell where each partition starts, its size, and the type of partition.

Metadata   Data about data, such as who created a file and the last time it was opened.

N

National CSIRT and CERTs   Numerous countries have their own Computer Emergency Response (or Readiness) Teams. These national CERTs and CSIRTs aim to protect their citizens by providing security vulnerability information, security awareness training, best practices, and other information.

Network address translation (NAT)   A method for remapping one IP address space into another by modifying network address information.

Network baseline   Normal network throughput levels.

NTFS   NTFS is the default file system in Microsoft Windows since Windows NT, and it is a more secure, scalable, and advanced file system when compared to FAT. NTFS has several components. The boot sector is the first sector in the partition, and it contains information about the file system itself, such as start code, sector size, cluster size in sectors, and the number of reserved sectors. The file system area contains many files, including the master file table (MFT), which includes metadata of the files and directories in the partition. The data area holds the actual contents of the files, and it is divided into clusters with a size assigned during formatting and recorded in the boot sector.

P

Payment Card Industry Data Security Standard (PCI DSS)   Program designed to protect the customer cardholder data when it's processed, stored, or transmitted. PCI DSS is required for any merchant, processor, acquirer, issuer, or service provider that handles payment card processing, along with outsourced or third parties involved with payment card processing.

Port scanner   Probes a host system running TCP/IP to determine which TCP and UDP ports are open and listening.

PSIRT   Software and hardware vendors may have separate teams that handle the investigation, resolution, and disclosure of security vulnerabilities in their products and services. Typically, these teams are called Product Security Incident Response Teams (PSIRTs).

Public Company Accounting Oversight Board (PCAOB)   Develops auditing standards and trains auditors on best practices for assessing a company's internal controls.

Q

Quality of Service (QoS)   Tools designed to define different priority levels for applications, users, or data flows, with the goal of guaranteeing a certain level of performance to that data.

R

Reconnaissance   Research on a target, such as available network ports, data on social media sources, learning about people at an organization, and so on.

Regular expression   A regular expression (sometimes referred to as "regex") is a text string for describing a search pattern.

S

Sarbanes-Oxley Act of 2002 (SOX)   Forces any publicly held company to have internal controls and procedures for financial reporting to avoid future corporate fraud.

Security event   An event is any observable occurrence in a system or network. Events include a user connecting to a file share, a server receiving a request for a web page, a user sending email, and a firewall blocking a connection attempt. Adverse events are events with a negative consequence, such as system crashes, packet floods, unauthorized use of system privileges, unauthorized access to sensitive data, and execution of malware that destroys data.

Security incident   A computer security incident is a violation or imminent threat of violation of computer security policies, acceptable use policies, or standard security practices.

Session duration   In network access terms, session duration is the total time a user or device connects to a network and later disconnects from a network.

Sniffer   A full packet capture software.

Standard operating procedure   A delineation of the specific technical processes, techniques, checklists, and forms used by the incident response team.

Stream Control Transmission Protocol (SCTP)   Protocol used by IPFIX that provides a packet transport service designed to support several features beyond TCP and UDP capabilities.

STRIDE   STRIDE stands for spoofing, tampering, repudiation, information disclosure, denial of service, and elevation of privilege. STRIDE was created by Loren Kohnfelder and Praerit Garg. It is a framework designed to help software developers identify the types of threats against the applications they are creating.

Swap space   Extra memory on the hard disk drive or SSD that is an expansion of the system's physical memory.

Switch port security   Provides a method to limit what devices will be permitted to access and send traffic on individual switch ports within a switched network.

T

True negative   A true negative is when the intrusion detection device identifies an activity as acceptable behavior and the activity is actually acceptable.

True positive   A true positive is a successful identification of a security attack or a malicious event.

W

Weaponization   The process of developing and testing how an attack will be executed.

Index

D

S

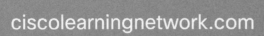